$\mathcal{O}$BJECTS
OF REMEMBRANCE

OBJECTS
OF REMEMBRANCE

A MEMOIR OF AMERICAN OPPORTUNITIES AND VIENNESE DREAMS

BY

MONROE E. PRICE

For Eric Kandel-
The true representative
of this story,

Monroe Price
1/21/10

CMCS ❯ CENTER FOR MEDIA
& COMMUNICATION STUDIES

CEU PRESS

CENTRAL EUROPEAN UNIVERSITY PRESS
NEW YORK • BUDAPEST

Published in 2009 by
Center for Media and Communications Studies (CMCS)
Central European University, Budapest

Distributed by
Central European University Press
An imprint of the
Central European University Share Company
Nádor utca 11, H-1051 Budapest, Hungary
Tel: +36-1-327-3138 or 327-3000
Fax: +36-1-327-3183
E-mail: ceupress@ceu.hu
Website: www.ceupress.com

400 West 59th Street, New York NY 10019, USA
Tel: +1-212-547-6932
Fax: +1-646-557-2416
E-mail: mgreenwald@sorosny.org

ISBN 978-963-9776-59-3 Paperback

Library of Congress Cataloging-in-Publication Data

Price, Monroe Edwin, 1938-
Objects of remembrance : a memoir of American opportunities and Viennese dreams
/ by Monroe E. Price.
p. cm.
Includes bibliographical references.
ISBN 978-9639776524 (hardcover)
1. Price, Monroe Edwin, 1938- 2. Jewish refugees--United States--Biography. 3. Jews--United States-
-Identity. 4. Jews, Austrian--United States--Biography. 5. Jews--United States--Biography. 6. Jews--
Austria--Identity. I. Title.
E134.87.P75A3 2009
981'.05092--dc22
[B]
2009028503

Printed by Akadémiai Nyomda, Martonvásár

CONTENTS

1

REFUGEE, OR HOW AUSTRIAN AM I?

I was one of the last Jewish infants conceived in Vienna as it once had been. At the beginning of my mother's pregnancy, Austria was a sovereign state. By March 1938, when my mother was a third through her term, the country had been violently swallowed into Greater Germany. When I issued from my mother's loins that August, Austria was fully integrated into the Third Reich. The Vienna in which I was created, as it were, was Austrian; the Vienna into which I was born was German. Vienna was literally my birthplace, but in a searing way that makes the word inadequate. The ambiguity, for me, of "place of birth" involves more than the legal status of Austria at the time I was there. There should be a more descriptive phrase: expulsion place or place of uncomfortable origin. My physical tie to Austria was brutally (and mercifully) short. Only seven months after my birth, in March 1939, my family, finally having the proper permits, departed for the United States. We left, the three of us (my 27 year old mother, my 32 year old father and me), by train to Paris and Cherbourg and by ship to the United States.

But here I am already playing into a special trope of birth and flight, the move from stasis to dynamic, from fixedness to entry into the whirlpool of events. Why is so much narrative weight given to the circumstances of birth? The subject of biographies is almost immediately defined by date and place of entry into the world. The reader, the historian and the critic require these ordinary markers that tie a person to continent, country, town or city, block, and house. These facts are set out first, often, as if they are the necessary backdrop and prerequisites for the emotional dramas to follow. Tying person to location provides a comforting anchor. And birthplace has a mysterious legal significance. Blood sometimes determines citizenship, but earth or territory does so more insistently. The US Constitution disqualifies almost all foreign-born citizens, certainly naturalized citizens, me included, from the Presidency. That may seem like a small matter, but for a child growing up, it is like saying you can have all the candy in the store, except for that one most wonderful piece.

Birthplace is the beginning of many stories. It hovers over narratives and is an essential element of obituaries. X was born in a small town and became rich and powerful in the metropolis. Y was a child of the slums and could never overcome her heritage. Z was Pakistani, or born in Russia, or from South Africa or Gaza. These are determinants. It's not only where the subject was born, but often where his or her parents were as well. Think of how newspaper obituaries revel in these stories of origin, going to great lengths to mention that a noted subject's parents had been born in a small Eastern European village or a rural hamlet. And not only is birthplace a fundamental of the narrative. Regularly disclosing and reciting it is a condition of existence. Almost every official form demands its disclosure as if place of birth is a defining characteristic like height and weight and eye-color. It is ineradicable. Financial documents, certificates of entry, applications for driver's licenses and for insurance plans, for jobs or schools, much of the machinery of one's dossier, asks for place of birth. Origin, in this sense, can be falsified, it can be misunderstood, it can be politically confusing, but it is hard to obliterate. Place of birth is one of those givens, a fact, something that can fix identity in a sea of relativity. It is our geographical DNA.

Flight vies with origin in the dynamic of these tales. Refugee stories revel in a uniqueness of escape: the drama of the last train from Berlin, the last boat from Hamburg, or the triumph of being on a ship that made it to Palestine but sank the next time out. It is odd that so many want to make it into the Refugee Book of Guinness World Records even if it's the World

Record of horrible possibilities. Refugee books have genres, but what defines them as a category is rude and dangerous expulsion. They tell and retell the myth of an Eden in which the rules suddenly change. And a particular and meaningful aspect involves the exigencies of exit. It is not only the semi-paradise lost, not only the search for refuge, but the circumstances of leaving that provide the details that rivet. We have images in our mind of clutching for a place on a departing helicopter in Saigon or catching the last flight from Casablanca or assaulting the sea between Cuba and Miami. The closer one is to being "saved" in so chilling a way, the closer, implicitly, to divine intervention (like the many stories of churches saved from destruction in bombing, tornado or fire).

At times—perhaps in varying extent in all cases—one result of the miraculous escape story is a notion of special responsibility. Prayer is accompanied by promise: save me, God, and I will serve you. Cure my disease and I will dedicate my life to society. The seeming arbitrariness of who lives and who dies can only make sense if those who live use their existence to fulfill a meaningful goal. One's duty is to make up for those who are lost, to be a living memorial to them, to re-people their cause.

Because, in 1939, I could leave with my parents and without physical harm and because we had succeeded in gaining access to the United States, my narrative is as undramatic as is possible in the range of stories of the Holocaust. All forced leavings and all expulsions are cruel, but ours, anguishing in many ways, was far less so. How are these things measured? My mother's parents, and much of her family, were left behind and killed. Our assets and my family's way of life were wiped out and our course in the world brought to a kind of abrupt and jagged caesura. But my father had American relatives who provided an affidavit sufficiently early to assure us a visa, and our passage to New York was in the comparative luxury of the Queen Mary. We did not have the tales of hiding in attics or fleeing to the forests. It was not us who endured or died in labor and concentration camps. I do not have the drama of the Kindertransport, shipped off, parentless, to the United Kingdom, or the tragedy of the children of France, first protected and then rounded up in the later part of the War. I may have endured, I may have had a close call, but I am not a "survivor" in the class entitled by circumstance to use that term. Mine is unlike the tale of Jakov Lind who, as an eleven-year-old boy, fled Austria, found temporary refuge in Holland, and succeeded in surviving inside Nazi Germany by assuming a Dutch identity.[1]

Indeed, the absence of these events in my relatively placid life may mean, for some, that I am disenfranchised from writing about this period in any significant sense. In 2002, the Jewish Museum in New York City mounted an exhibition called "Mirrors of Evil," a controversial event in which younger artists, some German and Polish, showed artwork that focused not so much on the victims of the concentration camps but on the perpetrators of the Holocaust, often with a novel kind of distance or attempt at post-modern fantasy. Keepers of the Holocaust flame (and I am not using an ironic tone) protested the exhibition, arguing against the dilution of memory through this kind of distancing art. They threatened to picket the show and bring their unique political power to bear to cut off municipal funding to the Museum and encourage a boycott by donors. I was asked to moderate a heated debate between victims and museum staff that preceded the show's opening. Little in common discourse was achieved, but the first question on the table was an interesting one: who was privileged, if anyone, to speak for survivors? One thing was clear to me: I was not.

But that leaves the question of who I was, in this continuum of Holocaust narrative. In 1997, five years before the Mirrors of Evil exhibition, sixty years after I left Vienna in swaddling clothes, the Austrian government granted me Austrian citizenship and issued a passport to me (I had applied under a recently passed Austrian law). I had voluntarily signed up to be associated with a place from which, as a Jewish infant, I had been expelled. I had to reflect on some complex questions put to me by friends: Why extend oneself to gain what might be deemed a stained and ill-starred status? Was gaining Austrian citizenship a form of after-the-fact collaboration? Was it an act of legitimation, however insignificant, of a state that, with so many of its citizens, had acted in such a beastly fashion? When I started the process, Kurt Waldheim was the president of Austria, his Nazi past had been exposed, and he and his country were being vilified. Perhaps a simple reason for applying was that Austria had pro-

---

[1] Andrea Hammel, Silke Hassler and Edward Timms (eds.), *Writing after Hitler: The Work of Jakov Lind*, Cardiff: University of Wales Press, 2001.

vided a legal box into which I fit, a description in which the exact concatenation of facts and personality meant that I was eligible. Filling out a piece of paper, I could gain a legislated foothold on who I was. And I could do so, under the then rules of the game, without peril: I was adding some sort of official Austrian-ness to my fundamental and remaining status as a citizen of the United States.

At any rate, I clutch my Austrian passport, hold it close to the one from the United States, and am puzzled by this combination. Indeed, I write in this self-exploratory form to increase my Austrian quotient, to bring some unity of person and acquired passport, to legitimate the act of calling myself, in small part, Austrian. Perhaps, too, I write as a mode of justification to cope with the argument that applying for Austrian citizenship (and the passport that accompanies that status) was reprehensible. As it turns out, I am grudgingly satisfied with the result of my legal transaction and new definition of status. As an Austrian citizen, I am a citizen of the European Union. I can hold a job anywhere in that official Europe. I fantasize that when I am truly old, I can be in a sanatorium in the Austrian Alps rather than a less pleasant place in the Bronx or Queens. Most important, as a holder of a European passport, I can bypass the long queues for "others" at the airports of Member States. I can dream of additional attributes of this new identity, but they are not as yet clear to me. Sometimes I think my halting German has improved, and I am more prepared to single out Austrians I meet and engage them in conversation.

Applying for and gaining a passport and citizenship, however, accentuated an old question for me: How Austrian am I? Of course, just as I was *not* a survivor, I was never really Austrian. But just as I had literally "survived," I was always Austrian to some extent. Austria was the indelible initiation of my existence. But how Austrian, in what ways, and with what consequences, had long been one part of the puzzle. I could, probably with more profit, ask how Viennese I am, on the assumption that the category of Austrian-ness is too broad, too foreign (for many of those in Vienna), just as later, much later, one could ask intelligently, how much of a New Yorker am I rather than how much of an American. I could find, through a process of reduction, ever more narrow, and possibly more productive niches of identity and ask how much of a Viennese Jew or, to recreate a category of the past, how much of a Jew? With persistence, I learn that it may be more relevant to explore my Slovakian roots and those of the Burgenland than my relationship to Vienna.

Whatever the approximate and hard-to-fathom answers to these questions of identity, this book, then, is not a "survivor" account. Nor is it, strictly speaking, a "second generation" narrative of a child of survivors. It is partly about being a refugee in America, but a particular kind of refugee, circumscribed by origins and circumstances. It is about being the child of Viennese Jewish parents and growing up in the American Midwest. It queries whether any hard-wiring from my circumstances of birth influenced my behavior in later life. To write this required (or perhaps reflected) a psychological remove, a physical distance, a diffidence. It's a half-generation question, not an emotion-pulling story of flight and suffering (though there are such stories), not quite a story of assimilation and total distance.

For much of my life, I saw myself as singular (perhaps all children see themselves that way). I did not think of myself as distinctively part of that very large class of refugees from Europe of the nineteenth and twentieth century. I thought of myself as someone quite specifically from Vienna, and somehow bearing the special crest of the Vienna that produced refugees who transformed arts, culture, universities, movements, films around the world. The "chosenness" of the Jews was melded with the chosenness of persecution, the specific chosenness of being Viennese and a Viennese Jewish refugee. It is only later, and insufficiently, that this idea of uniqueness was cruelly undermined as the public universe of refugees expanded to include Kosovars in the UK, Hmong in Minnesota, Serbs in Australia, Indian refugees from Uganda in Mississippi, Russian Jews in New York, Cubans in Florida. This remapping of populations should change many people's sense of self, but I'm not certain that it does so adequately for me or for others similarly placed.

The world is so full of refugees now (or at least it seems that way because of the emphasis in public discourse) that my very own history is being redefined for me by events of the late twentieth and early twenty-first centuries. Nations, belligerents, even nature itself, conspire to make my condition—born in one country, citizen of another—more a matter of course than the exception. Identity—its definition, its meaning, its relationship to power and history and family and religion—this is what populates novels by young writers from India, films from Iran, music from everywhere. So why can't I indulge myself in trying to measure my own? I have an American name and what now looks like a long American history. I'm virtually monolingual. I lead a privileged life. But within this envelope of identity is my Austrian birth, my derived and distinctive practice of Jewishness, and a kind of puzzling quirkiness that may be attributable to these mildly subordinated themes. My brand of self includes some odd and contradictory elements: anti-authoritarianism, anti-foundationalism, a habit of creating new things (ideas, institutions, fabrications) to prove that I exist, a mild sense of responsibility to participate in healing the world, a need to avoid conflict, one eye out for opportunities to escape if necessary, a penchant for hard work but not taking myself seriously, some underlying notion that all is illusion, that the world is a glittering Vienna about to dissolve, empty beneath the palaces and light.

Even in the face of the constancy of diasporas, it is hard to give up the notion of being part of a special story. Each aggregation of wandering and floating extensions has its overarching drama, patterns, often convertible into stereotypes, residuals or exaggerations of what went before. These matters of identity are especially vital in the battered suitcases of asylum where so little of material sustenance might be found. And in all migrations, the drama of expulsion is burnished by the circumstances of where people landed. In the case of the Jewish dispersion of the 1930s, so much turned on avenues of entry, the complex narrative of finding a place to go (including of course, the unusual place of Palestine as alternative homeland). And much turned, as well, on exacting particulars of individual family circumstances: how old the exiles were, who and how much they lost, how much they were professionally, personally and psychologically prepared to gain, how coherent was the residual family unit and the economic conditions it faced. One way to ask how much of an Austrian I am is to ask with whom I identify, what strangers, who has my sympathies, and with whom I empathize. On the whole, I do not think of myself as a citizen or descendant of the musical Vienna or the cultural Vienna, the painterly Vienna, the psychoanalytical Vienna or the imperial Vienna. I buy a VHS of Strauss's *Die Fledermaus* in German for my mother or go to the Neue Gallerie in New York City, and realize that I am supposed to sense something in my cultural nerve-endings. But, at times, I feel closer to Harlem, home of persistent refugees, puzzled by centuries of flight, poverty, resettlement, redefinition. I identify with corners of striving such as Edgware Road in London, where there is a string of Lebanese cafes. I have gone around to them at night, where middle-aged men sit at tables, smoking feverishly, sucking at their hookahs. I imagine them, in my mind's eye, plotting for their return to Lebanon. The markets are filled with Lebanese foods, gleaming, dripping masses of shawarma, lamb and chicken. The newspaper stands have only Middle Eastern newspapers, the streets women wearing burkas and men in sheikh's clothing. I envy slightly their capacity to carry their homelands with them, to have so intensely recreated it in the land to which they have come. There's something appealing about this quality of group-ness, but it is not mine. If I empathize, it is only from a distance, as is the case with all empathy.

Truer refugees from Vienna (the refugees of my parents' cohort) are now a nearly extinct species. A few years ago, one could spot a table of ancient women, gossiping in German, at the café of the old Museum of Modern Art in New York after a walk among the paintings, or at a neighborhood food place in Forest Hills, Queens, Au Bon Pain or even Wendy's, converted by habit and clientele into a very pale imitation of a European gathering point, or with a croissant and coffee at a restaurant in some artificial Florida. They, these artifacts of the past, exist now only in ones and twos, seriously endangered. Self-help associations, created in New York for the German and Austrian refugees of the 1930s, become more generalized spaces for the elderly from China and Korea and India. I, and those like me, more likely to still survive, are unrecognizable as refugees, no trace of accent or groping for vocabulary, no stride or walk characteristic of my origins, no style of clothes. I cannot find my cohort, or when I do the ties are tenuous and hard to develop.

Can it be said, then, that I was merely born in Austria? Is there really enough of a hold to think about, to reflect upon, to write about? One can say that in my case, birth plus seven months of infancy can hardly be determinative of anything. Yet I have to write down Vienna, Austria (I don't write Vienna, Germany, though that was my place of birth), on visa applications or landing cards and on document after document. And there is a set of more psychological questions. Through my childhood and even now I am asked "where are you from?" This question—usually meant as a simple introduction like "how are you"—occasionally had chilling self-evaluative consequences. Was there supposed to be a right answer to this question? The literal answer always seemed troublesome to me, not a sufficient picture, not a whole story, too misleading. It implied more of a connection between me and Europe than actually existed, something much too romantic and lovely (Vienna, the City of Dreams). Answering that I was from Vienna implied something erroneously grandiose, but hauntingly true. I was not wholly American, because of that answer, but that made me slightly uncomfortable. I *had* been born in Austria, and I was a refugee. I was different, but how?

CARING AND COMMITMENT

We, the children of the refugees, through our immersion into the language and cultural universe of our parents and their fellow immigrants, ...came to feel a certain nostalgia for places and lifeways that most of us had never known in their actual setting—places we encountered only as already nostalgic reconstructions in a situation of displacement. I now recognize that the nostalgic memory engendered in me and others of the "second generation" was indeed what might be identified as *rootless nostalgia—nostalgia about nostalgia*, so to speak. Unlike our parents' our nostalgia was not a classical *Heimweh*, "homesickness"—a pained longing for an estranged native land or lost origin. It was also certainly not a yearning for irretrievable youth—for some better time in a bygone past, or for a world of yesterday. But it did reflect a desire to establish a connection between a past known only secondhand and a lived present. It represented, I think, our need to repair the ruptured fabric of a painfully discontinuous, fragmentary history, even while acknowledging the impossibility of such reparation.

And yet, the "Over There" European world that was explicitly or implicitly conveyed to us children also came laced with strong feelings of ambivalence and negativity. The critical, negative memories carried by our parents and their fellow refugees—their anger, bitterness, insecurity, fright, and sense of estrangement were also transmitted to us. It couldn't have been otherwise. How would it have been possible for recent refugees from Nazi terror to insulate the traumatic aspects of their past experiences in Europe, and their intense fears about the future, from their children? The people around me, with whom I had the most intimate contact, spoke with one another and in my presence about cruelty and persecution, about the war and relatives left behind, about loss and destruction, about Nazis and Hitler. I was a young boy during the war years: certainly I didn't understand much of what they said at the time. But something about the darkness of their tone and the strain in their voices did not escape me. The truly frightening, violent, and sadistic aspects of a world reflected in whispered adult conversation became, for a child of refugees in the early 1940s, a shadow within my imagination. Europe, the culture of Europe, was a lost origin steeped in nostalgia. It was also a fount for my nightmares.[2]

I've been puzzled, from time to time, by a verbal usage that has plagued me much of my life. Often (even if it is not a true description of my sensations) I say, like Maurice Sendak's Pierre, that "I don't care" in a context where most normal people would express a strong feeling. My style is, more often than would be expected, one of indifference, remove, and distance. It's pretty obvious to me that I do care about many things, and I seem, objectively, to have worked hard at a variety of goals as if their accomplishment meant a great deal to me. But there is this existential gulf between doing and representing, perhaps between doing and thinking. I've justified this condition, in part, on the basis that my sense of the world and my place in it comes from my refugee-ness. I'm not sure this is fair, either to myself or to those for whom this appearance of indifference may be puzzling or harmful. But my hypothesis is that "caring" in the sense of the opposite of the child's phrase "I don't care" requires, as a basis, a structure of solidity in the world. And for some, me included, such a structure may not be present. Put differently, meaningfully caring (or the opposite of "not caring") might depend on a calculus of what events in the world are within one's potential control or where one's contribution might be sufficient to alter events in a material way.

---

2   Leo Spitzer, "Rootless Nostalgia: Vienna in La Paz, La Paz in Elsewhere," *Shofar: An Interdisciplinary Journal of Jewish Studies*, Vol. 19, No. 3, 12–13, Spring 2001.

The result of my "not caring" had implications for me that were both ontological and trivial. Take environmental concerns, for example, and the problems posed by global warming, warping a planet and endangering species, including humans. I have been able to rationalize my lack of passion about this issue by thinking of glacial time, or geological time and the built-in notion that species change, disappear, evolve, that there may be millions of years of ice and millions of years of fire. What privileges the specific moment in which we live and what conceit is involved in thinking of governing its duration? Or take a question my much younger and more engaged sister has put to me: why were you not on the streets in the 1960s, why were you not active? Why did you come to the edge of concern, why was there always a level of distance in your relationship to civil rights or the Vietnam War? I had the problem (at least I thought of it sometimes as a problem) of no battle being precisely mine, no context being absolutely my own. These worlds were occurring largely outside me and, in vital respects, were worlds that, if I affected them, if I engaged, I wanted to do so indirectly.

Another embodiment of the condition of "not caring" is a lack of attachment to things or objects, a willingness to give things up, surrender them, resign oneself to their absence. Many is the time I have been caught out, as it were, throwing away too many papers, not sorting, not valuing things properly before disposing of them. I gain strength from surrendering, a sort of personal reaction of non-violence to the banal violence of life. I can make a list of meaningful things that I have lost: the letter from my great-uncle A.D. Engelsman, to my parents that welcomed them to the United States saying what a great moment it must have been when the boy (me), had his first sight of the Statue of Liberty; a photo, the only one I had, of my grandmother who then died in the concentration camps, as she held me in Vienna, the only part of her visible being her hand against my body; an elaborate family tree worked out with my father, and in his writing, on a five-foot collage, carefully assembled; the electronic files of my family history using a software program I bought in a store, holding interviews I had with my mother, my now-dead cousin Herbert, and other relatives; a briefcase containing a collection of unique copies of writings of my son Gabriel. These are the dramatic examples. But "losing" things may be a way of life, a different way of valuing objects or experiences. Things are temporary. Their permanence, or the permanence of the relationship of thing to person (or even person to person) is an illusion. Even accumulations of things—even museums—are monuments, though unknowing ones—to transience.

The importance of self-reliance was drummed into me, undergirding the condition of not caring. It was my mother's mantra that I should be self-reliant, not dependent on anyone outside our nuclear family (and not always people within). One of the principles of refugee status was understanding the tricks that trust of others can play with one's life. My mother's religion of independence arose in large part from the fact that those around her in Austria or Slovakia, who should have cared for their fellows, and who might have professed loyalty, ended up killing or allowing killing to take place. It was the self, very narrowly expanded, in whom one must depend. "Caring," at least caring in the grandest and broadest sense, rests on a sense of broad mutual obligations, mutually entertained and mutually sustained. A story in which dependence on others is a necessary evil, to be reduced and circumscribed, is inconsistent with a story of charity.

On the other hand, this idea of "I don't care" fails adequately to explain me to myself. Once I was seized with the insight that I was like a small child in a sandbox. What is gratifying to such a child, and what, translated, was gratifying to me, was digging holes, packing sand in pails or boxes, and turning the containers over to create beautiful temporary structures. The child in the sandbox makes things feverishly and with intense pleasure, knowing (perhaps reveling in the fact) that they are ephemeral. It's the temporariness of the thing, as much as the fact that it was made, that is cause for rejoicing. The glory is in the process of assembling, and there is satisfaction too in the thrill of disappearance. Not yet is there the vanity of permanent accomplishment, the illusion of monument. This metaphor of the sandbox celebrates the habit of making things without attachment, and trying to pile them on, to make lots of them, the ideal of repetitive achievement without dependence. But this is achievement not for the amassing of wealth or of fame and reputation (though some equivalents exist even in the sandbox). It is a means of assuring that one exists. The metaphor is not wholly satisfactory for capturing my particular residue of diffidence. The act of merely imagining, thinking of connections, new formulations, varied and altered modes of composition—those are the aesthetic of the sandbox. But something in my particular refugee past made me act on these ideas, force them into the world. I created a trap for myself: sandbox into commitments, the imaginary into something else, something that entailed assumed, often gratuitously assumed, obligations or repercussions. And I always intensified the trap by making representations to others as to what would be done. And when my thoughts became entangled with another's reality and no longer purely the outflow of my imagination, I was caught or committed.

I could ask whether my distant idealized notion of Vienna—the Vienna before my birth—was that of this sandbox metaphor: a place of imaginings and pleasures without consequences. But sandboxes fade away, paradises are lost. One version of being Viennese was that you shouldn't wear your work on your sleeve. You shouldn't be preoccupied by money or achievement. You should think about the life of the Crown Prince and emulate it to some extent. When I was a child, I was told about a much-celebrated relative, my father's Uncle Emil, a paragon of sorts, a well-known fiaker driver, with his top hat and formal coat, much like successors in Central Park, in business with his horse and carriage. His task, highly appreciated, was to bring beauty and pleasure into people's existence. The Vienna of the fiaker driver should be a model for life. It was the operetta, not the opera, that should be the goal of existence. On the other hand, I had before me the plain fact that day-to-day existence was struggle, hard-scrabble struggle, and that life was a constant process of thinking and scheming. The myth of my refugee foundation was the focus, the source of sheer determination that allowed escape to be possible.

These aspects of self reflected a division between my father's view in which work, at best, was turned into a form of pleasure, and my mother's preoccupation with saving, storing, accumulating, ensuring command of all possible information so the best decision could be made, and coming up with constantly new ways of balancing all the family's needs and interests. I had to integrate a Vienna of pre-war carefree existence in which my mother's comforting Orthodoxy and my father's free and open secularity lay in uneasy conjunction.

CONFIDENCE MAN, FAITH HEALER

I read Thomas Mann's *Confessions of Felix Krull, Confidence Man* when I was about 16. I hardly recall the circumstances, only the impression. The essence of Krull, for me, was his supreme adaptability. He was able wholly to remake himself, even if as a total, amoral and overwhelming fraud. He gained for himself by playing on his understanding of the psychology of others. I seized on the book because there was something in Krull's attitude toward life that, in a radically exaggerated way, explained my own actions and yearnings. Though Krull was an inherently unappealing figure, on the border of criminality, his narrative reminded me of my efforts to determine who I was and could be. For Krull (and, perhaps for me as well), each step, each job, however menial, was a training ground for the psychological armament critical to his existence. He absorbed every detail necessary to perfect his expertise. He examined the details of the every day, learning the behavior of the crowd so he could turn it to his advantage. Krull epitomized the art of ingratiation. As a waiter, "how well I knew how to counsel the indecisive, employing the soft, discreetly reserved tone appropriate to my station, and how to avoid any appearance of indifference in arranging and serving the dishes, giving each motion the quality of loving personal service." Krull triumphed in his discovery of the universality of deception. "What unanimity in agreeing to let oneself be deceived! Here quite clearly there is in operation a general human need, implanted by God himself in human nature...." I loved Krull's pact with his friend, the Marquis de Venosta, to leave his job as an exploited waiter in a Paris hotel to take the young nobleman's place for a year and live the nobleman's life. He says of the transaction: "[I]t was the change and renewal of my worn-out self, the fact that I had been able to put off the old Adam and slip on a new, that gave me such a sense of fulfillment and happiness....[There was] a sort of emptying out of my inmost being—that is, I had to banish from my soul all memories that belonged to my no longer valid past."

My identification with Krull must have been just for this, not to banish a no longer valid past, but perhaps to overbuild a past that did not seem relevant; and, from that, the need for the skill to become someone else, to recognize qualities of human experience that allowed an ease of personal transformation. Krull was my adaptation of Horatio Alger. I could not embody the exact philosophy of Alger, because he was so very American and so devoid of irony. I would not and could not be Krull, but he was an appealing substitute. He was adjusting by manipulating reality, striving, seizing opportunities for himself, watching, quickly learning and processing information about the world. I could read into Felix Krull a common refugee experience of fabricating as part of the process of escape. I could have been finding my own substitute for the routinely dramatic refugee tales of the War, tales that have, at their heart, the resourcefulness to trick, tricking those particularly who were charged with maintaining order against deception. Perhaps I recognized that refugees frequently sought to mask their origins as part of the process of adjustment, to "slip on a new"—in Mann's phrase—as they tried to pick and choose what parts of their past they would keep and what discard.

Deception is probably too strong a word for what I felt when I was asked where I was from. But some elements of deception always seemed intrinsic in the transaction. Even as I was not really from Vienna, I was not really from anywhere else. Any answer disguised vital facts or overemphasized others. I could negotiate with the world in my imagination, pushing to become less Austrian and less superficially a refugee, in part through what might be called the Felix Krull factor. My adjustment was a kind of camouflage. I could engage in the process because of skills that flowed from my history, not from an authentic belonging. When I failed, or felt awkward, I could consider that it was because I had not learned, well enough, the lessons of Felix Krull.

Later in my life I was an undergraduate at Yale and a few fabulous events in my young life there reinforced my Krull-like tendencies. In 1959, when I was a college junior and full of intensity as a young writer at the college newspaper, I was seized by the fact that Castro had led the Cuban Revolution and that this could be my opportunity to be a journalistic star. I noticed that plane travel to Cuba had fallen precipitously and that college students who regularly would have gone to Cuba for spring vacation were threatening to stay away in droves. I wrote National Airlines and its principal stockholder, a Yale graduate named Juan Trippe, and convinced the company that a series of articles by me in the *Yale Daily* and in *Ivy Magazine* might do wonders for student ardor to visit Cuba despite the events there. They sent me a ticket. As I came off the plane in Havana, a minor official asked me whether I was there as part of the journalist delegation invited to observe the post-revolutionary trials in a vast Havana stadium as a guest of the government. I had read enough of Felix Krull to know that the right answer was yes.

Flush with my novel-like conquest, I sought additional proof I could carry off such a venture. Pan American Airlines had just introduced the 707 jet dramatically reducing travel time from Europe to the United States. Again, I wrote Trippe, also the Chairman of Pan American Airlines, proposing that I be flown to Paris and return, and that I write about the experience, with the tag line that I could be in Paris for lunch and be back in New Haven for an afternoon class. Much to my amazement, Pan Am agreed. Krull-like, I wanted to compound the achievement and I decided to try to stretch the trip so I could spend time in Russia and write from there. I persuaded Cosmos Travel, the agency that had a virtual monopoly on the Soviet trade, to underwrite my travel and help arrange a week's stay so I could write about the handful of American students then living in Moscow. I did all this, feeling, of course, triumphant when I succeeded, yet slightly and happily fraudulent.

I have found elements of myself, too, in several related literary creations: the title character of Brian Friel's "The Faith Healer," Sinclair Lewis's Elmer Gantry, and the figure played by Jason Robards in Eugene O'Neill's "The Ice Man Cometh." Krull deceived for his own sake. These others did something quite different. In Friel's play, for example, Frank Hardy trudges about his daily work, a drama of deliverance among the sick and the emotionally needy in Ireland, with a mutual dependence on belief. He is dependent on their faith that he can provide a cure for them and they are dependent on his capacity to engender that faith. He ultimately dies, killed by local toughs, when he no longer has the power to persuade, no longer has sufficient belief in himself to convince others. I remember being moved especially by Robards's portrayal of the itinerant figure in O'Neill who annually visits a bar and makes people feel so different about themselves that the effect lasts until he comes again. And then, all of a sudden, it doesn't work. "What did you do to the booze?" is the plaintive cry of the regulars deprived of their illusion.

I came to see myself not, as I did when I was younger, solely as Felix Krull, the Confidence Man, but more in the tradition of the Faith Healer. I wanted to orchestrate perceptions, use the leverage of accumulated efforts of others to reach some concerted goal. In 1982, I became dean of the very young Benjamin N. Cardozo School of Law in New York, a law school that had been in existence for just four years. I told the admissions director to put a sign high on the inside of her door so she could remember it: "This is a place where hopes become truths." I wanted people to believe that this law school could be a significant place and I wanted to act in such a way that it would come to be so. I had a variety of conceptions of what could be accomplished through a kind of group levitation: always on too little money and the wobbly force of an idea. In Los Angeles, where I lived before moving to New York, teaching law at UCLA, I invented, one day, the Jewish Television Network, not out of some degree of belief in its virtue, but, as it happened, because I wanted to levitate an idea. I wanted to take advantage of the need of a local cable company to increase subscribers and use an opportunity to convince them to dedicate time and resources to demonstrate (unsuccessfully, I believe) that cable television could, actually, develop programs for minority groups in which they would produce their own material and develop their own genres and formats. I sought a group of avid volunteers from around the city who would get equipment, produce programs, raise money, figure out promotion, and create something out of nothing. Why did I do this? I wanted to make a reality out of a kind of benign deception.

A metaphor occurred to me that has explanatory value. I saw the world around me as a series of jigsaw pieces from which I could help create an overall puzzle. No one could put together the old, pre-existing outcome. My immediate world was a series of oddly shaped elements that existed, seemingly at random, without any objective possibility that one piece had a relationship to other segments. Of course, there was a universe that had been fragmented into pieces. The inventive task—part deception, certainly creation—was to make a new aggregation, the finished product being the outcome of the pieces available.

Perhaps this idea of puzzles and pieces arises from the multi-colored puzzle-like representation of pre-War Europe. The Austro-Hungarian Empire was an array of irregular blocks that had patterns of consolidation and decomposition. My history, the history told to me, was the history of convulsions of pieces changing shapes, changing names. Once upon a time there was the Austro-Hungarian Empire, and it dissolved. Once upon a time, the Austro-Hungarian Empire provided security and opportunity for its Jewish subjects, but that vanished. In 1919, idealism, in the form of President Wilson's Fourteen Points, shook boundaries and transformed national and personal histories. Twenty years later, the rise of an obscure Austrian amateur artist led to further wild dislocations and the tumbling of our family. What can one, what did I, carry away from this? That arrangements, idealistic, historically determined, or personally constructed, are temporary? Or that it's all up for grabs, but elements of the outcome—at least in the short run—are not the product of chance, but of deliberate planning and manipulation? Or that it's all something of a joke, in which we don't quite know the punch line? The Faith Healer, the Confidence Man and the idealist in me were all paying attention. I could cherish the child in the sandbox, knowingly creating only temporary phenomena; I could be Felix Krull, at least in my heart, with a gulf between what was proclaimed and what was believed. I was the puzzle-maker, creating the puzzle of my own life.

2

LEAVING VIENNA, 1938–1939

My mother and father married on March 15, 1936. They settled on Tabor-strasse in a comfortable apartment that my father, semi-orphaned, had inherited from his uncle, Isidor Preis. During the first two years of their marriage, despite the anti-Semitism of much of Austrian politics, my parents had no thought of leaving Vienna. They were beginning a life, and notwithstanding what was going on in neighboring Germany, they did not consider that life in crisis. As they started a household together, they felt promise, not danger. My father saw himself as devolved from an old Burgenlander family in which at least one of my great grandfathers had been in the military. My father was a loyal citizen, a person of trust. He believed Austria would remain independent and free from Germany, as guaranteed by the Entente, and immune from the explicit, government-sponsored anti-Semitic violence of the Third Reich. My mother comfortably trusted in the continued familiarity of her deep network of relatives—parents, cousins, aunts, uncles, grandparents—spread through Vienna, Hungary and Slovakia.

I have scraps of evidence of these happier days of the 1930s and before. There are the photographs of my mother traveling around Europe with her mother. A sketchbook of delightful drawings shows Uncle Isidor poking fun at himself and his family on a splendid birthday. Somewhere, there is a special, satiric edition of the newspaper, published by my grand-father's small freight forwarding company, to celebrate his marriage to my grandmother. There are fading portraits, almost mocking in their reflection of a Jewish Vienna now incapable of reconstruction. These mementos were brought out from closets when, as I was growing up, my father and mother talked of their pre-War lives. My mother cherished her summers growing up in Nyitra, in Slovakia, my father his travels to the corners of the former Habsburg Empire on behalf of his family's spinning factories. They would love to recount adventures, sometimes lost romances, contra-dictions and eccentricities of families in the complexities of twentieth cen-tury change. What was harder was to talk with me, as a young boy grow-ing up, about the overwhelming, unbounded, unprecedented events of the period after March 1938. In the 1940s and early 1950s, their emphasis for me was on living a new life, even though it was impossible not, simul-taneously, to relive the old one. My sense of the time and circumstance is conditioned through the voices of others. With no memories of my own, and only a patchwork retelling by my parents, I was unclear how, if at all, to stake out my own entitlement or exact connection to the drama of es-cape or to the narrative of Viennese normalcy. I could not, and probably still cannot, tell what story is or should be my own and what I draw from others.

Once, I talked somewhat idly about issues of memory with Franz Al-lina, a refugee from Vienna and human rights activist in New York. My casualness with him arose because I thought of him as a contemporary, our stories similar, our lives forged in circumstances that were proximate. But he reacted quite sharply when I mentioned this notion of similarity. He re-minded me that he had been seven years (not seven months) old when he left Vienna and had been in a camp for much of the war. Mortified by the distance between his experience and my lack of one, the conversation cast doubt on my capacity to write about a subject that seared him and others so deeply, but was just a shadow for me.

I compensated for my own lack of direct observation by reading such memoirs or recollections as George Clare's *Last Waltz in Vienna*, David Weiss's *Reluctant Return*, Lore Segal's *Other People's Houses*, Richard Ber-czeller's *A Trip into the Blue* and Peter Gay's *My German Question* to find voices that would educate me and with whom I can, in my mind, converse.

I tried to learn from such stories what life in those critical days was like for my mother and father. These describe aspects of Vienna I cannot derive from memories and conversations: the complexities of class, the influence of urbanism and modernity in polarizing the population, the impact of World War I and the end of the Habsburg period. I cannot even enter the accounts of Austrian hatred. I knew of aphorisms and would repeat them, but not necessarily understand them (for example, the writer Alfred Polgar wrote that "[t]he Germans are first-class Nazis, but lousy anti-Semites, the Austrians are lousy Nazis, but by God what first class anti-Semites they are"). The consequence is that there's a bit of memory-acrobatics involved: my perceptions have become an amalgam of historical accounts, memoirs of authors, similarly and differently situated, and the stories of my mother and father (mostly my mother).

How this works might be illustrated by my interaction with Richard Berczeller's book. When I was about twelve, in 1950, my parents and I went to a refugee-packed Adirondacks resort for our annual vacation, and we met the Berczellers among the other Austrian and German guests. Some years later, Berczeller's stories about being a Jewish doctor in Austria and his escape were printed in the *New Yorker*, then collected in a book first published in 1963. I read stories from this book to my son when he was ten, and when I started writing about my own childhood, he reminded me how moved I had been by them.

In the title story, "A Trip into the Blue," Berczeller tells of a 1940 meeting in Paris with two brothers who, like him, were refugees from a country town in Austria. The boys had been the *feschen Brüder*, the "dashing brothers" in the hamlet. In the usual small talk of recollection that takes place among refugees, the doctor and his friends spoke of the *Reisen ins Blaue*, a special promotion that the Austrian railroads had developed to promote passenger traffic in the early 1930s. People would buy tickets for a Sunday adventure not knowing the destination nor the entertainment to be provided. The two brothers, as children, saved their money, got dressed up, and went to Vienna to get on the train for one of these weekend adventures. The blinds were drawn and the train pulled out of the station. When the train arrived at its surprise destination, townspeople in the square and bands playing, it turned out, embarrassingly, to be Eisenstadt, their very home town. The *feschen Brüder* wanted to disappear from sight.

After the war, Berczeller, now a doctor at Beth Israel in New York, had a patient from the region of the pair. He asked after them. The patient recounted a dramatic ending: "One day," the two brothers were arrested in France and, ultimately, "herded into a freight car headed for Auschwitz. As the SS troops lowered the sliding panels to lock them in, he heard Bruno say to Otto, "Well, another trip into the blue.""

I embraced this story for many reasons. I thought of my father as being, or wanting to be, at the same age as these boys, *fesch* or dashing. I thought of the nice pleasures of pre-war Vienna, the designed but humble fantasies. There was the way in which refugees remembered, got together, told stories about themselves and others. There were the various passages, stages of escape and recognition. And finally, of course, there was the irony, the way of wrapping tragedy in a turn of phrase, the bitterness of a certain kind of wit.

Other memoirs have augmented my practical void of personal remembrance. The book by George Clare fulfills a part of my memory that is always gnawing to be satisfied: how my parents negotiated the months of decision-making between the Anschluss and flight. Clare recreates the day-to-day anguish of his parents, whether to stay or leave, how to get an affidavit, how to adjust to the dramatically altered life of Vienna. Clare was younger than my father in 1938, still on the cusp of responsibility, not married, but old enough, and experienced enough to record the experiences of his family. He could measure and assess his father's desperation, the regrets about failure to act earlier, the depression and then intensity of action to find a solution and a means of leaving. I could try to imagine the various scenarios of his family—race to the border, leaving an aging parent behind, arrests and death—all reflected in tales of my relatives.

Reading David Weiss's memoir was significant for another reason. His story seemed more like mine would have been had I been a young boy born ten or twelve years earlier. He was not from Vienna, but from Wiener Neustadt, yet I identified more with his parents than with the Clares. He wrote intelligently and personally of the "bimodality of Jewish existence" of Austria in the 1930s, of being "a Jew in the full meaning of the word" and "a wildly patriotic Austrian." I could identify with his experiences as a teen-ager, trying to help his parents during the crises of forced departure. I could empathize with his perceptions of an increasingly anti-

Semitic school system. "It was said," Weiss wrote with a touch of irony, "that the Nazi movement was the uprising of physical education instructors; these were embittered men who had lost their military commissions with the monarchy's defeat at the hands of the international 'communist-capitalist cabal' and who entered their new profession as a stopgap until a greater Germany would once again recognize their worthiness."[1] I understood his ambivalence—central to his narrative—about returning to Austria, much, much later.

ANSCHLUSS AND AFTER

There were 220,000 Jews in Austria in 1938 at the time of the Anschluss. By 1940, only 50,000 remained. The Vienna of 1938 to 1939 was, for our family, as for so many others, a hiatus of anguished dispersal. For me, though only in retrospect, it was the narrow ledge of early identity and the fulcrum of my legal personality. In reconstructing that time—in thinking about major ways the critical months in 1938 and 1939 affected my parents (and through them me)—the inevitable markers, the markers in every memoir, are the Anschluss itself in March 1938 (the crossing of German forces into Austria), Kristallnacht in November, and, for each refugee, the moment of departure. This third date, in our case, was March 1939, when, finally extricated, we departed for France by train and then to New York by ship.

A radio broadcast by Chancellor Schuschnigg, on the evening of the Anschluss, is engraved in the memory of almost everyone who writes of the time. Here is an account of it (as I read the passage, I thought of our family, anxious in the Taborstrasse apartment):

> You remember that Chancellor Schuschnigg intended to hold a plebiscite in Austria about the Anschluss with Germany. This seemed to me encouraging, and we were all excited about the possible results. Then, on the Friday evening before it was to take place, as we were sitting and listening to music on the radio, the announcement came suddenly that the chancellor was going to make a speech to us. Immediately his

---

[1] David W. Weiss, *Reluctant Return. A Survivor's Journey to an Austrian Town.* Indiana University Press, 1999, p. 29.

voice followed, and you could tell from his tone that he was unusually strained and excited. Everybody knows the speech now—how he had "tried to find peace" for the country, and was now resigning to spare Austria violence and bloodshed. We were stunned. When he ended, the station started to play music again, and what they were playing was actually Haydn's *Kaiserquartett* which contains the melody of the Austrian national anthem...[2]

I approached the reality of the Anschluss from the recollections of Clare, in *Last Waltz in Vienna*. He asked:

Who were these men and women who surged through the streets, breaking into Jewish homes and shops, looting and stealing? What were they like, the creatures who dragged Jewish men, women and children out into the streets, forced them to their knees and ordered them to scrub away the Schuschnigg plebiscite slogans which had been painted on the pavements and the walls of houses, often by the very people who were now falling about with laughter as they watched their Jewish victim.[3] The city behaved like an aroused woman: vibrating, writhing, moaning and sighing lustfully for orgasm and release. This is not purple writing: it is an exact description of what Vienna was and felt like on Monday, 14 March 1938, as Hitler entered her.[4]

My mother, as I spoke with her in 2002, could finally talk with me more freely about these events, perhaps because I had prepared myself, and was not asking out of idleness or curiosity, but rather to elicit her specialized knowledge as part of accomplishing a specific task. On that day of Anschluss my mother was four months pregnant. What she saw then, she would see, in some form or other, every day for another year in Vienna, for five months while she was carrying a child and then seven months before we had all the permissions to leave. At any rate, she recalled March 11, the day of the Anschluss itself, with an eloquence of fresh remembrance:

---

[2] Mark M. Anderson (ed.) *Hitler's Exiles: Personal Stories of the Flight from Nazi Germany to America.* New York: The New Press, 1998, p. 84 (From the collection We Escaped, 1941).

[3] Ibid., pp. 223–224.

[4] Ibid., p. 230.

A dam broke, hell broke loose, repressed anti-Semitism poured forth. It was a Friday night. We always had dinner at my parents. Afterwards, we walked home, terrified. People were running through the streets like crazy. They were tramping like a herd of horses. When we came back to our flat in the Taborstrasse, the force of the crowd on the streets below was so great that the houses shook, and the very mirror on our wall fell and smashed. The Viennese showed a hatred accumulated over centuries. Men and women could harbor spite and anger and manifest it in many ways, but before this date they couldn't actually notoriously kill or plunder. Now, finally they could open their heart and do what they wanted to do: humiliate, rob, and persecute. The state wasn't in it before, endorsing, encouraging. Now there was official sanction. Almost every house suddenly had swastika flags. So great was the transformation of the city, so different was it from one day to the next, that it was like being transferred to the moon. People were like hyenas.[5]

The sheer madness of the time comes through in account after account. My father's uncle, Gabor Engelsman, was at his newspaper, where he was an editor, on the day of the Anschluss. It was a famous newspaper in Vienna, the *Sonn und Montag Zeitung*, that had a reputation for news and satire discomfiting to the Austrian authorities and hardly respectful of the Germans. (One example: in 1936, when Hans Knappertsbusch, a Munich opera conductor who opposed the Hitler regime, had his passport taken away so he could not fulfill foreign engagements, his friends turned to Engelsman's newspaper to gain favorable publicity.[6]) Now, with the Anschluss, Engelsman saw what would occur. The Germans were coming to arrest him. He jumped from a window in his apartment, one of many committing suicide in those weeks. His wife Helene witnessed it (she later died in Auschwitz).

The German policy of forcing a wholesale emigration of the Jews began. Vienna was now part of Greater Germany and so was Hitler's program of *Entjudung*, expelling the Jews. A few days after the Anschluss, one of the ambitious henchmen of the Security Service Branch of the SS, Adolph

---

[5]   Marjorie Perloff also quotes her mother on the Anschluss in her *The Vienna Paradox: A Memoir*, New York: New Directions, 2004, p. 35.

[6]   "Nazis Said to Curb Opera Conductor; Knappertsbusch of Munich Is Reported to Have Been Deprived of Passport. Has Opposed Hitlerites. Month's Sick Leave Extended—Friends Fear He Will Be Unable to Make Tour." Wireless to The New York Times; New York Times (1857-Current file), New York, NY; Jan 28, 1936.

Eichmann, was placed in charge of the emigration of Austrian Jews. This was his chance to demonstrate his skill, to succeed as a manager, to be effective. Eichmann put in place three basic principles: emigration was not a choice for Jews but compulsory; Jewish agencies involved with any aspect of emigration would have to operate through a centralized organization under the supervision of the Security Police; and emigrating Jews would be stripped of all their assets except the minimum amount of money required to enter the countries receiving them.[7] The strange mathematics of Annexation served as an additional reason for an accelerated policy of expulsion. Hitler had sworn to reduce the Jewish population in Germany, but now, with Anschluss, the number of Jews in Germany was even greater than it had been in 1933. Of the approximately 220,000 in Austria, 80 percent were in Vienna, and the efforts to drive Jews to leave needed to be intense and accelerated. The method used and perfected in Vienna was a "continuous and increasingly severe economic and physical persecution…its operations rationalized and centralized."[8] The obsession to gain the total departure of the Jewish community was complicated by the existence of obstacle after obstacle to the ability of individuals and families to comply.

In June of 1938, when my mother was seven months pregnant, this world of Vienna was described, with terrifying accuracy, in the *New York Times*. The specific physical violence, public humiliation and robberies in broad daylight that immediately followed Nazi entry had come to an end, the reporter said, and in its stead there was a "more considered policy" of "systematic maintenance of economic destruction and systematic panic for the whole Jewish population." Field Marshal Goering, arriving triumphantly in Vienna, had declared that Vienna should be made a German city and the Jews should be evicted within four years. But, as the journalist noted, "the action that has followed looks as if the local authority were trying to complete the ruin in four months."

With ingenious refinement of cynicism, a Jew whose property is confiscated is even required to pay an emigrant tax of one-fourth of the capital value of the confiscated property; so that if he has property

---

[7] Leo Spitzer, *Hotel Bolivia. The Culture of Memory in a Refuge from Nazism*. New York: Hill and Wang, 1999, pp. 30–31.

[8] Ibid.

abroad he must sell it in order to pay the tax before he can leave the country. By another ingenious refinement Jews are charged for the paint used in writing upon their premises that it is a Jewish business. Demoralization is pursued by constant arrest of the Jewish population. No specific charge is made, but men and women, young and old, are taken each day and each night from their houses or in the streets and carried off, the more fortunate to Austrian prisons, and the rest to Dachau and other concentration camps in Germany. …The authorities demand rapid and impossible emigration. The Jews would welcome evacuation, but for most it is impossible…[9]

Jewish families like mine moved from the already urgent panic of leaving to the desperate effort of getting the proper papers or assuring that all the papers were in place. We were fortunate. My parents immediately sought and obtained an affidavit of support from my father's US relatives and prepared a filing with the American Embassy for a visa. They simultaneously started the process of liquidating assets (or having them involuntarily liquidated). Their lives were infused with the tragic insanity of the process. In the months between Anschluss and my birth in August, my mother's best friend had left for Palestine. The sister of one of her friends had a child who was killed at birth. Three of my mother's obstetrician-doctors in succession had been arrested or injured because they were Jewish. My mother, in labor, took a taxi to the Auersperg sanitorium where she had arranged, finally, for a fourth. Outside the window of the hospital room where my mother recovered, the Hitler Jugend paraded, singing a newly popular song: "From the point of the knife, Jewish blood should spurt." My father arrived later in the day in the three-wheeled delivery vehicle of his Speditiongesellschaft, the family company that shipped goods within the city limits.

I was brought home to Taborstrasse for my circumcision. I could be taken, in the next weeks, for walks. But by police order my mother and her Jewish child were banned from most public parks and gardens. Had I been older, I would have been prohibited—as was my cousin Herbert—from using playing fields or wearing any of the traditional Austrian Al-

<hr>

[9]   "Vienna Nazis Widen Drive on Jews; Every Family Reported Suffering," *New York Times,* June 20, 1938, p.1.

pine clothing: lederhosen, dirndl, Alpine kneesocks, or styrian hats, clothes I would learn to know because my father packed and brought a few examples to the United States.

KRISTALLNACHT

Whatever the madness of German Vienna was for my parents that summer of my birth, it must have been intensified beyond the stretching point by Kristallnacht, November 10, 1938. On that night there was a general roundup of Jews in Vienna. Over 6,500 hundred Jews were arrested in the capital and about 1,200 in the rest of Austria. Of these, 3,700 hundred were sent to Dachau,[10] very few of whom returned.[11] One Gestapo agent in Vienna later reported that he and his colleagues had difficulty in preventing crowds from manhandling still more Jews. Almost 700 Viennese Jews committed suicide in the days and weeks following Kristallnacht. Another 27 were murdered and 88 seriously injured.[12] A reporter wrote, "Many of the actions carried out by the SA were nothing more than pure sadism." Jewish men who were arrested were placed in quickly appropriated buildings including the Spanish Riding School next to the Habsburg Hofburg Palace and forced to go without food and sleep.

My father was one of those arrested. The officials came to our apartment and took him away. In the moment or two before he was marched off, he wrote a short note to his American uncle in Oklahoma, asking him to take care of his wife and infant if he did not return. My father was held for twelve days in a facility in Kariangasse, in Vienna, a building once a school, now adapted to hold Jewish prisoners. Eichmann, himself, was there, determined to bring home personally the message that Jews must be removed from the city. Those days, and the nature of the beatings and mistreatment there, were never described to me by my father. I was told that he was re-

---

[10]   Gertrude Schneider, in her *Exile and Destruction: The Fate of Austrian Jews, 1938–1945* (Westport, CT: Praeger Publishers, 1995) traces who was sent to what destination from Austria. In an Appendix, on p. 169, she lists those who went to Dachau and Buchenwald. Between April 1938 and August 1939, 7,958 men were sent to Dachau. Of those about 5,000 were released. Of the approximately 3,000 who remained (including a few sent between 1942 and 1945), only 71 returned alive. Schneider publishes the names of the 71 who survived. One is Heinrich Preis, born 1923, a cousin of my father who later emigrated to Ecuador.

[11]   Bruce F. Pauley, *From Prejudice to Persecution: A History of Austrian Anti-Semitism*, University of North Carolina Press, 1992, p. 680.

[12]   Ibid.

leased on the condition that he sign a document agreeing to leave Austria within six weeks or be under Gestapo supervision if he did not. I was told another story, too. As he was questioned in the holding facility, his interrogator asked him who had inflicted the horrid bruises on his head and eye. Instinctively, he said "I hit myself." That answer satisfied those in power.

That defining night, Kristallnacht, the night of my father's arrest, my mother's parents came to our apartment. My mother took her infant son into the bathroom, locked the door, sat in the dark and cried. During the following days, while my father was imprisoned, we lived in the apartment of my mother's mother. My mother sought, desperately, to find out, during those long ten days, the whereabouts of my father, then to try to send him food or money or whatever he needed. I am certain her experience was like that of her counterpart who wrote of "long queues of women who did not know where their husbands or sons or brothers were... Wherever I went, they all said... that he would be back in a few days. But when I asked on what charge he had been arrested, they did not give me any answer. When I said, *Why, why?* They would shrug their shoulders. There had been no decree explaining the arrests, and nobody could give me any reasons."[13] Many were the wives searching for husbands, seeking information in endless lines, crowded in narrow corridors. "Nobody dared to speak. And when somehow they made only the slightest noise, some stupid young rascal would come and scream, 'If it isn't absolutely quiet here immediately, I'll throw this whole god-damned Jewish circus down the stairs!' Then the women would creep close to one another like frightened hens. They do not speak any longer, but looking at their faces one could see they were praying that they would succeed in helping their husbands..."[14]

My father's brief arrest was only a tiny detail in the sudden narrative of extinction of the Vienna that had been. Eichmann's thorough and systematic pressure to create total Jewish emigration from Vienna "came to be viewed with such great favor by high Nazi officials in Germany that his Austrian model served as the basis for the establishment there of an emigration center ground on similar principles, procedures and institutional arrangements."[15] When Hitler went through any street, no Jew could be

---

[13] Anderson (ed.) *Hitler's Exiles*, pp. 92–93.
[14] Ibid., p. 79.
[15] Spitzer, *Hotel Bolivia*, pp. 30–31.

near the window, and when he went through the street where we lived, an SS man was posted in our apartment building. Confiscation of Jewish homes had begun immediately after the Anschluss in March. What Germany had done over a five or six year period, in terms of a regime of legal exclusion and prohibition, Austrian laws and regulations and practices performed in a matter of months.

EXIT

The American Consul in Austria was responsible for the issuance of immigration visas to individuals and families who wanted to come to the United States for permanent residence. He had the unilateral life and death decision over whether an applicant was "admissible." There was no process for appeal. The Consul made the decision based on papers and a physical examination of each individual and family. Earlier in the 1930s, after the onset of the Depression, President Hoover had instructed American consuls to inquire carefully into the likelihood of prospective immigrants becoming public charges. The intensity of a humanitarian crisis did not alter the American concern that welfare burdens could inflate. Indeed, this was a preoccupation not only of the consular officials, but also of significant Jewish groups in the United States. They saw themselves as part of an immigration process in which families should quickly become self-sufficient, and certainly not a burden on the general public; they did not wish to open the way for a charge that poor Jewish families would be on the dole when or after they arrived.

As I tried to reconstruct this time, I looked for families who had come from Vienna and whose stories in some ways paralleled our own. I use Anne Hammermann as an example because she, as we did, settled in Cincinnati, Ohio. She and her sister were young women in Vienna who, after the Anschluss, had written blindly to as many people as possible in the United States with their surname. The Hammermann sisters hoped (this was not an uncommon response to the desperateness of the situation) that someone in the US might respond and provide the invaluable affidavit—warranting that the refugees would be supported if necessary—that was prerequisite for a visa. In fact, one unrelated Hammermann family in Brooklyn, recipient of a random letter, passed it on to their son, then a medical student in Cincinnati. He was living in a large boarding house and the owner of the house provided the Hammermann girls with the requisite guarantee; they received their papers, and arriving in Cincinnati, rented a room from him.[16]

Gaining an acceptable affidavit was a highly complex process. Not only was there the problem Anne Hammermann and so many others faced of finding a person willing to provide the requisite assurances, but there was the bureaucratic issue of how the precious document would be evaluated. There was help available from people like Cecilia Razovsky, a dedicated and extraordinary officer of one of the American groups that helped in getting the necessary paperwork and negotiating the US bureaucracy. She wrote, at the time: "For these affidavits the applicant is dependent upon the interest, ability and good-will of his American relatives, and any one who reads the list of documents which the Consuls insist must accompany the affidavits from the United States will understand why many applicants fearfully and hesitatingly write to their relatives for these papers."[17] The affidavit required what might be expected: name, address, citizenship, relationship, age, occupation or business or profession, number of dependents and the affiant's financial worth. But to be convincing these had to be supplemented by documentary proof of income, such as a certified copy of an income tax return or proof of employment or interest in a business.

Razovsky was a heartening and determined figure at an American organization called the National Coordinating Committee for Aid to Refugees and Emigrants Coming from Germany (later the National Refugee Service). She had worked with Jewish immigration questions most of her life and tried to explain to Jewish groups throughout the United States the difficulties departing Austrian and German Jews faced. About the period during which my father was coping with the US and German bureaucracy in Vienna, she wrote:

The applicant appears at the Consular Office. He is given instructions and information as to the documents he must bring to the Consul. ...

---

[16] Abraham J. Peck and Uri D. Herscher (eds.), *Queen City Refuge: An Oral History of Cincinnati's Jewish Refugees from Nazi Germany*, Springfield, NJ: Behrman House Publishing, 1989, pp. 73–74.

[17] Material for this section was found in the Archives of the National Refugee Service held at the Center for Jewish History.

Before the applicant is prepared to come to the American consul with the documents requested of him, he must arrange to secure a passport from the German officials which will permit him to leave the country. To obtain this passport, it is necessary for him to pass through the hands of at least twenty-five different German governmental agencies or officials. In the course of this procedure the prospective immigrant parts with at least 80 percent of whatever fortune he has left after having paid the fine imposed upon all Jews in connection with the notorious Van Rath case, the "flight" or escape tax, and all the other "contributions" which must be made to various departments by Jews. This procedure is likely to cause a delay of several months.

In addition to this passport, the applicant must present to the American Consul in duplicate for every member of his family birth certificates; military certificates; police certificates, preferably from each city in which he has lived since his sixteenth birthday; marriage certificates; divorce and or death certificates...Finally he must have Affidavits of Support from relatives or friends in the United States to establish to the satisfaction of the American Consul that he and his family will not become public charges after their admission to the United States.

Cecilia Razovsky was writing about people like my father. He had acted quickly. He was fortunate to have supportive, cooperative and prosperous American relatives who understood well how to respond to the system. He initiated the process of applying for a visa very soon after Anschluss. By the end of April 1938, he (and his mother and sister) had registered and therefore had a favorable or low number in the quota queue. My father's uncle, A.D. Engelsman, was a public-spirited, well established Oklahoma insurance executive and he sent the required affidavits as soon as they were requested. He was able to provide convincing and adequately documented affidavits for my parents, my father's sister and her family, and my mother's aunt and uncle. He provided them, also, to no avail, for my mother's parents whose fate was determined by a different and harsher quota. On July 11, 1938, with my birth imminent, he sent a confirming telegram both to the Consul General and to his sister (my grandmother) at Paracelsusgasse 7. It stated "my affidavit binding and effective...for new born child" in Vienna.

"Affidavit" became one of those talismans of survival, but not the only one. Obtaining an affidavit was a critical step in gaining freedom from present persecution and the impending fear of shipment to a concentration camp. For us it was a step toward getting to freedom. But the way was still filled with gigantic obstacles. Though my father had completed much of the process, there were still hurdles that required cooperation from the Consulate. Until July 1, 1938, the quota of greater Germany (as it was called) had not been completely filled. Prospective immigrants, if they were able to fulfill all the requirements and produce all the documents required, could expect a positive result, even if they confronted what seemed like unending delay. Cecilia Razovsky's comments underscore how much the Consul's individual judgment mattered (though in these particular matters we were mostly in the clear):

> The Consul may feel that the applicant is…not employable, or his relatives are too poor; they have not evinced enough interest in the applicant; they have too many responsibilities of their own in the United States; they have no bank account; they paid no income tax; their bank deposit was made at one time and not over an extended period of time; the mortgage on their property is too great; they are too distantly related to the applicant, or they have already given a number of affidavits for other relatives and they are assuming too much responsibility. So additional documents are required, such as a copy of the latest income tax statement, and a detailed letter from the American relatives specifying exactly what their plans are for the care of the family after their arrival. Cables and letters fly back and forth over a period of months.

Most of our papers were filed before July 1, but we had not received our visa and the tension was great. On September 9, 1938, my father wrote a polite but pleading letter to the American Vice Consul. He had to couch panic in the tone of obsequiousness that comes when peril faces bureaucratic authority:

> *I take the liberty to hand you enclosed copies of a part of your correspondence with my uncle…who has sent longtime ago the affidavit of support to the*

Consulate General. You will see from this letter that these affidavits are also valid for me and my wife and child. In the meantime my mother, Mrs. Gella Miller, received already the visa and has left Vienna. My sister and brother in law, Mr. and Mrs. Gustav Zellnik and their son Herbert Zellnik have received last week the invitation to call on your physician the 21st of September. Though we received our affidavits from the same sources and our applications were registered by Mr. Reinhart on the same day, the 29th of April, as those of the Zellniks, I have not received the invitation until now. I request you herewith to be so kind to invite me and my wife Alice Mary Preis for the same date as we belong all together and are also obliged to leave this country together.

Each day staying in Vienna was crisis-ridden, anticipation of disaster. And a month later, on November 10, 1938, in the whirlwind of Kristallnacht, my father was arrested, as I have already recounted. Twelve days later, when he was miraculously released, his efforts to gain the documentation to leave reached an even more frenzied pace. He obtained, from the German authorities, his passport on February 9, 1939. It was valid for one year. The all-important visa, issued by the United States, was stamped into the passport on February 14, 1939. Yet in the nightmare that was Vienna, obtaining the passport and the visa did not end the Kafka-like processes. The last necessary step was gaining an exit pass from the German authorities. My parents had booked a February passage to New York on the Aquitaine, but the requisite pass remained unissued. My father, the German officials asserted, had not given adequate proof of sale of stock in business that had already passed to Aryan hands. New responsibilities of proof, new legal requirements, were raised.

More than that, when the authorities denied us exit, they imposed an additional psychological and legal nightmare: they withheld their indispensable passport with its extraordinarily valuable, almost magical American visa. My father paid an agent, Mr. Zeisel, to bribe an SS officer to get our passport back. My mother had to line up, for days, in a tightly disciplined queue outside the Rothschild Palace to get the documents. Finally, all papers approved, the exit pass was issued. But the Aquitaine had already sailed.

Fortunately, my parents, documents in hand, gained berths on the Queen Mary, sailing from Cherbourg in mid-March, 1939. As the day of leaving approached, several crates of belongings were packed, to be

shipped to us in New York. We were assisted, even in these days, by workers at my father's forwarding firm, Brüder Preis Zoll und Speditionsge-
sellschaft. Family silver and jewels were mixed with linen. Paintings and
portraits were packed. Sixty years later (in 2002, actually), I saw "Nowhere in Africa," a film about a family that leaves Nazi Germany for Ke-
nya. The film shows packing crates—much like those our family used—
and the process of filling them. When I saw, in the film, the trunks of the
Redlichs on the sidewalk outside their door, it seemed the virtual simula-
crum of our own departure. A shot of the crate, alone, awaiting its fate on
a German street seemed an extraordinary image: as if objects, like people,
had become refugees subject to flight. And it was as if a photo of my past
had been miraculously set before me.

The packing and shipping done, our family took a train from Vienna
to Paris on March 15, 1939. We stayed in Paris for two days, went to Cherbourg and embarked. The Queen Mary had entered service in 1936 and
ours was one of the last passages before it was converted to a troop ship.
The liner had a small synagogue, designed by the architect, Cecil Jacob
Epril, lined with wood from Palestine. In the 1970s, when I lived in Los
Angeles, the Queen Mary, vessel of my deliverance, was permanently
docked near Long Beach as a tourist attraction. The synagogue's pews had
been salvaged by a Long Beach temple and the ark for the Torah had been
sent to the Magnes Museum in San Francisco. I bought a ticket to tour the
ship, but for me the visit was unsatisfactory. The Queen Mary had become
about luxury and transportation, not refuge. I could not adequately imagine its connection to my past.

3

MACON, GEORGIA

For the first year of our American life, from the spring of 1939 until June 1940, we lived in New York City. My father's mother and his other American relatives found a temporary apartment for us near the American Museum of Natural History on the Upper West Side, near the apartment of my grandmother and her husband and not too far from where I live now. In the summer of 1939, we moved to rooms in Lawrence, Long Island for its infant-friendly clean air, and then to Flushing, closer to the City, where a place was available on a short-term basis. But my parents, especially my mother, became restless in New York in those pre-War, tail-end days of the Depression. She was under an unbearable emotional strain. Her parents were stranded in Vienna, hostage to a US quota system that would have allowed her mother, but not her father (officially from Czechoslovakia, not Austria), to leave. They had decided to stay together, and in those days and the months afterwards, my mother must have been consumed with the frustrating and unsuccessful task of trying to extricate her parents from peril. It is hard to believe any living arrangement could be wholly adequate to mitigate the day in and day out powerlessness and uncertainty she faced concerning her mother and her father, leading to overpowering and dramatic swings of emotion.

Also important was the fact that job prospects in the New York region were not promising. My father was fairly young and flexible to a point. But he had the refugee's classic problem of self-definition. He had been a relatively secure, middle class owner of his family business in Vienna. He was not an entrepreneur who could recreate for himself in New York what he had inherited in Austria. Now he was close to poverty. He had found one job sorting rags, and another as a representative for a company selling waste textile material, but he could not sell enough to cover the $15 weekly advance made to him by his employer to purchase the goods to sell. Of course, he was relatively fortunate. He spoke English well, he was charming and he had a guarantee of a small amount of monthly support from A.D. Engelsman, his prosperous Oklahoma uncle. He knew he would not be out on the streets.

My mother's response to these circumstances was to advocate leaving New York, to strike out to a broader, more open United States. She was more of a risk-taker than my father. Our benefactor, the same A.D. Engelsman, had, almost a half-century before, moved from New York to Oklahoma and made his life there, and he vigorously supported my mother's view that my father should work outside the traditional refugee gathering points. And there were other factors. My mother's longing for her parents must have underscored a hurting difference between her situation and that of my father. His family was safely around him; my mother's closest family member, those she deeply and desperately loved, were trapped in Vienna and other of her close relatives in Czechoslovakia and Hungary. Perhaps she wanted to be in a place where the reminders of old ties would be diminished. Whatever the mixture between psychological and economic reasons, my parents started investigating opportunities to settle elsewhere in the United States.

RESETTLEMENT

In 1940, we boarded a train from New York City to Atlanta, Georgia. My father had the hint of potential employment and some promise of community support for his resettlement. We did not know that our final destination would be a town about 100 miles from Atlanta, called Macon, where we would stay until 1943 when our family would move to Cincinnati, Ohio. The shift to Georgia not only illuminated private tensions and adjustments. It was an example of how one family's circumstances meshed with historic attitudes in the Jewish world of New York and the United

States. And it illustrated the manner in which the American Jewish community managed the refugee influx. We had become part of a system, a modest machine designed to help immigrants to America find economic independence by distributing them far and wide throughout the country.

To understand this requires starting with segments of a different history, not of the Jews of Austria, but of the Jewish movers and shakers in the United States. In 1896, at the time of the great influx from Eastern Europe into New York, Jacob Riis had written about patterns of accommodation among the many ethnic groups of New York City. Already a noted photographer, sociologist and social worker, Riis studied ways in which groups were organized, supported themselves, set objectives for communal action. About the Jews, he wrote that "It is more than 240 years since the Jews were first admitted, by special license as it were, to the New Netherlands, on the express condition that 'the poor among them should not become a burden to the company or to the community, but be supported by their own nation,' and most loyally have they kept the compact that long since ceased to have force to bind."

What especially intrigued Riis was the growth within the Jewish community of social organizations that fulfilled this pledge (certainly not a legal obligation) and the motivation among its leaders to ensure that the Jewish poor would not be a public charge. Riis admired not only the existence of this web of interdependency, but the efficiency with which it operated. "The Jewish charities are supported with a generosity and managed with a success which Christians have good cause to envy. They are not run by boards of directors who stretch their legs under the table in the board room while they leave the actual management of affairs to paid superintendents and officials. The Jew as a charity director directs. And he brings to the management of his trust the same qualities of business sagacity, of unerring judgment and practical common sense with which he runs his store on Broadway. Naturally the result is the same."[1]

When our nuclear family decided to launch out, this time not from Vienna to the United States but beyond New York into a more unknown America, we were in the hands of just such a Jewish charity. It was probably the awkwardly named Resettlement Division of the National Coor-

---

[1] Jacob Riis, "The Jews of New York," *Review of Reviews* 13, 1896: 58–62.

dinating Committee for Aid to Refugees and Emigrants Coming from Germany. The group had been founded in June 1934, and I have already recounted its role in providing information on the complex process of preparing affidavits. It also helped in matching those trapped in Europe with sponsors in the United States and worked with federal agencies to facilitate entry, protesting when US enforcement methods were especially onerous and irrational (as was often the case). As the 1930's unfurled in all its complexity, as the number of refugees arriving in the United States mounted, relief agencies added another focus, the needs of those who had landed and could use support in settlement. A National Coordinating Committee Fund was established to assist organizations that "engaged or intend to engage in furnishing advice, information or guidance and financial or other assistance to Jewish or non-Jewish persons who have immigrated or intended to immigrate, or who are about to immigrate, to the United States of America, its territories or possessions, as refugees from political, religious or economic oppression." The range of participating agencies shows the pockets of interest: the Emergency Committee in Aid of Displaced Foreign Physicians, the Emergency Committee in Aid of Displaced German Scholars, the German Jewish Children's Aid and the Greater New York Coordinating Committee.

In October 1936, the board members of the Coordinating Committee started a program that would ultimately touch our lives. It was the project of resettling refugees away from New York. There was demand for such a service from the émigrés themselves. As my father would experience several years later, unemployment seemed most severe in the metropolis. Refugees were competing against one another for the few jobs available. Because we had relatives in New York and were from Vienna, the city was, otherwise, a logical place for us to be. But for many refugees, the very complexity of New York was an additional burden. Not all refugees were from Vienna, Berlin or Hamburg, and, for many of them, cosmopolitan New York contrasted greatly with the manner of living in the German town or city from which they had come.

There were other pressures. Community leaders and assistance agencies articulated the danger that a further massing of immigrants would enhance American anti-Semitism or inflame disruptive and divisive tendencies within New York City itself. Here, the late 1930s echoed concerns of the Jewish society of Riis's time when a huge wave of immigrants from Eastern Europe had arrived at New York harbors. Also, US entry into war had not yet occurred, and isolationism and even pro-German sentiment was still a force. Decisions of where to move and settle turned also on refugee dreams of what they might do in the future. As the 1940s arrived, these dreams changed. Earlier, some thought of the 1930s immigration as temporary. Jews from Antwerp and elsewhere refrained from teaching their children English because they thought it was only a matter of months before they would return to Belgium. By the late 1930s and early 1940s it became clear that almost none of the recent refugees would return to Europe. They would have to make lives in the United States.

As a result of these forces, William Rosenwald, Vice-Chairman of the National Coordinating Committee, took on the responsibility of forming a Resettlement Division. He had precedents. The idea of Jewish resettlement, of trying to reduce immigrant Jewish population density in New York City, was not a new one. The initial staff of the Resettlement Division was trained during the larger and earlier wave of migration from Eastern Europe at the turn of the century. Then, fears in the American Jewish community were more substantial and actions more radical. In 1907, for example, Jacob H. Schiff, one of the pillars of the older New York Jewish establishment, set up the Galveston Immigration Plan.[2] The idea was to encourage Jews coming from Eastern Europe and elsewhere to land in Texas, rather than in New York City, and to have them be dispersed from there (35 years later, when I was a young special assistant to Secretary of Labor W. Willard Wirtz in Washington, DC, I worked briefly on ways of "dispersing" to other parts of the United States Cuban refugees then overwhelming Miami).

This earlier resettlement effort had a more extensive administrative structure in Europe than would have been possible in the turmoil of the 1930s. The Galveston Plan faced far different political and economic factors than the refugee surge of the Nazi era. The Galveston Plan was built on an extensive interrelated system of persuasion, financing, and transportation. An Immigration Information Bureau sent pamphlets to Europe to convince

---

[2] Gary Dean Best, "Jacob H. Schiff's Galveston Movement: An Experiment in Immigration Deflection, 1907–1914," *American Jewish Archives* (April 1978): 48, 62, 78.

Russian Jews to come to the United States through Texas instead of New York City. The Jewish Territorial Organization there helped the Jewish emigrants get from Russia to Bremen in Germany. At that point, another entity, the Hilfsverein der Deutschen Juden, cared for the Jewish emigrants and put them on ships for Galveston. Once the Jews got to Texas, the Jewish Immigration Information Bureau provided them with initial financial assistance and dispersed them throughout communities in the United States.

An important and related part of this effort—the direct forerunner of our bureaucratic benefactors—was the Industrial Removal Office in New York City. It had been formed in 1901 by the United Hebrew Charities of New York, B'nai B'rith, the Baron de Hirsch Fund, and other Jewish immigrant aid agencies, and its central purpose was "the systematic diversion of Jewish immigrants, on an individual basis, to smaller Jewish communities throughout the United States."[3] The Removal Office aimed to lessen the burden of Jewish immigrants on charity organizations in New York City. It also was designed to provided a defensive answer if nativist arguments were raised emphasizing the local demographic implications of further immigration. The Galveston Plan lasted scarcely ten years. Convincing immigrants to come through Texas was a hard sell. Still, more than 10,000 Jews came through Galveston and were helped by the cadre of agencies. After 1914, the office in Galveston still functioned as a branch of the Industrial Removal Office to help Jewish immigrants who had already been brought over to America through the Galveston Immigration Plan.

The bureaucratic and organizational approach to dispersal in the late 1930s was different from that of the Galveston Plan. Because refugees were gasping to leave Europe, and were operating in as hostile an environment as possible, there could be little coordination of their manner of entry into the United States. And the numbers were far smaller. Entry was dispersed but by historical accident, not design: my great aunt, for example, Irene Goldstein, arrived in Seattle in 1940 after a trans-Siberian railroad trip and embarkation from Yokohama. But the main focus would be to encourage some refugees in New York to think about moving elsewhere. As in the earlier efforts, propaganda and persuasion played a role. My parents might have read a brochure published in the late 1930s by the

---

[3] See http://www.cjh.org/nhprc/JIIBGalveston02.html

National Coordinating Committee. It was entitled "New York Ist Gross, Amerika Ist Grösser (New York is Large, but the United States is Even More Spacious)." Capturing the mood of the time (and, to some extent, touching the concerns of my parents), the brochure evoked a refugee who "with unending patience, waits in New York for the 'job:"

> The terrible number of people without jobs, which he read about in Europe but did not believe, now strikes him before the eyes. He doubts that he will be able to make a living. He becomes tired, depressed. But does he have to reach that point...? Don't stay in New York, but go into the other states, the Middle West, the South, the Far West or New England. There you will find a home and a way of life for you and yours, there you will find the beginning and the way to the future. What about unemployment in the other States? The people in the smaller cities and towns are not yet so weary of the constant coming of the refugees; their relationship is closer and therefore the possibilities are better than in the metropolitan New York.[4]

The Resettlement Division inherited some of the staff as well as the philosophy of the Industrial Removal Office. The first director, for example, was Dr. Jacob Billkopf, who had been associated with the work of the Industrial Removal Office as well as the Galveston Bureau. Billkopf distinguished the problems of the new German and Austrian émigrés from the Jewish immigrants who had come to the United States earlier in the century. In his view, "this new immigrant was from a cultured, fairly well-to-do, middle-class group. The majority spoke English; had some funds, at least for temporary support; and was concentrated in the business and professional fields." Billkopf's main job, as he saw it, was to establish a network of leaders in cities and towns spread through the country. He would travel to the participating towns and cities and help locate possible jobs. He would wire the results of his meetings there to the New York office where his assistant would interview refugees and their families, write histories, choose nominees and provide summaries of his interviews for referral to the potential destination cities and towns.

---

[4]   Archives, Center for Jewish History.

Many of the records of these travels are at the archives of the American Jewish Historical Society and at Yivo (both located at the Center for Jewish History in New York). I looked through them as a way of understanding the machinery that affected us in 1940. While much of the later writing and scholarship about the refugees of the 1930s emphasizes the rescue and resettlement of the great physicians, scientists and writers coming from Germany and Austria, the day-in and day-out work, including the efforts concerning my father, dealt with more quotidian middle-class and worker families. Roughly a year before my father relocated to Georgia, the Coordinating Committee was making placements in Massachusetts and the notes of the administrators are illustrative. For example, in August 1939, I can find a report of several resettlements to practical, more or less entry-level jobs. Max Creutzberger was sent to the Fitchburg Shoe Company in Fitchburg, Joseph Seliger was assigned to the Commonwealth Plastic Company in Leominster, and Erwin Breth was placed at the Worcester Paper Box Company in Medford. In the Boston area, Mary Mohrer got a job at The Window Shop, Mrs. Isabella Karplus was employed at The Jack and Jill Shop, Isidor Silberstein at the Shapiro Drug Company in Nashua, New Hampshire. These were not the Albert Einsteins or "illustrious immigrants" who are among the legends of the decade.[5] (One German immigrant boy who *did* become such a legend was Henry Kissinger, then called Heinz. In 1938, the Kissinger family—the father had been a grocer in Germany—sought assistance, in New York, from the Resettlement Division. The Kissingers had arrived in New York on September 5, 1938 from Furth. Robert Dolins, a member of the Resettlement Committee's staff, wrote Evelyn Isaacs in Cincinnati, an employee of the United Jewish Social Agencies: "we are referring to you for assistance in employment or business placement, Mr. Louis Kissinger. Family is Louis, 51, Paula, 37, Heinz, 15 and Walter, 14…The family will be leaving for Cincinnati on November 20 at 4:05 p.m. and will arrive there on November 21 at 8:15").[6]

In 1937, with much effort and innumerable bureaucratic difficulties, about 225 families, totaling 400 individuals, had been resettled in various parts of the United States. The Resettlement Division of the Coordinating

---

[5] See, e.g. Laura Fermi, *Illustrious Immigrants: The Intellectual Migration from Europe 1930–1941,* Chicago: University of Chicago Press, 1968.

[6] Abraham Peck and Uri Herscher (eds.), *Queen City Refuge,* p. 52.

Committee, like all record keepers of their own actions, found their work successful, at least publicly: "Of this number, over 90 percent of the employable members were located in jobs within less than a month after their transfer from New York City. Approximately 50 percent of these were placed in employment related to the kind of work they had done abroad."

When Jacob Billkopf resigned as director in 1938 he was replaced by S.C. Kohs whose policies were in effect when my parents were mulling over their alternatives. Kohs realized that the pace of work needed to be intensified, partly because of the Austrian Anschluss. He could have been thinking of families like mine when he argued to his board of directors (the kind of efficient business leaders that Riis had earlier praised) that it was necessary to accelerate the group's efforts. To think in terms of resettling a few hundred individuals each year would not meet the needs created by the massive push of Jews from Europe. Kohs's analysis of immigration figures showed that approximately two-thirds of all émigrés entering the country were remaining in New York City. It was his view that if this concentration were allowed to continue, it would make for an "extremely unhealthy situation."

At the May 1938 meeting of the National Conference of Jewish Social Welfare, Kohs successfully pressed for a strengthened program. It included organization of the country on a regional basis, with the larger communities assuming responsibilities for surrounding smaller communities and rural regions; and the setting of a definite quota of émigrés which each region would be requested to absorb. These various regional committees would be expected to absorb one refugee family per thousand Jewish residents. To meet this expanded program, the Resettlement Division added to its staff two social workers and the Coordinating Committee took on renewed responsibility for interviewing and preparing individuals and families for resettlement. The aspirations were substantial: "5,000 Require Resettlement During Year, Plan for Regional Responsibility Adopted by Community Leaders" one newsletter of the period proclaimed. "A good resettlement program would be one of the best defensive measures against anti-Semitism." The office chided the cooperating groups in the field: "Many local committees tended to slow down the work of the national office of the Resettlement Division, rather than speed it, by insisting upon accepting refugees on a selective basis instead of being willing to take them as their cases reached the national office." This would have to be changed.[7]

By the end of 1937, there were almost 50 communities participating in the work of the Coordinating Committee. In 1938, the NCC had referred about 2,000 families to communities outside New York. About 800 families with about 1,250 people were resettled. Noteworthy was the fact that of these, 225 families had been receiving some form of relief in New York City. Our eventual passage to Georgia was part of this intensified but still difficult process. We had been swept up in the American and Jewish machinery of geographical dispersion.

MACON

Like all those helped by the Resettlement Process, our family had been offered various geographical and occupational alternatives. In our case, it came down to Corpus Christi, Texas or Atlanta, Georgia. Corpus Christi seemed, to my mother and father, too far, though tempting, and my parents selected the South over the Southwest. Georgia was a destination (as would have been Corpus Christi) that could help my mother make a more certain break with the past, allowed something closer to "forgetting" Vienna, though that was, of course, impossible. And, as war seemed imminent, there was a pragmatic reason Georgia seemed appealing. The textile companies were engaged in essential war production, contributing to the manufacture of uniforms; my father, so went the hope, could be deferred from the draft and stay with his wife and child.

As was their practice, the New York Coordinating Committee must have sent a request to its Atlanta counterpart, the Georgia Farm School and Resettlement Bureau, so named because among its goals was the recruitment of potential Jewish farmers in connection with a New Deal program. And, after determining that there might be an opportunity for my father, the New York office must have sent notice as to when we would arrive (sad to say I have not been able to find the records of the correspondence in the relevant archives). When our train pulled into the Atlanta rail-

---

7   Source N.C.C. Bulletin (News Letter of the National Coordinating Committee for Aid to Refugees and Emigrants Coming from Germany, vol. 1. no.1. September 12, 1938. (AJHS, Kohs papers), Center for Jewish History.

road station in June 1940, we were met by the representatives of the Jewish community and immediately taken to the rooming house of a Jewish family to spend the night. The Bureau helped my father find a job almost the next day. It had received a request from the Bibb Manufacturing Company in Macon, 100 miles away, for a textile engineer, skills my father had from Vienna. He went for an interview and was immediately accepted. Within the week, we had a new address, my father had a new job, and some of the complexities of life had, at least for the moment, been resolved.

We were the second refugee family from Europe to be resettled in Macon, more than the national "quota" would have demanded. Ultimately, the town would have a tiny colony with five and sometimes six such families. Nathan Kessler, a clockmaker from Vienna, was the pioneer, and he and his wife became my parents' best friends. When he first arrived in Macon and wore lederhosen, he was an object of public curiosity. In those days of 1940, there was a small Jewish community with two congregations, one Reform, one Orthodox. Despite my mother's traditional Orthodoxy, in this new environment a new approach could be given a chance. The members of the Reform Temple, located not too far from Cherry Street, where we were living, seemed more welcoming to the young refugee families. Yet the experiment ended badly. The modernity of Reform, the American and probably Southern quality of the service underscored for my mother how far removed she was from her protected and familiar Vienna. With everything else going on in her life, the extent of change and foreignness was too much for her. The Reform service caused her to break down in tears. She immediately left and never returned for religious services there (she participated actively, however, in the temple's community activities).

When we first settled in Macon, we felt fortunate to have a small room with a window and kitchen. My mother, in that initial home, put up a white sheet that stretched across the room, making a separate sleeping space for me. I remembered that arrangement when, several years later, my mother read a story to me about a child, in a similar arrangement, who awakened in horror to see a bear's shadow against the white, backlit divider. The happy ending in the story was that it was not really a bear, but a person whose shape made the fearful image. The window screen in the first Macon flat was often broken, mosquitoes would stream in, and mice came through the chimney. We soon moved to a better apartment,

47

across Cherry Street, to a place with three rooms, including adequate bedroom space, and we stayed there for the remainder of our Macon existence. Behind our yard—though it could have been miles away—were wooden houses where poor blacks lived, sang spirituals and had outside fires to keep them warm.

I am sure that my three years in Macon were important to me, though I am not able adequately to reconstruct them. As a father and grandfather, I am often astonished at how much of children's personalities and their attitude toward the world seems fixed so early in their lives. I might have skipped over these formative times in my life partly because I have so little personal memory of them (perhaps the formative times were my seven months in Vienna or the little more than a year in New York). Yet I know these years must be plumbed. The feelings and their impact have to be recreated from letters, circumstances, general writings, and photographs. How my young parents coped with the very specific and harsh complexities of their transition from Austria to the United States affected me in ways muffled by time. I can repeat the stories I was told about these early years in Macon or absorbed over the years. But what I would really like to know was how my father adjusted to this new environment and how it affected him. And what I wanted to know even more was how my mother, so torn about her parents' still pending status, went about her daily life, protecting me, if she could, from her own emotional turmoil. My father has died, and my mother still cannot discuss these questions, so I can never fully discover the answers. But, while writing this book, I found a set of letters that are partial witness, letters that my mother wrote from Macon to her aunt Irene Goldstein with whom she was extremely close and who had just recently arrived in the United States. In them, she reported many of her feelings. When Irene died, these letters made their way, with her heavy Cuban-made furniture, to my mother's basement in Forest Hills.

Though only in Macon for a matter of months, she urged her aunt to join her. "I think it would be much better for you," she wrote Irene (in German) in early November 1940, to settle in Macon rather than go to New York City. "Life is less expensive and the opportunities to make money are better. We have our own apartment now and have purchased furniture. I could buy a bed that opens and closes and we could live together here until you find something. There is kashruth and an Orthodox temple." A week later on November 11, she balanced her earlier enthusiasm with caution: "I wouldn't be annoyed if you went somewhere other than Macon. No one knows where good fortune is to be found. We came here by chance. As if we were blind, we traveled to Atlanta and the Jewish Council then brought us here to Macon. Should we look for a job for Alfred [her aunt's husband] here? They would take him, perhaps, in a Jewish department store or factory. The job would pay 11–12 dollars a week. Alfred would learn the American mentality and he wouldn't have to live off his capital. Next week I could speak with the Committee that occupies itself with getting positions for refugees."

My mother dreamed of starting a small business and sought to persuade her aunt to join her in the effort. Doing so would redefine our family. It would provide a chance to add to savings (even in these hard times my mother was putting away small amounts of money each week), and try for a more prosperous life. My mother expressed this urge in a letter to her Aunt Irene in December 1940, showing, as well, how thoroughly she had considered what was at stake. "There is no doubt that labor is cheaper here and the climate is better and so it is more favorable for business. That is why the textile factories leave New England and Philadelphia and come to Georgia and Alabama. Please don't believe that I want to talk you into the rag business. It is certainly not easy. But you don't have to make a big investment and if you buy the rags from those who gather them, then sort and clean them employing a used machine, there is a market for waterproof roof covers and other applications. I know a potential partner and a yard where the materials could be stored, as we learn the business." My mother was momentarily persuasive: Irene and Alfred came to Macon from New York City. But the Georgia environment, to which my mother was adjusting herself, was too distant and difficult for the older Irene and Alfred. They did not think they could adapt. Besides, while they found a possible partner in Macon and tried to negotiate an arrangement, the percentage they would gain in the business was, they thought, too small. They returned to New York City where they would live for the rest of their lives. And my mother's hope to begin investing and building capital would have to wait another decade.

Our days in Macon were during the War, and my mother was proud of her work helping the Jewish boys from New York and elsewhere, often refugees themselves, who had enlisted or had been subject to the draft and were stationed there. A special USO-like canteen was established for Jewish young men. My mother found there an outlet for her energies, perhaps some notion of making a contribution, and certainly a link with a Jewish world, by participating in this effort. My father often took care of me while my mother went to serve food to these boys, even dance with them. Perhaps in association with black and white films of the 1940s, the romance of these USO moments lingered in my imagination. It was nourished by a photograph of my young mother helping to make young soldiers (not much younger than she was) feel at home. She described, in a letter to her aunt, how she divided tasks with her friend from Vienna, Mrs. Kessler. "The evenings are in our apartment. In the bedroom there is dancing and in the living room there's eating." Among the soldiers were refugees from Vienna, Cologne, Ulm, and Hamburg, "You can hardly imagine what happens here during a Saturday afternoon or Sunday. Weekdays after five, people come as well." She was particularly concerned about religious young soldiers. "There are around 10 Jewish boys at Camp Wheeler," she wrote in late 1941, "who are so Orthodox they haven't eaten any meat for three weeks. I will invite one or two of them every Sunday. All of them want a good Jewish home cooked meal. Thursday, a shochet [the person who supervises the appropriate slaughter of animals] was here from Atlanta. I already ordered beef and veal. I plan to bake two cakes, and I bought 25 pounds of pears for compote as well as potatoes, fresh carrots and honey."

The social relations between the few Jewish families in town and the young Jewish men in the military was close. The Kessler daughter, Emily, married a young Jewish German refugee who had been a soldier at Camp Wheeler. Many of the Jewish young girls in the town met matrimony in the same way. At least one sergeant must have had a crush on my 30-year-old mother: after he was shipped out, my mother received a box of candy with a heart painted on the outside. The gift was a practical joke. The Kesslers, our Viennese friends there, had arranged to have the package sent with a false return address. Of course, the times were pretty deadly serious. Because we had German passports, and Macon had active, important Army facilities (Camp Wheeler and an Air Force establishment at Robbins Field), we were required by the federal government to register with the government as "enemy aliens." After war was declared, our house was searched, and our binoculars confiscated (among the papers we have saved,

I have a typed letter, sent to my parents in Cincinnati in the early 1950s from the FBI office in Atlanta, asking if the government could keep or purchase the binoculars they had seized).

My father was probably the only Jewish employee among the hundreds at the Bibb Manufacturing Company. In a way, Macon was a company town, very much dominated by Bibb. When we arrived the president of Bibb assigned a person to show my parents around Macon and to help us find a place to live. He wanted us to know about the legacy of the Civil War, and he personally gave my parents their first Southern history lesson. The talk surprised my mother in the analogy he drew: the Northerners, in the Civil War, could be compared to Hitler in terms of Sherman's purposeful and willful destruction in his March to Atlanta. Some months after we settled in, a group from Bibb asked my mother to give her impressions—as an outsider, as a European—of Macon and Georgia. She gave a short speech in which she described what, for her, was an uncomfortable reminder of Vienna and the post-Anschluss treatment of the Jews, namely segregated park benches and the segregated water fountains. She spoke in a diplomatic way in a talk otherwise filled with praise for our hosts, and our status in the community remained intact.

There were opportunities for advancement and recognition at Bibb, but it proved not the ideal place for us. My father received increased responsibility and bonuses. He was liked by management and many of his fellow employees. But there were dangers too. One day, he tried to fix a moving part and his fingers were almost severed. That would have been just a passing accident, but an event more worrisome to my mother occurred soon after. My father criticized a worker for not properly cleaning a machine and the worker retaliated. He threw a heavy piece of machinery at my father, injuring him in his shoulder. When my father came home, my mother, whether over-reacting or not, read latent anti-Semitism into this incident and saw post-Anschluss Vienna before her eyes. On the spot she made up her mind that Bibb, and with it Macon, would have to be abandoned.

My mother's letters of this period, mostly to her Aunt Irene, now settled in New York, have a pattern. They tell of the daily activities in Macon, the price of food or clothing, how my father was progressing at Bibb Manufacturing, small vacations we took to nearby lakes, the comings and goings of young Jewish soldiers. She always had a line about me, telling whether I had had a slight sickness, what new words I was using, how I was adjusting to Macon, and describing new appliances that she bought. She wrote about my father's family and the advice that they gave her. But each letter, or almost every one, contained a plaintive and sometimes panicky note about her mother and her father trapped in Europe. She had to conduct her life in Macon, be a wife to my father and a mother to me. But each day she tried to do something that would make it likely that her parents could escape. And she tried to protect me from her anxieties. On March 27, 1941 she wrote:

> Today I sent what was required for the affidavit, but I had to leave the document with the notary and Harold had to be there, so, yet again, there was a delaying strategy. I had hoped to send the affidavit on Sunday with God's help. I have just received a letter from my mother in law and her husband. They write that the Jews in Slovakia must vacate their rooms and must move to the ghetto. Mueller says that his brother in Bratislava has already been moved. I am out of my mind about these developments (*ganz weg*). What will my parents do if they really have to leave Vienna? It would have been better for me to die there (*in Wien zu verekommen*), than always to exist with such trembling here. I have written in the affidavit that it could be used by mother alone [if she chooses to come without her husband]. I also wrote the Council in New York asking if my parents could come outside the quota, and what happens when one is rendered stateless because of the Hungarian quota. I haven't yet received any answer. Mama cannot make any effective queries in Vienna because they do not give any answers at the consulate. Where this will lead, I have no sense. Monroe is so sweet. He always wants to console me (*trösten*).

A few months later, her parents, as my mother feared, had to leave Vienna for Slovakia. She wrote Aunt Irene on May 21, 1941 as follows:

> I received a letter from Mama on May 2, saying that on May 15 she will go to Nytra (in Slovakia). She sold the dining room set. I can feel with what a heavy heart she must have done that. It is not a minor thing what she has to endure. I wish she wouldn't be so attached to her things.

I have a letter she wrote her aunt on February 13, 1942 describing her mother's condition and her own growing desperation:

Mama laments that she is so cut off from the outside world (*Aussenwelt*). She is always in the house on the Zobor. It is very cold and damp and when she goes out she wears a hood that Fraulein made out of Papa's winter coat material (*Wintermantelstoff*). My mother finds herself sometimes driven to despair. I can certainly understand this. If only summer were already here, then life would be somewhat easier for them.

On August 29, 1942:

I have constant and terrifying worries about my mother and, there is no rest or pleasure for me. I think of Mama always and the circumstances that bind her. I think of her when I eat, when I sleep, whatever I am doing. I cannot get any reliable information at all. News from Slovakia is discouraging. It is enough, often, to drive one crazy. Sometimes I am so nervous that the child, unfortunately, suffers as a result. I cannot summon up enough patience. And who knows what is happening with my other relatives. Visions of them are always in my mind.

I have only these fragments, merely fragments, from my mother's efforts to make a life in a town in Georgia while consumed with the fate of her parents in Vienna and Slovakia. I know my mother. She must have considered every possibility, everything that was remotely available to her in a world in which distance, borders, histories, time, mindless, hateful strategies, were conspiring against her lone efforts. Even then, and over time, she was amazingly resilient, but the burden of these moments was always with her, and the thoughts of her mother and father never subsided. In later years, I could see the outcroppings of her grief, in many ways, but most clearly during the four times each year that *yizkor* commands mourners to light a candle for those close to them who have died. One thing was certain: because my grandparents did not escape from Vienna, my mother did not either.

4

NEW YORK CITY

In Cincinnati, where I would come to live, and Macon, Georgia before that, our family was in a double exile. We were, of course, in a painful exile from Vienna; but we were also hundreds of miles from the center of our diaspora, New York City. After the war, in the 1940s and 1950s, there was no question of visiting Austria. The grinding facts of the 1930s were still too raw, too horrific. Austria was a site of tragic memory. One could associate with its past, not its future or its present. If there would be a place for recreating, aggregating and rebuilding the idea of Vienna, it would be in New York City where so many refugees lived. For us, and for many like us, New York was a homeland, the concentrated locus of Jewish-Viennese culture. It was there that we had relatives. A year after my mother and father had arrived in New York, they had restlessly left for a new economic life, temporarily in the South. But almost as soon as she left New York in 1940, my mother also dreamed of moving back.

New York was the source for information about refugee life, refugee aspirations, news about the missing, news about reparations, news about Austria. The *Aufbau*, published there, was the newspaper of German and Austrian Jewish refugees in the United States and for many throughout the refugee world. I didn't exactly read the *Aufbau*—it was in German only until the 1970s—but it entered my bloodstream by osmosis. I knew of its existence, its weekly arrival in our household; the importance it had for my parents. My father would sit in a chair in our various domiciles in Cincinnati and quietly read it. It would lie around the house like a friend. I could see it as a conscious and vital link to other families like ours, to men and women who wanted news about each other and about the things that they cared about. In the years after 1945, it was in the pages of the *Aufbau* that one looked for notices about family members who had been taken to camps, but might show up as displaced persons. The *Aufbau* was among the first newspapers to report on the death camps. After the war, many pages of each issue were devoted to search lists and death notices, including from members of our family. An example from an advertisement placed in 1946: "It has not been until now that we received the sad news that our dear parents, brother, sister, brother-in-law, sister-in-law, uncle and aunt, Hugo and Else Rohrbach, born Frank, formerly from F'urth, Bavaria, were gassed in Poland in 1942." I still have the invoice sent to my mother's aunt for $6 to run a search for members of the Ehrenfeld family. And I have the well-meaning, but cruelly misleading letter sent to my mother in November 1945 from a cousin, Frieda Wunsch, in Sydney. Wunsch wrote to say that her friend in Zurich, Grete Bergmann, had "managed to obtain the information that your mother is now living in Brunn (Bratislava). If I were you I would apply to the Jewish Community there. I hope you will have luck to find my dear aunt Hilda. Weeks ago, I found your address in *Aufbau* and wrote still in the same moment to you and so I hope you will already have got it."

Later, it was in the pages of the *Aufbau* that my parents and thousands like them gained knowledge of changed reparations policies by Austria and Germany. The *Aufbau* carried intelligent foreign policy discussions about Europe and the United States and the development of Israel. The *Aufbau* was an agent of identity. It was a demonstration of what Benedict Anderson meant, in his brilliant *Imagined Communities*, when he described the role of the newspaper in buttressing the cohesiveness of a diaspora.[1] The *Aufbau* could be purchased at every newsstand on the Upper West Side. It was a fixture at every coffee house frequented by refugees not only in New York (in the coffee houses of 72nd Street on the Upper West Side and 86th Street on the East) but in Buenos Aires, Quito, Sydney, Johan-

---

[1] Benedict Anderson, *Imagined Communities*, London: Verso, 1991.

56

nesburg, London, Los Angeles. The *Aufbau* was civilized Jewish Europe transplanted to New York. It was the guide to culture and patterns of adjustment. It was a social glue when the world was falling apart.

The cosmopolitan wit of the *Aufbau* carried my parents and others through hard times. One article from 1936, entitled "Ten Commandments for New Immigrants," captures the sardonic recognition of Austrian and German refugee personalities: "When you're invited for dinner," declared one "commandment," "make fun of the poor American cuisine, the cheap Woolworth knives, the poor table manners of the Americans who even cut their potatoes with a knife, and do not forget to mention that you used to have sterling silverware at home." "In every conversation," stated another, "make sure that you are the center of attention. Please tell your audience for hours and hours how well off you and your relatives were in Germany, do not forget to make a point that people in Germany know how to live better than the Americans do, and please don't forget to mention that the entire American culture has been imported from Europe."

VESTIGES

New York was where many of our most significant relatives lived. It was where my father's mother, Gella, was born and returned after her marriage, after the death of her husband, after the bringing up of two children in Vienna. It was the home of my mother's closest surviving relative, Irene Goldstein. My father's sister, Alice, and her family lived near New York. And New York was, for me, the site of an alternate history of my family life, because of a nineteenth-century migration of other relatives from Europe. New York was a place of stories, an incubus of relationships, a focused and intense place for remembrances. Nowhere else was home. New York was a place of vestiges, and it was through them, and the stories my parents told me about them, that much of my sense of Vienna emerged.

IRENE

Irene Goldstein was my great aunt, the only survivor, in the United States, of my mother's family. She was the link to the most Eden-like period of my mother's past, her summers in Slovakia. To my mother, she was cousin, sister, aunt, confidante. To me she was a surrogate grandparent. Irene and my grandmother, Hilda, had been sisters, in a large, traditional and important family in the provincial town of Nytra. Hilda was the first to move to Vienna. She had married Josef Diamant, a textile goods merchant who was from her home town. They settled in the capital and Irene, her younger sister, came to visit her frequently. On one such trip, she was introduced to a severe and serious man named Alfred Goldstein and they married when she was 30 in 1926. Both couples, the Diamants and the Goldsteins, lived in the fortress of Jewish Orthodoxy in Vienna's Jewish Second District.

Irene and Alfred remained longer in Vienna than we did. In 1940, quite late, they secured a visa to the US and were able to leave. Like us, they had been the beneficiaries of affidavits from my American great uncle A.D. Engelsman. Not by choice, as I have mentioned, they took the complicated Eastern route to freedom, journeying across Russia, to Japan, and then from Japan to the west coast of the United States. After this long trip they were greeted, on their arrival in Seattle, in November 1940 with this bit of advice from my father's New York relative, Ralph Engelsman: "As you have probably heard, New York is overcrowded with refugees, and there is great difficulty in getting established here." He cautioned them against spending "all the money necessary to come to New York under present conditions" and encouraged them to consult with the Jewish relief organizations helping to find jobs for refugees elsewhere in the country. The warning did not deter them. They had saved and secreted a little money and, still in Vienna, asked my mother how it could be preserved. She suggested that they send it for safekeeping to the Engelsmans and the nest egg, however small, emboldened them. After the very brief foray to Macon to the business venture with my mother, New York became their permanent home.

There, at the beginning, they struggled in the rag business. To supplement their income, Irene, clever and ambitious, learned to be a diamond cutter. She bought her own machine and worked as an independent contractor. After the War, the diamond business changed. Skills sufficient during a time of great demand were now inadequate, and, now, more professionalism than she had (or could master) was required. Flexible, responsive, alert to opportunities, she began working in the garment district fixing clasps on the backs of brassieres. Alfred and Irene shaped a life in the

Bronx, secure, not triumphant, enterprising but hugging the margin, engaging the world around them, but hardly released from their Central European past.

Every year after I was six, my parents and I spent a week in New York City living with Irene and her husband Alfred. Visiting them was like looking through a long telescope, far away to a different world, and absorbing and reveling in it. Our first trip to the Bronx was in the last year of World War II, and we came by train from Cincinnati. The Goldsteins lived at 1186 Grant Avenue in the Bronx, a street in which a block of attached two family houses were signs of aspiration in a sea of bulky apartment buildings. Grant was near, but not of, the Grand Concourse, the big Art Deco experiment in florid architecture and expansive style that was, still, a place for more middle class Jewish families. The neighborhood, around 186th Street, provided the thick urban experience of New York 40's imagery, the overpowering elevated subway, the intense struggles of massed refugee hustle and coping. For a young boy from Cincinnati, these summers provided a sharp contrast and a strong notion of some distant habit of home.

This two-family house where they lived was like no other, or so it seemed and still seems to me. The building was owned by a fiercely proud, highly esteemed *misnaged* (a movement of ultra-orthodox Jews who were opposed to mystical Chassidism), named Rabbi Baruch Rokeach, who lived upstairs with his family. But this capsule dramatically understates his dominance of the building and his personal and psychological occupation of its space. On the ground level, Irene and Alfred lived squeezed into two rooms; the apartment's living room and entry had been converted to a small synagogue, an intense shtiebel or place of public prayer. This shtiebel was a center of life in the neighborhood. Each morning at 6:30, old men and a few younger ones would shuffle in and say their morning prayers, wearing, on appropriate days, a tallis (creamy and fading prayer shawls, many brought from Europe) and putting on tefillin (the phylacterics that, according to Orthodox law, each Jewish male is obliged to place on his forehead and arm every morning save the Sabbath and special holidays). Each evening they would return for afternoon and evening services, establishing what became a familiar drone with a precise rhythm that permeated Irene and Alfred's living accommodations.

To get to the rooms of my relatives from the street, one had to pass through the austere space of the shul, past the chairs and tables arranged for study and prayer, past the simple but forbidding ark holding the Torah. When services were in session, I would either scurry through, avoiding the narrow section in the back where women could sit if and when any came, or I would go down dark steps into the basement and up another set to emerge in my Aunt's apartment. It was a custom, when the shul was empty, that I would kiss the tapestry covering the wooden ark. In the early mornings, if there were not ten men for a minyan, the required number for communal prayer, my father would be summoned from his bed. If that was not enough, I would sometimes be dispatched to the little street outside to collar someone passing by. I became used to the old men sighing and the daily lifting of the glass of schnapps with any excuse for celebration. I learned to carry the *pushta*, the brass vessel in which coins would be deposited to assist the poor (those poorer, even, than the members of the congregation).

Near the ark, at the front of the shul, was a doorway that led to the apartment: a small kitchen, a bathroom where the facilities never functioned properly, a dining room, and the Goldsteins' sleeping chamber. The rooms were dark, stuffed with large wooden furniture. I thought the massive carved armoires and other pieces had been shipped from Europe, but they were not. As part of a typically bizarre New York refugee story, the thick and ornate table and heavy cabinets had been made in Cuba and purchased there in the early 1940s by the sister of the upstairs Rebbetzin (the wife of Rabbi Rokeach) when she fled from Poland to Havana. Now they landed in New York and my clever aunt, seeing a bargain, purchased the set when she arrived on Grand Street. The furniture overwhelmed the room, crowding out space for maneuver.

When I visited, the immense table groaned with food, the vitrine was packed with European dishes and silver, the tables were covered with evidence of Irene and Alfred's most recent business efforts, and the long couch allowed me to sleep during long hours of talk in which the times and people in Vienna and Nytra and Budapest were discussed. Bottle after bottle of home-made muscatel would be produced. The meats, prepared in the Hungarian tradition, were rich and savory. There would be delicious salads and abundant servings of poppy-strudel and other cakes. Being with

Irene was of immense importance for my mother. She and Irene spoke not only of the past, of the farm in Nyitra, of each member of their family, but of the practical aspects of the present and the future. Ultimately, my father and I would escape from the intensity of these Ehrenfeld rooms for long walks in the neighborhood, going in and out of as many local news agents and candy stores as we could visit, buying newspapers, sometimes sneaking off for a brief meal at a not very kosher diner.

Irene was not particularly handsome. She was strong, loose cheeked, slightly bewhiskered. She was innately more beautiful than she exhibited to the outside world. She was not indifferent to her womanhood. Signs of it, small jewels, objects for the hair, excellent swaths of cloth, filled the apartment. Her clothes were fine but plain, purchased, certainly, because of their price, not their fashion. She made many of her dresses, using her skills as a seamstress. It was not her style to wear, as the upstairs Rebbetzin did, a wig or sheitel, to cover her hair when she went into the street. Irene was a highly observant, but not necessarily a profoundly religious person. Her husband, a workhorse of Orthodoxy, was a daily participant in Rabbi Rokeach's minyan. Irene maintained the discipline of Judaism completely and with total favor. But she did so as an extension of her environment at home in Vienna, and she was tolerant of my mother's pragmatic and laxer set of practices.

Throughout her life Irene worked, and after she was a diamond cutter and sewing machine operator, she helped her husband Alfred develop a small export-import business with counterparts in Japan. She had an unmistakable sense of duty and loyalty to the family. The rooms in the Bronx were an archaeology of her activities during her life in America. From her life as a seamstress, there were hooks and needles and other contraptions, as well as scraps of cloth and spindles of thread. From her life as a diamond cutter, there were loose and imperfect stones, gathered up and placed in tiny sacks. From the life of Irene and Alfred as export-import agents, there were tattered envelopes with foreign stamps exciting to my eye, samples of ladies' fans and other small objects that might be from China or Japan.

After Alfred's death, Irene took over the export business, at least to wind it down in an orderly way. My mother helped Irene write the necessary letters and think through strategies. In the 1950s, Irene, with an old friend from Vienna as a partner, began to buy real estate, large, rent-controlled, hard to manage apartment complexes in the Bronx. She taught my mother the economics of purchasing, managing and selling buildings (information my mother put to use wisely and almost immediately). After 1956, when my parents moved back to New York, the two women conspired daily.

During the time we lived in Cincinnati, the small apartment on Grant was our home in New York, where we slept, where we ate. For that intense week each year, I was bombarded with sensations of different claims to truth, new modes of living, intensified ideas of duty. Between 1945 and 1950, in the darkest economic days after the War, Irene sent money and care packages each week to her two surviving sisters and her surviving brother in Budapest. I learned to pack these boxes, neatly arranging foods and clothes and other small items. Another responsibility gained from our Bronx visits was to save ration stamps to be given to Rabbi Rokeach. He had a weakness for sugar cubes in his tea, and the allocation for his family was not sufficient to meet his voracious needs.

The impact of my annual visits to New York was enlarged because I was surprisingly close to two of the three children of Rabbi Rokeach: Shloimy, who was about my age, and Chaiku, a year or so younger. We each saw something exotic in the other. Shloimy wore tsisis, the halachically required tassels that show outside one's trousers. He had pais, the long sideburns and, of course, wore a yarmulke or skullcap at all times. There may have been boys like him in Cincinnati, but I had rarely seen them there. Beneath Shloimy's dedicated, religious life beat the heart of a regular young New York boy who wanted to play stoop ball endlessly, talk about sports, walk around the neighborhood. Beneath my secular, urban Cincinnati life, there was a curiosity about my friend, what he did, his mastery of baseball statistics, and how he was dealing with the world. We played and talked intensely together and we quizzed each other about our respective experiences. On a rare outing for Shloimy, my parents took us to Orchard Beach in the Bronx, where the paleness of his skin reflected his life of study. He was to be trained to be a great thinker, in the tradition of his father and his father's father before him. When he was about twelve years old, our friendship dissolved. He was obliged to devote himself to becoming a wise man, a leader, knowledgeable about the most exacting details of Talmudic instruction. His time of frivolity or detours was more or less over. I was as close as I could be as well to Chaiku. She was shy, with downward casting eyes and was frequently in the house with my aunt. One of her life tasks was taking care of her younger sister who was mentally retarded. I had a crush on Chaiku, as we used to say, when I was ten or so. I'm not sure of the extent to which her spiritual remove, her modesty and unattainability contributed to my feelings.

The Vienna of Grant Avenue was not the Vienna of my parents' life, not the urbane and sophisticated Vienna that was the passed-on public myth. But it was a Vienna rooted in the family network in Slovakia and Hungary. These visits to the Bronx were an immersion for me in a seemingly authentic past. Grant Avenue connected me to a world in which religious practices were engraved in the every day, in which rabbinical dynasties had meaning, in which the signs and customs of American desire—as I was learning them in Cincinnati—held little sway. The tastes, the smells, the density of Grant Avenue stayed with me as a different aesthetic and tied me to a longer history of refugee life in the United States. Did these visits make me more Viennese or more Austrian? Irene, and the dense combination of objects, flavors and reminiscences that were her apartment, allowed me to find a more complicated sense of self and origins, a richer Vienna, in a way, than the Vienna that was the City of Dreams. These times allowed me to appreciate, more readily, the decision of my son, Gabriel, very much later, to become a *ba'al teshuva,* a deeply orthodox person. Grant Avenue provided an alternative idea of what constituted a "normal" practice of life and Judaism that forever put our customs in Cincinnati and elsewhere in a new perspective. After the Bronx, I could see our family's religious habits as an ironic adaptation of a set of customs already modified in Vienna.

COUSIN

My only first cousin was Herbert Zellnik. He and his parents left Vienna at the same time we did. But he was eight in 1939, and this difference in ages, among other things, was one important determinant in our patterns of becoming American. Mainly he was a reference point for me. I could observe him, from time to time, or hear about him, and get a sense of his mode of adjustment, the extent to which he represented either Vienna of some sort, or a lack of it, what it meant for him to transact the process of assimilation.

The Zellnik–Price relationship was a stormy one. I thought of it when I read Isaac Bashevis Singer's *Shadows on the Hudson* many years later. The novel is about refugees from Poland on the Upper West Side of New York in the 1940s, living in the buildings we now occupy or pass by daily. For many of those inhabiting Singer's world, their lives in New York were intense continuations of the relations, conversations, animosities and romances that had occurred in Warsaw or Krakow or wherever they had lived prior to the War. The discourse between my parents and Herbert's was certainly a continuation of words and actions, insults and warmth that began in Vienna. Herbert's mother Alice was only three years older than my father, but had the visage and bearing of a somewhat dominating older sister. His father, my Uncle Gus, was a severe and exacting man, the son of the cantor and organist in Vienna's most important Neolog or "progressive" synagogue. Gus's profession in the United States was "consulting engineer," and he sought to make money by managing patents and advising companies on how better to organize their factories. My aunt Alice had been married and divorced very early in her life (a surprising and relatively innocuous secret that I did not fully comprehend as a child), and, at one time, in the late 1920s, before her marriage to Gus, had been sent from Vienna to Oklahoma, with the possibility of discovering an American life. Instead, after a short stay, she had returned to Austria.

After the death of my father's Uncle Isidor, in the early 1930s, the two brothers-in-law had jointly taken over the management of the family business, Brüder Preis. When my father married, the two Alices, my mother and my aunt, each fervently supported the point of view of her spouse. The short years before the Anschluss were somewhat rancorous with disputes about the course of the business. The controversies between them over management spilled into their personal lives, persisted as they left Vienna and came to New York, and then continued into the issue of claims for reparations for the business after the war. I never understood the details, but they were not so important as the existence and continued drama of the arguments. Even in the throes of leaving Vienna, the two families disputed who would take which possessions; who, for example would gain the valuable piano, or which part of Uncle Isidor's legacy of silver and china each should claim (if they could ever receive the shipment when it got to New York). Later, when my grandmother died, in New York, similar questions arose (which painting would go to whom, which letters, which mementos).

Herbert, as a reference point for me, was different from the few refugee children I knew in Cincinnati, at the South Warwick or in my classes at Avondale School and later, Walnut Hills High School. He differed, too, from what an older brother would have been. He represented a repository of some remote, not understood but common experience. He was my most solid connection with a child of the Viennese past who shared my history. Yet I don't recall talking with him about what his life was like there and of the thoughts that occupied him when he was required to leave. I never spoke with him about the complexities he might have had in adjusting to the new environment. Far more important was the fact that Herbert and I were bound in a way not of our choosing. We were, to some extent, competitive entrants in an unusual horse race: one vital aspect of how each family had fared in the sweepstakes of exile. Each family, of course, rejoiced in the achievements of the other. But each family closely and critically observed what was occurring in this other wing. This was underscored by the fact that we were (my sister was not born until 1949) each an only child, and a male child at that. Comparisons were rife, my mother harshly assessing the Zellniks and their economic and child-rearing practices. And I am sure that the Zellniks reciprocated, thinking that our branch of the family was beyond hope, off in Cincinnati, and that my mother was not instilling in me the right set of values, that my modest father was not doing the necessary things to advance.

In retrospect and understandably, Herbert was, much more than I, shaped by his Viennese heritage. But, at the same time, he seemed more forced into an American identity. His parents maintained the external trappings of Viennese life to a far greater extent than we did, partly because they lived in or near New York City. They went to concerts, they had a Bösendorfer piano (they prevailed on that score) imported from Vienna. Simultaneously, they were more ambitious for the visible signs of Americanization. My parents more persistently struggled to achieve economic stability, They were more significantly hewing to a continuing refugee path, still unsettled as to city or even region of the country. The Zellniks lived, when I visited them in my childhood, in a house—an actual private house—in Newburgh, New York (they moved later to Jackson Heights, in Queens, a short subway ride from Manhattan). I remember Herbert as doing things that 13 or 14-year-old American boys are supposed to do growing up: he made model airplanes and ships, he understood about fixing cars, and he had a hose to water the lawn (and he had a lawn to water).

The Zellniks seemed to know more about what was going on in the United States. I remember visiting them and hearing all about Dr. Carleton Fredericks, one of the first successful radio nutritionists, who had a detailed program about what one should eat to retain one's health. We didn't seem to know, even, that there was a problem that needed attention. One day, at the Zellniks for an afternoon tea, after they moved to Jackson Heights, the adults talked about Henry George and the Single Tax Movement popular in the nineteenth century. Henry George had been a visionary who claimed that government could and should support itself only by a tax on the appreciated value of land. It turned out that Gella had been a foot-soldier in the movement during or after her college years at Hunter in the 1880s. Her daughter, Alice, saw herself as an inheritor of these interests, someone whose salon was, in this way, part Vienna, and part old New York.

Perhaps it's a contradiction, but the Zellniks seemed both more Austrian and more American than we. True, they had a house, and sophistication about American political movements and were, in many ways, a continuation of my grandmother's American self. But their apartment in Jackson Heights was a small museum of a remembered Austrian life. Visits there were ritual occasions for silver Viennese sugar tongs and Viennese porcelain cups, Viennese pastries and Viennese formalities. Herbert and the Zellniks seemed closer, indeed close, to my grandmother, whom I hardly knew, but whom Herbert, of course, knew well both in Vienna and New York. From a distance, I was interested in who she was and her seemingly distant relationship to her children. My father seemed to have been closer to his governess and to his Uncle Isidor than to his mother. I am sure that my grandmother passed judgment on both Alices—her daughter, and her daughter-in law—but my mother took care to remove herself, by hundreds of miles, from the weight of her criticism. Gella's Americanizing hand must have always been felt by her daughter, and, through her, by Herbert.

If a competition existed between the two families and through them the two cousins, one could ask what criteria there were for measuring success. These criteria could be seen as a vocabulary of adjustment, a mode of assessing the balance between being Viennese and being American. One involved music. There the Zellniks far outstripped us. Music was part of the Zellnik household in a serious way. Herbert trained, and almost became, a concert pianist and was once engaged to be married to an accomplished professional performer. He met his actual wife-to-be at rehearsals of a Gilbert and Sullivan Society. Music was a mode—an important mode—of bridging the American and Viennese worlds, of recreating or continuing a European practice. As it turned out, not only was Herbert talented, but his two sons, David and Joseph, became composers (in the 1990s they wrote a musical, performed in workshops in New York, called City of Dreams, about the psycho-sexual history of Rudolf, the Habsburg Crown Prince, and his mistress with whom he had what appeared to be a mutual suicide pact). In contrast, my piano lessons with Mrs. Levy in the South Warwick apartments (she was a German refugee) were far less satisfying. I barely could master the metronome, much less the piano itself. I studied five or seven years, one day a week or more, at great sacrifice to my parents, but to little avail. We did not live in a world of serious performance and attendance at concerts. Our music from Vienna was sheet music of playful songs and Strauss waltzes and my father's eager banging away at the piano.

Each family, in its own way, must have felt itself superior when it came to the question of Jewishness. Ours was clearly more observant of Orthodox traditions. I was obedient, following in my mother's footsteps, but I experimented in finding my own balance between tradition and modernity (as if a balance were necessary). For the Zellniks religion played a far different role. They had started from a Viennese Neolog tradition from which ritual had largely been stripped as irrational. They could see their version of Jewishness as allowing them to come to grips with modernity, rejecting the insistences on difference that might have caused misunderstandings and prejudice in the past. They were of the view that religion was primarily a cultural phenomenon that could be shaped for such purposes as are warranted in the circumstances. I doubt that my Aunt Alice or Uncle Gus had much time or respect for my mother's struggle to define some corner in which ancient practices could be maintained and her fight to ensure that her son preserved a significant part of that tradition.

Educational achievement and inherent smarts was another measure. When I was about ten, Herbert went off to college, to Rennselaer Polytechnic Institute, eventually to become a nuclear engineer. This underscored, at the time, the distance between the Prices and the Zellniks. I was still at South Avondale School, still somewhat incorrigible, still a subject for discipline by the teachers and the principal. Herbert was a model and something of a reproach. To go to RPI, then to go off to get a doctorate at Michigan, to be a brilliant analyst, to be an engineer, to understand all that mathematics, to deal in the world of major corporations—that was achievement.

One thing that had never been clear to me was the legacy, for our family, of patterns of knowledge, culture and education in Vienna as experienced by our fathers. My father had not gone to university, but Herbert's father had done so. Somehow, in ways that still evade me, these differences in Vienna influenced the way the two of us were brought up in the United States. Herbert was destined to be an accomplished student and PhD. For me, a strong education was always an assumption, but the nature of my path and its ultimate reach was less predictable. We were not going to replicate, in my generation, the patterns of our parents, yet some elements of those tenuous antecedents were relevant.

Economic security and material achievements were a major measure of the differences between our families. My mother was big on saving, building for the future. The Zellniks were bigger on manifestation. We lived below our means, they lived above theirs. Our summer vacations were more modest than theirs. We went to the Bronx and to the Catskills. The Zellniks explored America, including its vast West. They wished to be abreast of the most recent developments, particularly culturally. We were indifferent. We underrepresented ourselves to the world around us. They put on airs, or at least that was my mother's view. We never had new furniture. They did. My mother used the Zellniks for constant instructional purposes. If *Struwwelpeter* was the text for learning manners and behavior, the Zellniks were the textbook for trying to understand the importance of conservative economic practice. We were refugees once; we could be refugees again. We were financially needy once, we could be financially needy again. In the issue of successful adaptation, this was not the only measure that mattered, for her, but it was close.

These are races—these intrafamilial competitions—that never end. They are assessed in marriages, in children, in grandchildren. The judges may have died or given up, even the horses may themselves have expired as has, sadly, my cousin Herbert; but the process of transition and its capacity to be evaluated, continue over time.

ENGELSMANS IN AMERICA

As a child and into teenagehood, I was consciously or subconsciously wrestling with what it meant to be emerging from the thin post-Viennese cocoon that was my parents' house into a much thicker American world. Obviously, change was inevitable and proper. It was inevitable because American society as a transforming culture was overpowering, and I and my family were more than willing. In the 1950s, without question, the dominant narrative was assimilation. This meant not necessarily "melting," but adapting and preserving (how many, and how dreary were the long articles on melting pot versus mosaic). For each refugee family, the terms of transformation were individually negotiated, the tenure of respect for the past mediated against the demands of the present and the hopes for the future. And this process of negotiation was influenced by available models of behavior.

For me, one such relevant model, in terms of my narrative sense of self, was the quite distinct and puzzling American branch of my father's family. These Engelsmans had given us affidavits and furnished financial support for us in the early days. They had played out most of their lives in New York (except for my grandmother who had gone to Vienna for a visit—and stayed—and her brother who moved to Oklahoma City just after the Territory had been "opened"). They had been in the United States for a long nineteenth and twentieth century generation or two and they exhibited, to me, a very advanced idea of being an American. They had never been, even approximately, refugees or immigrants.

The representative I knew best was my grandmother's nephew, Ralph Engelsman. He was the same generation and almost the same age as my father. But his life trajectory did not include being expelled from his native land. He was, it seemed to me, authentically American or as American as one could neatly imagine. He was a celebrated insurance executive; he helped develop and direct the War Bonds effort in Washington during World War II and had a sophisticated New York existence. His brother-in-law, Alan Barth, was a prominent author and editorial writer for the *Washington Post*. For me, Ralph was a remote tutor, his life an idea available to me through a side mirror as I grew up. His existence was some sort of opposite: comfortable wealth, leisure, a quality of being at home in American business, and an apparent effortlessness that was beyond assimilation.

Ralph was the son of Monroe Engelsman, for whom I had been named. Through Ralph, I could imagine an alternative story of my existence, a story that was somewhere in the back of my mind, namely that I was actually not fully and totally a refugee and that I was part of a family, even though a distant part, reasonably prosperous and adjusted, that had been in the United States for a very long and settled time.

The forebears of Ralph and this version of my American family were two brothers Engelsmann, Bernhard (born in Prussia, October 8, 1838, died in New York, September 20, 1897) and Gustave (born in Prussia three years earlier, March 17, 1835). (The name was spelled this way, or Engelsman as well). A group of New Yorkers had invited them, still in their twenties, to move to the United States as experts in a revolutionary technique for the education of young deaf-mutes. In 1857, a story appeared in the *New York Times* about them and the school they were about to launch. "The Messrs. Engelsmann have established at 28 West 27th Street an institution where they teach the deaf and dumb to express themselves in gutturals. The pupils comprehend with facility common words and phrases by observing movements of the lips, teeth and tongue of the speaker. This means of teaching the deaf and dumb is not by any means new; it was known and practiced in the seventeenth century. But for reasons that have not been well explained, it fell into disuse, and was recently revived. There are several schools in Europe like the one of the Messrs. Engelsmann."

The techniques of these precocious brothers became part of the history of education for the hearing-impaired in the United States. One insight into their role arises from an account of teaching at the Pennsylvania Institution for the Deaf and Dumb during its shift from dependence on the manual or Sicard system of instruction to an emphasis on cultivating speech articulation. In 1870, the Board of Directors of the Pennsylvania school, impressed by the reports of the success of the New York experiment, sent a committee to inspect the Engelsmanns' school. "This committee was so favorably impressed that upon its return it recommended that arrangements be at once made for giving instruction in articulation to all semi-mute and semi-deaf children. Miss Rebecca Cropper was sent to New York for instruction under Professor Bernhard Engelsmann, and upon her return was placed in charge of the articulation class. In 1876 Mr. Edward Crane, a pupil of Alexander Graham Bell, was placed at the head of the articulation department. The success attending this form of instruction was so marked that the Board was led to consider the advisability of introducing separate oral instruction for such pupils as retained a considerable command of speech, and, incidentally, as a means of testing the practicability of teaching speech to the congenitally deaf. When, therefore, the day-school was established it was decided to employ the oral method exclusively."[2]

I wish I knew more about these brothers. I want to know how they came to be interested in these methods of teaching the deaf in Germany, how they emerged from a deeply religious family, how they integrated into New York life. Of the two, I descend, not from Bernhard, who remained a bachelor, but from Gustave. It's hard for me to recognize that Gustave was my great-grandfather, so remote is his life in the United States from my own sense of my heritage. Indeed, I am creating this family as I research and write this manuscript. I discovered that of the four children born to Gustave and his wife Betty Rosenberg,[3] the oldest, Gabriel, was a distinguished academic. He graduated from City College in 1880 and was a learned scholar and a philologist.[4] The two other sons of Gustave and

---

[2] H. Van Allen, *A Brief History Of The Pennsylvania Institution For The Deaf And Dumb*, fn 50. A good account on the importance of school and training is "Deaf Mutes, Improved Methods of Instruction, The Institution on Broadway," *New York Times*, August 7, 1870 p. 5. See also J.F. Richmond, *New York and its Institutions, 1609–1872. A Library of information pertaining to the great metropolis, past and present*, New York: E.B. Treat, 1871, pp. 285–287.

[3] She was born June 15, 1843 and died May 2, 1887.

[4] According to the *American Jewish Yearbook, 1904–1905*, Gabriel Engelsman was Instructor in Classics, College City of New York. Born February 5, 1862, Maco, Hungary. Son of Gustave Engelsman and Betty Rosenberg. A. B., 1880, College City of New York. Pursued post-graduate course in Classical and Oriental Languages, Yale and Harvard Universities, 1880–1881; studied comparative philology and linguistics at Leipzig, Berlin, and Vienna; Ph.D., 1885, University of Vienna. Married Celestine Bader. Was private secretary to Rev. Dr. Adolf Jellinek, Vienna; assistant foreign editor New York

Betty were Adolph (A.D.) and Monroe, whose immediacy in my life was far greater. It was Adolph who ultimately provided us with the affidavits of support that allowed us to come to the United States. A.D. was born in Austria in 1865 (perhaps his mother had gone back to Austria to have him and Gabriel there), returned as an infant, and lived in New York[5] and, at some point, probably around 1889, moved to Oklahoma to make a career there in insurance and in oil. He was a civic figure in Oklahoma City, and the AZA chapter (a fraternal organization for young Jewish high school students) was named after him. A.D. was long a bachelor and did not get married until his sister, widowed early, married a second time.

Monroe, the first of Gustave and Betty's children born in the United States,[6] was in the jewelry business and also involved more widely in trade. In 1914, he was President and Manager of World Novelty Display, Inc., publishers and distributors at 71–73 Nassau Street near Wall Street.[7] More relevant to me (as I learned about him in my youth), he was a habitual writer. The archives of the *New York Times* include a Letter to the Editor from him on March 22, 1903 called "On the Status of the Negro." Monroe wrote, for reasons lost in history, that "The discussion of the Negro problem, which appears to be an absorbing topic...should rest until existing prejudice should have moderated through time and experience. There is a general lack of comprehension of the conditions to which the Negro must necessarily submit." He was not shy with his opinions. I have a pamphlet by Monroe, printed in 1912 and called "A Few Thoughts and Reminiscences." He was, by the looks of the pamphlet, frequently called upon to speak at funerals and liked writing about his philosophy of salesmanship. One essay is a eulogy to his brother Gabriel in which he included a riff on the family tradition: "The moulding of [Gabriel's] career can be greatly attributed to the influence and great efforts of his father who was (like his

---

Herald; revising editor Jewish Encyclopedia. Delivered course of 30 lectures on comparative philology with special reference to the modern languages at College City of New York, 1901–1902. Address: 232 W. 120th, New York. His wife was Celestine, who died on February 2, 1933. They had three children, Gustave, Edgar and Walter.

5   A.D. Engelsman was part of group called George White's Boys that had attended Grammar School No. 70 on the Upper East Side, E. 75th, and he returned to speak to a reunion at the school as reported in the *New York Times* on February 15, 1903.

6   He was born August 1, 1866 and died in August, 1937.

7   Back Page, Essays, by Monroe Engelsman (privately printed, 1912).

forefathers) a learned man, possessed of the noblest ideals of life. In fact the name of Engelsman is synonymous of the word teacher."[8]

The only daughter of Gustave and Betty was my grandmother. I know little about Gella's childhood, but she attended Hunter College (when it was a Normal School preparing women for careers in schools) and became a teacher. Shortly after graduating, she went on a trip to Vienna to visit her relatives there and fell in love with her cousin, Salomon Preis. They were married in 1899.[10] I have a photo of Salomon, the very handsome Viennese cousin, taken at his country house in the company of friends and family. He must have made a dashing impression on the young American girl. Twelve years after they married, he died, perhaps of the flu, perhaps of another illness, a tragedy, of course, not the least for my 6-year-old father. A.D., as successful older brother, insisted that Gella come to Oklahoma for a visit, and she did so, leaving her young son, my father, in Vienna. Possibly because of her children, Gella spurned the life of Oklahoma and New York, and soon returned to Vienna, where she remarried and stayed until she left, this time, in 1939, for refuge among her American brothers.

It is difficult for me to retrieve how Bernhard and Gustave adjusted to the United States in the mid-nineteenth century, what kind of family produced Gabriel, Adolph, Monroe and Gella, and, in some significant sense, produced me. I could look at change in profession, in status, in perception of the world. As to many of these factors, I'm impaired by lack of available information. They quickly became part of a rising middle class, as

---

[8] The eulogy also said: "At an early period of his life, he was an unusually young student in the City College of New York, where he manifested a great inclination towards mastering the ancient and modern languages, and before he received abroad the degree of Ph.D. he had acquired a great knowledge of the Sanskrit, Arabic, Persian, Turkish, Chinese and Hebrew languages, and also of Greek and Latin. Of the latter two languages, he was honored here by receiving the Greek and Latin medals, at the time he graduated from the City College of New York. He was also a good English, German, French and Spanish scholar. In other words, he was recognized as a great philologist; and through this proficiency he acquired and gained a better insight into religious, political and scientific history."

[9] Among my papers is the transcript of Gella's birth certificate prepared for the Austrian authorities at the time of her marriage to my grandfather in Vienna. She was born Cornelia Engelsmann on July 30, 1873 according to her wedding certificate. The certificate states that her mother was Betty Rosenberg Engelsmann, born in Nunkirchen (Funfkirchen), Hungary. The certificate lists her father with the occupation of Kassier or cashier. Her birth residence was 300 55th Street, not clear whether it is East or West in New York City. According to the certificate, Gella's mother was born June 15, 1843 and died May 2, 1887.

scholar or businessman. I'm naturally drawn to looking at their various approaches to being Jewish as a point of reference. A.D. was a stalwart of the Reform Temple in Oklahoma City and was instrumental in establishing a Reform outpost in late-nineteenth century Tulsa.[10] It is family gossip that the oldest son, the philologist Gabriel, married outside the faith. The other children, Monroe and Gella, seem to have embraced, either as an adjunct or a substitute for Jewish practice, the modern ideas of Ethical Culture and universalism. In one of Monroe's writings, he says, "in order to reach nearer to ethical and moral truths, we must put aside all traditional beliefs and accept only the beliefs which appeal to us as being reasonable, logical and comprehensible."

A central place in Monroe's pamphlet of essays is given to an article he had written on anti-Semitism, designed to attack prevailing ideas of prejudice. The essay tries to demonstrate that the Jews were not responsible for the crucifixion of Christ and draws on biblical texts to show the importance of Judaism for Christianity. In the essay, Monroe writes: "It is a positive fact that, notwithstanding the merit or worthiness of the individual Jew, he is socially ostracized by his Christian brethren. And when aspiring to some political position or responsibility, he is conscious of that feeling of anti-Semitism which prevails; and in consequence of that intolerance, the Jews are restrained from accepting or from obtaining any large share of great political responsibilities or honors." Printed together with the essay is a letter from Nathan Straus, the New York philanthropist and co-owner of Macy's, complimenting Monroe and ordering 100 copies of the essay. In a phrase that could have multiple interpretations, the letter says "It is gratifying to see Justice to the Jews advocated by one who does it from a sense of justice and not because he is one of their own."[11]

A.D. fathered no children. Gabriel's sons had children and grandchildren but I do not know much about them. So, for me, studying the chain of adjustment and change of this American cohort is tied to Monroe, his

---

[10] "Unlike Oklahoma City where Reform Jews were the first to organize, the Orthodox Jews led the way in Tulsa. The Reform Jews were not far behind. Rabbi Blatt [the Reform Rabbi in Oklahoma City] and A.D. Engelsman, an important communal and civic leader in Oklahoma City, aided and encouraged them." Henry J. Tobias, *The Jews in Oklahoma*, Norman: University of Oklahoma Press, 1981, p. 31.

[11] At the New York Public Library, the Dictionary Catalogue of the Research Libraries for 1912 reprints the card listing for Monroe Engelsman's 1912 pamphlet "anti-Semitism." The category marked at the bottom left of the card is Jews-Apologetics.

son Ralph, and Ralph's sons, Ralph Jr. and Alan. Ralph was born in 1899 and was in his mid 50s when I came to know him. His life was one that combined ease and profession in a way that was distant but intriguing to me. I could see Ralph as an important executive, very much emblematic of the 1940s and 1950s as I might have read his existence through the prism of Hollywood films. When Ralph was about 18, he left Townsend Harris High School, in Brooklyn, and enlisted in the Navy as the United States entered the First World War. When Monroe, his father, died, he was returned to civilian status as the sole surviving son.

Soon, he married Naomi Lauchheimer, important to my later imaginings, because it transformed Ralph into a figure within New York German-Jewish society. As I saw him through the corner of my growing-up eye, he represented something apart, apart certainly from our refugee existence, but apart, as well, from the typical patterns of mobility and achievement. Nao, as his wife was called, raised Ralph to a new level of social practice. In New York, in the 1930s and later, Ralph (I learned all this later) was part of the Akron Club, a group, including Richard Rodgers, that was involved in the making of Broadway musicals. He lived, at times, in Far Rockaway, with a country house in Maine, and, later, a swell apartment in New York. Ralph was a public business success. He was the subject of articles in the *New York Times*. In the enthusiastic language of industry friends writing after his death, he was "the Babe Ruth of ideas in the area of life insurance marketing." He was president of the Life Underwriters Association in the 1930s. He was the youngest member of the Million Dollar Roundtable, an elite within the industry. He was immensely successful in developing new plans and ideas for selling, so successful that he made a second fortune writing and consulting about the process of selling.[12]

Ralph absorbed a great deal from his father in terms of his facility with phrases, techniques, stories, anecdotes. When reading of Ralph's prowess, I could only think of Monroe's homilies and essays and stories about selling, and the reputation he seemed to nourish as a man who understood the psychology of the customer. When, in the 1940s, Ralph went to Washington to help establish the War Bonds Program, he used techniques from in-

---

[12] E.g. Vincent B. Coffin, and Ralph G. Engelsman, *Sensible Selling*. Indianapolis: Rough Notes, 1933.

surance marketing to promote the sale of these patriotic instruments. And then, when the war was over, he took the new techniques developed from the selling of War Bonds, like payroll deductions, and adapted them to increase the sale of life insurance policies.

Ralph was five years older than my father. When we lived in Lawrence, Long Island, fresh from Austria, my father unemployed in the Depression, the Engelsmans, with their two sons, were living in Far Rockaway, with a butler and maid. There was no sense of envy on my parents' part, but rather a feeling of gratitude. The degree to which the household of Ralph and Nao and their two sons maintained a religious tradition was minimal. In their household, none of the Jewish festivals or holy days was celebrated. Christmas was their family holiday. The Far Rockaway in which they lived had a large number of Jewish families, but the family did not participate in organized religious activities. When the family moved to Washington, during World War II, the boys went to a private high school, Landon, which had a strongly Christian, Southern and American culture. I did not have the vocabulary to understand the Engelsmans during my visits to New York as a child. By the time I began college at Yale, their existence seemed more normal to me. From the perspective of New Haven, the idea of the comfortable executive was virtually the 1950s norm.

At the end of 2002, I had lunch with Ralph Jr. to gain his musings on the times. We were about the same generation, with common antecedents in Europe, but with the extremely diverged lives of parents and grandparents. I was hoping I could see in his life things that might have occurred in mine had the turn of fate's screw been different. A few months before, I played a mental game, during a visit to Austria, looking around the U-Bahn and trying to see in 20-year-olds what I might have been had I grown up in Austria. Now, in Ralph, I could try to see (preposterously, of course) what my life would have been like had my American-born grandmother stayed in the US and not gone to Vienna.

Ralph Jr. gave me notes about his father's childhood and youth that surprised me. While I thought of his father as worldly and sophisticated (which he was), his in-laws considered that he married above his station. "I didn't know until the late 1940s that Ralph had never graduated from Townsend Harris High School and instead enlisted in the US Navy in

1917....Dad's father was a jeweler and relatively comfortable in the finan-cial sense, but not in the same category as the Laucheimers." Nao was the daughter of a wealthy New York family that owned real estate on the Up-per East Side, part of the German-Jewish inner-circle parochially called "Our Crowd." She had gone to Smith as an undergraduate, and Ralph, for all his suaveness, had never gone to college.

Ralph Jr.'s notes about his world of Jewishness were also illuminating. "In the summer we would go to the Woodmere Club, a Jewish golf, ten-nis and swimming establishment. We went to Kennebec, a Jewish camp in the Maine woods. These were in no way religious places, but places that at-tracted primarily Jewish families. In many ways this was a social pattern of the times; Jews were frequently excluded from country clubs and other so-cial settings and so set up their own places, where they were pretty much as exclusive as the white Anglo-Saxons." There were sentences from Ralph Jr's own stab at a memoir:

When I moved to Washington and entered a public junior high school, I was certainly conscious of the fact that I was Jewish, coming from a setting where almost all of my compatriots had similar backgrounds, I wasn't sure what being Jewish meant. One of my key desires was to blend in, be liked and not make waves. I'd been aware of anti-Sem-itism but never experienced it, and wanted to avoid it. I was 12 years old, hormones starting to run, and I didn't want to be thought of as different. At Alice Deal Junior High, I found myself between two worlds. My parents introduced me to a Jewish boys' club. I seemed to work both sides of the aisle so to speak, but I worried about it and ba-sically kept my Jewishness light under a bushel. When we moved back to New York after the War, my parents got me involved with dancing class and a Jewish social group. The group was primarily liberal and re-formed Jewish in background and I don't recall any connection to re-ligious training or a temple. I was not in denial, but certainly not tell-ing the world. Since this pattern worked I continued to follow it for many years to come. Looking back, I think that there was some justi-fication for this in that I had no religion to speak of, I didn't practice, so in many ways I was nothing, and confused about what a response should be that encompassed my experience.

When my father died in 1984, he was buried in the Engelsman family plot in the Hungarian Union Field Cemetery in Queens, acquired by Monroe and A.D. Engelsman in 1894. It is the burial place of the American side of my family, and it includes Bernhard, Gustave and his wife Betty, and three of their four children (Gabriel, Gella and Monroe). A.D. is buried in Oklahoma City.[13] I go to Hungarian Union Field Cemetery rarely, but I gaze around at the tombstones and think of how distant, but also how present for me is my American past, how loosely it lies in my own consciousness of myself. As a boy, a refugee with refugee parents, it was impossible to cleave to it, to produce a childhood in which I could construct myself as essentially American. But my life, oddly, has converged with this story. I could come to see my life trajectory as rooted in the United States with the accident that my grandmother was in Austria, married, stayed for 35 years and then, with her offspring and their families, returned to the United States when Hitler came to power.

---

[13]   The Hungarian Union Field Society was started in 1865 by 44 Hungarian immigrants who started acquiring land in 1867. The first burial of members of our family were Bette and Gustave in 1886 and Bernhard in 1897.

5

CINCINNATI, OHIO

From the time I was four until the time I was eighteen I lived in Cincinnati, Ohio. I did not know it then, but can see in retrospect what an ideal place it was for my basic education in becoming an American. It was there I fumbled with the questions of self, self and others, self and society. It was there that I had to try to figure out who my parents were, what institutions to respect and admire, how to define friends. It was there that I first wondered what it meant to come from Vienna to the United States, how Austrian I was, or Viennese, or American or Jewish. An essentially decent child and an assertive teen-ager, by the time I was in high school, I had seen many styles of adjusting refugee identities. I was fortunate to be in the Midwest, and I might have appreciated what Peter Gay later wrote of his good fortune to have settled as a refugee in Denver, Colorado, "far from the massive colonies of German refugees huddled together in New York and San Francisco."[1] Just as it made a difference to me to have American relatives, just as it made a difference to have left Vienna as an infant, it also was significant to have been brought up in Ohio rather than in the great metropolis where we had landed in 1939.

---

[1] Anderson, *Hitler's Exiles*, p. 333.

In the first years of our life in Cincinnati, the toll of the Holocaust on my mother's family became clear. She learned, finally, that her mother, Hilda, and her father Joseph, had been deported to Auschwitz and killed there. She had, of course, known that all of her aunts, uncles and first cousins (there were nine brothers and sisters in her mother's family) were at risk of death, but the extent of the grim reality rolled in, fact by awful fact, during 1945 and 1946. My mother's uncle (Hilda's oldest brother) Armin, his wife (Mitzi Gestetner) and their daughter Elizabeth who lived in Slovakia, had been deported to Auschwitz in 1942 at the same time as my grandparents. They were all killed. Hilda's oldest sister, Adele, was a survivor, but Adele's son Paul died in Auschwitz as did the wife and children of her son Bandi. My mother's aunt Margit (Braun) endured, living in Budapest, but her children, Edith and Imre, had been gassed. Another sister, Rozsi, was killed with her husband and their son, Bela, disappeared without a trace. Rozsi's daughter Judith was a survivor (and later moved to Palestine). A brother, Ignatz (and a sister Bianca), lived through the war in Budapest. Ignatz's daughter, Kato, escaped successfully into the fields as she was marched to Auschwitz and Bianca's daughter, Clari, survived as well. (I came to know both of them in later years). Hilda's youngest brother Eugene (Jenő) was hidden in a bathhouse in Budapest. His wife was in a labor camp in Czechoslovakia and his daughter kept by a hunter in Hungary (as a harsh postscript, the three—Jenő, his wife and daughter—were united after the war and Jenő and his wife had another child, a son named Milan. In 1951, the family was shot as they tried to walk across the border from Hungary to Austria fleeing Communism. Only the son, Milan, survived. He was adopted, became Milan Javor, and lives in Canada).

For me, and much later for my sister, one consequence of this gruesome history was juxtaposing the conventional theater of Cincinnati life and the drama my mother had to internalize. A key to this was the interaction between my mother and my father. My mother, understandably, would have sudden periods of depression or otherwise inexplicable rage. She would be easily excited at a slight to her, to me or to my father. My father became a peacemaker, a soother, a mediator, an avoider of conflict, qualities that very much influenced me. My mother prided herself on control, on coping, by herself, with the emotional demands placed on her by the destruction of so many of her family.

These years, while I was rising through childhood and adolescence in Cincinnati, my father was moving from age 35 to age 50. While I was scarcely aware of it, he was struggling with his identity at the same time I was defining myself. His personality, as a faithful employee, as well as husband and father, was being shaped. He was establishing his place in the workplace, defining his relationship with a distant mother in New York and his uncle A.D. in Oklahoma, while trying to help my mother deal with her sadness. Cincinnati provided the frame for these simultaneous and overlapping developments but always in the shadow of Vienna, of what it had been and how it had so violently and unexpectedly changed. Vienna and its consequences shaped his attitude toward his wife, his family, his job, his community. It affected the way I perceived him and, thus, the way I function in the world as an echo of him.

But still, the dominant frame was Cincinnati and a drilled-in context of American citizenship. Later, much of what I experienced would be the fodder for studies, as scholars (often refugees themselves) looked back on the lives of communities in the late 1940s and 1950s. Cincinnati had the strong underlay of citizenship (after all, it was named for the Roman Cincinnatus, the very incorporation of ideals of public dedication). But it also had the strains of race, class and economic transformation that made cities more complicated than appeared on the post-war surface. At one level, Cincinnati was about the grace of urban life. I doubt that I understood that Cincinnati was a place in which great families, over generations, had endowed civic treasures. But I began, just as an ordinary child, to wander among them. The city was the home of extensive parks and exceptional cultural institutions (the symphony, a large playhouse, a great zoological garden, and a beautiful art gallery). Around the time I was ten, I spent Sunday mornings studying mineralogy at a modest museum packed with stones and fossils that illustrated the prehistory of the region. Through the museum, I went on hikes to nearby Mount Baldy to collect additional specimens. I learned of the fantastic configurations, the Great Serpent Mound, that existed elsewhere in Ohio. There were storybook parts of my existence. When I was a small child, my mother took me to Fleischmann's Gardens, the former home of Charles Fleischmann, a typical Cincinnati leader, founder of the Fleischmann Yeast Company. The park had monumental ornamental iron gates topped with old-fashioned gaslight fixtures and a stone path flanked by holly trees that led down steps to an evergreen maze. As a child, I was mesmerized by the goldfish pond, by milkwoods and great cottonwood trees that exploded with fluff, by the ubiquity of grasshoppers, and by a mulberry tree, where I could hide, play with my friends and sing songs.

Over time, I was developing a bit of a civic life, in a Cincinnati way. I joined cub scouts and boy scouts, hiking groups and acting clubs, and I delivered newspapers. I was a soda jerk and started and ran a summer camp. I worked in summer stock, where I drove a truck, moved scenery, and chauffeured visiting actors. I mowed lawns. Later, in high school, I went for hay rides, ate at Frisch's Big Boy, and danced to fifties music. Cincinnati gave me an American youth. I didn't quite see that Cincinnati had invisible lines separating South Avondale from North Avondale, North Avondale from Bond Hill, Bond Hill from Roselawn, Roselawn from Amberly Village. Only on reflection did I realize how these neighborhoods accounted for fractures in American society, though it was probably not too long before I could see how this array of proximate communities posed ladders to some and barriers to others and how important it was to negotiate the distinctions.

There were close to a thousand German-Jewish (rarely Austrian) refugees in Cincinnati who had come in the period from 1935 to 1939. As was true in many exile communities, there was a social organization for the members of the group. For the refugees from the 1930s, in Cincinnati, it was the Gate Club, and my father was, at least for one year, an elected officer. I knew the community through its outings to local parks, such as Mt. Airy, where a field could be crowded with refugee families and their children, having a picnic, flying kites, having softball games, with the older men playing soccer. Vienna was not such a frequent point of origin: many of the refugee families to Cincinnati were from the Rhineland or Sudetenland, sponsored by Landsmänner of an earlier generation. One learned their tales, their pride and disappointments. On those fields of Mt. Airy, each immigrant family told a slightly different story, representing different pasts, reflecting different means, different ambitions, multiple threads of occupation and social arrangement.

That was one Cincinnati for me, but not its dominant side. The city was close to the once-significant frontier, bearing qualities of being Southern, and of being a border place. It once could have been defined as a river town, and the river still exerted some power over the physical space, the arrangement of downtown and the imagination. One of Cincinnati's most appealing features was taking a steamboat, the River Queen, up the Ohio to an amusement park (as I did, in the moonlight, on the evening of my high school prom). Kentucky, across the river, was a foreign country. Cincinnati was my classroom about ideals in politics and citizenship. It was governed by a Charter, benignly nonpartisan, that produced a largely liberal Republican ruling elite. The conscience of the city was the graciously named Murray Seasongood who had been mayor in the 1920s and whose legacy inspired idealistic sentiments. After he triumphed over a corrupt regime, he imposed a strong city-manager, apolitical administration. He proudly claimed that Cincinnati, during his administration, had been transformed from a rundown, shabby, despairing, boss-ridden city to a forward-looking, confident, clean and well-conducted municipal corporation. He summarized his work by saying that "in these two years we have seen the life of the city refreshed by the impulse flowing from the City Hall. A new courage has come to the people, and they go forward. The time may come when they will take a backward step ... but they will never go back all the way, for the hearts of the people beat to the tune of new ideals." We were urged to believe this idea of progress making its way in our urban life. I came to admire a Cincinnati of American nobility, of seeming patrician American heritage. I didn't know it then, of course, but roughly 20 years after I came to Cincinnati as a child, I would be working for Associate Justice Potter Stewart of the United States Supreme Court, who had been a member of the Cincinnati City Council and was an exemplar of Cincinnati's sense of civic responsibility.

My political maturation took place before the race riots of the 1960s, though the seeds of decay and frenzied race-based outmigration by whites was already taking place. Good government, I was taught to think, was not an oxymoron. As refugees we had before us this established civic life that, even if it did not embrace us, tolerated newcomers and seemed open to access. I must have made my own personal study of what it meant to be a refugee during this time. Not as a sociologist, not as an anthropologist, just as a nine or ten or 15-year-old boy trying to figure out where he fits in the world. I couldn't comprehend all of it then, of course, but, with the capacity of retrospect, a more defined picture emerges. I absorbed subtle distinctions that were emblems of place and status. These could be manifested through dress, or furnishings, or educational attainment; by marriage or friendship and, most pronouncedly, by moving from one house to another.

THE SOUTH WARWICK AND ROSELAWN

My cauldron for refugee life in Cincinnati was the apartment building where we lived from the time I was six until the time I was eleven. I remember the Warwick as a large, somewhat forbidding place. It was divided into two parts—the South and the North—and we lived in the South. The Warwick was faintly English in its architectural style, as the name implied. But its architectural husk obscured an elaborate network of complex and personal European alliances. The density of refugees in this apartment block made the Warwick a hothouse, a container of striving families, each of which was its own incubation unit.

Every child has his own mental map of the surroundings of his home, extensions of his family space. The Warwick was a fortress, in my memory, with an ill-maintained lawn in the back, sloping to a gravelly margin from which a steep and menacing hill emerged, covered with trees and snares, and capped with hostile forces (poor whites, people with whom we should not associate). Our lives inside were protected, but there were moral and physical hazards in the vicinity, tough boys who liked beating up obviously weaker kids, usually Jews (at least that was my belief). Treacherous tempters, representatives of threatening cultures, these boys also went to the White Castle, next door, where they ate hamburgers, treasures of America, but clearly off limits for me as violations of the laws of kashruth. Scattered along the hill there were strange structures that, in our imagination, might have been old and primitive prisons, or holding places for we knew not whom.

As one entered the South Warwick, marble steps led to three floors on the right and three floors to the left. We lived on the third floor on the left. So did another refugee family, the Kaelters. On the second floor there were three more refugee families: the Becks, the Oppenheims and the Raunheims. On the first floor were the Sasses and the Kramers (the father Leo, his wife Betty, their accent-plagued daughter Emily Ann, and Mrs.

Kramer's elderly mother). The Kramers, Kaelters, Sasses and Raunheims were from Germany, the Becks and Oppenheims from Czechoslovakia. We were the only family from Vienna. In the Warwick, in this instantly created village of past identities, refugee families were related by blood, by trade, by recently created or developed bonds. The building had its own refugee doctor (Dr. Abraham) and its own refugee piano teacher (Mrs. Levy). After the war, it had one Displaced Person, a woman who had been in the concentration camps, placed, when freed, in one of the transition camps by the Allies, and, ultimately, somehow adopted by an existing refugee family in the Warwick. She was disturbingly wan. She would occasionally visit our apartment, or I would see her, pallid, with her equally thin and sickly infant child.

My mother's closest friend in the Warwick was Mrs. Beck. The two of them shared joys and grief and the progress made and impediments faced by their husbands and their children. They gossiped about the other refugees in the building, and constituted a tiny Central European cabal in constant watch over the more snobbish German members of the building, or those too obviously upwardly mobile, too preoccupied with the next steps in Americanization. Both my mother and Mrs. Beck had worked as salesladies in Cincinnati, but they did not like the hours and the minor chances for advancement. For a time, the two of them had their own store on MacMillan Street, in what was then an Italian neighborhood about a fifteen minute bus ride from the Warwick. Their store, called the Gloria Shoppe, sold clothing and other sundries. It was a family affair: Mrs. Beck's husband, who was in the wholesale business, arranged for their inventory. While my mother was there, she arranged for me to be taken care of by another refugee family who lived a few blocks from the Warwick. Ultimately, the women decided that the business took too much time away from their children for what it produced and, after two seasons, they sold it.

While the adults of the Warwick were a big part of the cast of characters of my youth, I saw myself, mostly, in relation to the children of the refugees in the building. All of them, as it happened, were girls. Because my mother was so close to Mrs. Beck, I spent many evenings with her daughter Edith and Edith's cousin Ruth, each a half-generation older than I. Through them, I saw refugee struggling with courtship and refugee decisions about college, marriage and life. Edith's first serious boy-friend was a young man named Bill Cyrkin, significantly not the son of a refugee, who had a tiny shop that sold stamps and phonograph records. I used to go there after school to look through piles of material. I made my first major purchase from him, an ebony cabinet with a wind-up RCA Victrola. Edith and Bill did not marry. She became the wife, instead, of a responsible member of the Orthodox community and a pillar of Cincinnati Jewry (I've come to wonder about whether courtships by refugees are accentuated and intense stages in the process of assimilation or its rejection. Maybe it was for Edith; maybe later it was for me as well. Even today, on Sundays, I read the wedding announcements in the *New York Times*, and discuss them with my oldest friend and American Studies scholar Daniel Horowitz. Perhaps this is what I am looking for: signs of whom the refugee chooses, who chooses a refugee, and what attenuated part of refugee origin can be identified across the generations).

My closest peer in the South Warwick was Hanna Raunheim who lived downstairs from us. She was my age and went to the same elementary school and, from there, to the same high school. In my mind's eye, the Raunheims were more secure than we were, more knowing, more confident. In some murky way, I constantly compared myself and our family with the Raunheims. They were my main measure for trying to understand what it meant that some were German and we were Viennese. Also, I could begin to understand, by comparison, that though my father had been in business, he was not a businessman. I found out later that Hanna and her parents left Germany in November of 1939, lived in England for a few months and embarked for the United States in June 1940 (they sailed on the Cunard White Star Line's Scythia shortly before it was converted into a troopship). They lived in New York for several months, aided by the Jewish Agency, while Hanna's father looked for work. Like us, they were encouraged to leave the city and find opportunities elsewhere. Hanna's father researched opportunities in different states and thought that Ohio looked like a promising locus to make a new beginning. Of the three major cities in Ohio, he picked Cincinnati because he had a distant relative there. In Frankfurt, he had been involved in importing and exporting scrap metal, but in Cincinnati he became a traveling salesman, selling lines of costume jewelry through the Midwest. His wife had received a law degree in Germany, but, finding it impossible to get related work in the US, she eventually became a bookkeeper at Wise Temple, Cincinnati's major Reform synagogue (established with the goal of "molding Judaism to the times"). I had remembered the furniture in her apartment and compared it favorably to ours in terms of European influence. But Hanna told me that the Nazis had confiscated their container of furniture and belongings they had tried to send ahead. As a result, most of their furniture had come from a warehouse run by the Jewish Agency in Cincinnati.

For Mr. Raunheim, business was central to his existence. It was important that the Raunheims, unlike us, had been attracted to Cincinnati by specific elements of the German-Jewish community. They were much more tied to it, with geographical and cultural links to the previous generation of Jewish immigrants, families who had arrived in Cincinnati earlier and had established footholds in meat packing companies and other enterprises. Mine and Hanna's pattern of socialization differed. I was an awkward boy, prone to losing the coat off my back, not a leader in my group or an athlete, or particularly illustrious in our elementary school. Hanna was a very pretty girl, carefully dressed, socially adept, whose course through this critical part of life—defining one's possibilities as an American— would be affected by these characteristics. She seemed more confident, more capable of dealing with the transitions and adjustments that were required of us. (Not surprisingly, many Jewish girls of Cincinnati ended up marrying rabbinical students at Hebrew Union College. Hanna was one of them, and with her husband, Rabbi Mark Shapiro, helped shape a suburban congregation in Chicago.)

I could contrast myself, as well, with Marianne Kaelter, who lived on our floor, and whose pattern of assimilation and absorption was different still. Marianne was one year older than I; she was an athlete, and she seemed, at least to me, to be freer of the culture of the apartment building, with a different set of friends and already in a different (and more adjusted) league socially. Her parents' circle, though still within the German refugee community, was not so much centered on the Warwick. I hardly ever saw her as we were growing up. Much later in life she became mayor of a suburb of Cincinnati that was only farmland at the time we grew up and then a lawyer and assistant attorney general. "I learned to respect my parents and what they achieved," she told me when I was doing research for this book. "But at the time, as a young girl, I was embarrassed to have parents with a German accent. I did not want to be a foreigner with foreign parents." Her grandfather had been a chief rabbi in Danzig, and her uncle had been selected among top rabbinical students in Germany to participate in a special and vaunted program at Hebrew Union College in Cincinnati (designed to train a new generation of Reform rabbis for Germany if the War turned out sufficiently well). Because her uncle, Wolli Kaelter, was already in Ohio, her parents had come directly from Danzig to Cincinnati.

The Warwick, in ways that surely eluded many of us at the time, became a base point for its refugee families as they probed the space that was Cincinnati and America beyond. How these spaces were negotiated turned on many factors: the capacity to overcome or integrate the heavy baggage of the past, cultural background, saved wealth, pattern of ambition, physical health, ability to lose a confining accent, integration into the working world, the age of the children when they came to the Warwick, prospects for education and marriage. For most of the families, the Warwick (and one other building about five blocks north of us) was one step up from their initial housing in Cincinnati. We, for example, previously rented rooms from refugees of earlier crises and that pattern was common. The Kaelters had a slightly different story. Before they lived in the Warwick, Mrs. Kaelter was the caretaker for children of wealth in a large and beautiful home where the father had died and the mother was incapable, alone, of fulfilling parental duties. Strategies of advancement, change, improvement, all efforts to achieve a standard of living closer to the one in their European home, these were the agenda of all, debated within the bosom of the family, and to a lesser extent, among the floors of the Warwick. Hannah Raunheim later pointed out one rule to me about the Warwick crowd and others like us: those who left Europe before 1937, she said, came with funds as well as property; those, like us, who came in 1937–1939 were fortunate to leave with some goods, but no money; and those who came after 1940 came with just their lives and were fortunate to do so.

The Warwick—in these years—was a rich set of mysteries. In addition to the maids' rooms in the attic, relics of a more glorious past for the building, and massive lockers with unknown contents in the basement, there were, of course, families that were not Jewish. The most important to me, and to all the children, were a family called the Hagues. The Hagues had five daughters and, finally, one son. They were, for us, a living soap opera of what it meant to be an American family, a contradictory model of aspirations and dangers. They were always in and out of one scrape or another. They walked differently, they played differently. They bought different things from what we all bought. They had more fun. Each of the children from the refugee side of the building studied their habits and learned from them. Marianne became Alice Hague's best friend. We were warned against them from time to time by our parents as case studies of what we should avoid. But we also tried to understand and appreciate what it meant for the Hagues that they were free of any refugee identity. Alice's father was killed in an airplane accident, their lives changed and they moved from the building. When I was doing research for this memoir, I discovered that Alice had married James Lytle, descendant of one of Cincinnati's early leaders and for whom a small but elegant park was named in front of the Taft Museum. It was not only the refugees for whom Cincinnati was a structure for mobility.

The Warwick was my most intimate educational institution. I could watch the refugee children of the building as they each pursued their own path of moving from the network of the past into some network of the future. The Warwick was also a social place where my mother and father frequently invited friends, almost without exception refugees. The language of friendship at these events was more German than English. German records would be played, or Austrian and German music performed on the piano. One of my fondest memories was helping to assemble the appetizers for these parties, and these, for some reason, remain significant for me. My mother and I had a ritual, fixing open-faced sandwiches with Ritz crackers or white bread cut into squares. On top of the bread or cracker base, after they were buttered, we would arrange tiny pieces of lox, tomato, cheese, hard boiled eggs, and dabs of anchovy paste, always carefully rationing the amount. The crackers would have to be prepared in advance but there was always the danger that they would get soggy. For a special reminder of her Austro-Hungarian roots, my mother would mix a Liptauer, composed of Bryndza, a cheese made from sheep's milk, anchovies (or anchovy paste), caraway seeds, capers and paprika. I would love to blend the mixture and eat what was left in the mixing bowel. My mother would make a Guglhupf, a special Viennese cake using a fluted, spiral-patterned form that she had brought from Austria. Preparing for these evenings was important: it was about engaging with my mother, it was about my parents as hosts, it was about gathering together the remnants of a civilization in pain.

In 1949, my sister Vivian was born, and soon thereafter, when I was in the fifth grade, we moved to Roselawn, to a white stucco house, purchased for $13,000, with a walled patio in the middle and a large lawn behind. It was on Kenova Avenue, a name created by a real estate developer, an acronym for Kentucky, Ohio and Virginia. It was our move away from South Avondale, and we became, as it turned out, part of the massive migration of Jewish families from the inner city to the suburbs. For me, with a new school, a new environment, there was a totally changed atmosphere for the process of seeing myself. I was no longer a refugee child living among other refugee children. I had a bike, I would have a car, I would do suburban things, get suburban jobs, have a girlfriend, go to 50s drive-ins and drive-in theaters, dance to Elvis Presley and be moved by Bing Crosby.

SYNAGOGUES

Thinking back on Cincinnati and its role in the negotiation of my identity, religious schools and Jewish institutions loom larger than I would have expected. For some of my refugee peers, especially those where the family had decided that the goal for the children was to be "as American as you can be as quickly as possible," religion, at least Orthodoxy, was seen as a barrier. That was not true for us. At my mother's insistence, we kept a kosher home (with occasional breaches). But we were not unduly observant. We did not keep the Sabbath, and even the lighting of candles on Friday night was a private affair of my mother. Still our Jewishness, having been central to my mother's past, remained central to our present and would be an important part of the manner in which I would be constituted. I was always sent to some sort of religious school and made to see myself as belonging to a synagogue community. Paradoxically, belonging had its assimilating benefits. While these schools and institutions taught the history or practices of Judaism, they did so by finding and underscoring a resonance between biblical stories and current events, between portrayals of the Jewish people historically and ways of thinking about obligation and relationship to public life in the here and now. While the dominant text was biblical and historical, the subtext was American.

Our first synagogue in Cincinnati was Adath Israel, known in the vernacular as Feinberg Synagogue because of the rabbi who had helped build it. Adath Israel was a monumental edifice that looked like a Greek temple, with gray columns and classical forms. When the late nineteenth and early twentieth century Jewish population of Cincinnati had moved to Avondale from near the river, the synagogue followed. The Congregation opened its impressive pile on the corner of Lexington Avenue and Reading Road in 1927, before the advent of the refugees of the 1930s and 1940s. The rabbi who was the congregational head during my childhood was Fishel Goldfeder, who joined Adath Israel in 1945 and became the primary leader after Feinberg's death in 1949. I would see him as one model of religious leader throughout my life: the corporate rabbi, manager and executive-inspirer.

We were members of Feinberg even though a group of the refugees of the 1930s had specifically organized the aptly named New Hope Congregation for themselves. Perhaps New Hope was too strict for us, too Orthodox, too Germanic. Perhaps we did not join New Hope because it was not so much a vehicle of adjustment or a symbol of transition as was Feinberg. New Hope was modest, located in a converted residence. It could not afford grandeur and probably would not have been so ostentatious in display even if that were financially possible. Feinberg's architecture represented a particular form of pride in a community's achievement, an assertive and optimistic message about the important place of the Jewish community in Cincinnati life. Its massiveness seemed to imply a permanence for the Jewish community, permanence of place, constancy of impact. But there was an architectural irony: not too many years later, as Jews moved from South Avondale to the suburbs, the Feinberg community would have to move as well, abandoning its monumental building to another use, to house adherents of another religion, worshipers of another race. We could not or did not foretell that outcome.

While Feinberg represented the American Conservative movement in Judaism, New Hope was proudly of the school of Samson Raphael

Hirsch, the most gifted and broadly educated of the Orthodox rabbis of late nineteenth and early twentieth century Germany, centered in Frankfurt. The followers of Hirsch emigrated en masse in the 1930s and had established a replica of the home community in New York City (in Washington Heights) with Hirsch's son-in-law as the rabbi. New Hope was so devoted to the Hirschian ideals that when difficult issues of interpretation arose as to religious practice, questions of practice and behavior would be referred to the newly defined center.[2] The somewhat casual Orthodoxy that my parents practiced might have made them slightly uncomfortable there (my son, Gabriel, a half century later, would become a devout member of the Washington Heights community and receive ordination from them). Still, when it was time to have my bar mitzvah, it was held at New Hope. My parents may have decided to have it there because more of their friends might feel at home. More likely, however, New Hope was selected for economic reasons.

Feinberg was where I went for the High Holidays and for Sabbath with its children's services, and, when I was in kindergarten, for a twice-a-week religious school. In the summer, and in free time, I was parked at another community institution, the Jewish Community Center, a few blocks from the Warwick. The Center gathered in its commodious arms the unevenly assimilated Jewish children of Cincinnati and, through woodwork and theater, through songs and sports, went through the complex process of smoothing identities but making sure that religion or religious culture was part of the mix. That is where I learned to play softball, where I was hit by a swung bat, broke my glasses and was slightly scarred. I went later, for several seasons, to Camp Livingston, an 18-acre place near the Little Miami River established in memory of the son of a clothing merchant in Cincinnati (the son had died of influenza in 1918 and his father wanted to bring joy to other Cincinnati Jewish youth). In this summer day-camp with campfires and boating, and in these playgrounds and summer pastimes, the idea of a secular American Jewish identity was reinforced in a thousand ways. These institutions taught skills of adjustment, but did so within the comforting envelope of religious affiliation.

---

[2] A small history of the New Hope Congregation is Benny Kraut, *German-Jewish Orthodoxy*, New York: Markus Weiner Publishing, 1988.

In the first grade, I started attending the Talmud Torah, my religious school until the time we moved to the suburbs. Intense, the school was part of a national movement. Talmud Torah schools had been founded by a generation that wished their children to have a backbone of strong religiosity at the same time that they willingly and enthusiastically participated in public education. Supporters of the Talmud Torahs were inspired by the work of Mordecai Kaplan (whose Orthodox and Reconstructionist synagogues in New York I would later frequent). Kaplan had brought an American perspective to the Germanic ideal of creating Jews who could live fully in two contexts, the religious and the secular. Talmud Torah was designed for parents like my own who wanted their children to know religious practice well and appreciate the Jewish elements of their identity. The progenitors wanted to inoculate children against the baleful influences of the clearly powerful secular world. Parents thought of the frequent afternoon sessions at the Talmud Torah as a means of strengthening the resistance of children to the dangers that would crop up in their lives every morning. Less in Cincinnati than in New York and the East Coast, the Talmud Torah movement was also a reaction against the yeshivoth, the intense, total learning environments in which religious emphasis was almost the exclusive concern. My Talmud Torah, like its counterparts elsewhere, had two-hour classes every day during the week (save Friday) and on Sunday morning. I learned how to pray and to understand the meaning of customs and ceremonies. I was drilled in Biblical Hebrew and introduced to the modern vernacular. The founders of Talmud Torah were deeply Zionist. My education spanned the War of 1948 and the founding of the State of Israel. For the school, achieving national-cultural goals and motivating its students with a complex curriculum was integrally bound up with the restoration of Jewish national existence in Palestine. As a young refugee in Cincinnati, becoming American, I was also being educated in the duty to support a Jewish state. I was taught, at the Talmud Torah, that I was helping to reforest lands through the Jewish National Fund by selling stamps representing leaves of a tree until a complete tree, and then a few and then many were financed. I have a beautiful certificate, acquired later, issued to a group on behalf of the work they had done to fulfill the pioneering ideals of the Fund. It shows a young boy and girl reclaiming the swamps of Palestine, with flowering trees in the background.

Whatever the history and its hopes, my Talmud Torah—and, probably, its sister institutions throughout the country—found it difficult to achieve many of its theoretical goals. There was much in the Talmud Torah that was like an old world *cheder*, the institution that had existed for the poorer children of the community of Eastern Europe. Modernized, the goal would be to build an independent educational institution, headed and staffed by professional educators and dedicated to progressive methods of pedagogy. In fact, this goal could not easily be realized in Cincinnati or its many similar settings throughout the United States. Budgets were tiny. It was hard to get professional teachers. Children, having completed a full day at their secular school, were invariably restless.[3]

My Talmud Torah, if not educationally overwhelming, was enormously entertaining and also a place to misbehave with impunity. Just beyond the entrance was a gymnasium that doubled as the assembly room. Almost everyday, I played vigorous basketball with classmates, much the happiest part of my athletic life. There was an extraordinary drama teacher at Talmud Torah named Charles Becker. He manifested the idea of expressing religious identity in contemporary forms that would capture the attention of wayward students. Together children and teacher wrote plays and then enacted them. My favorite was the transfer of the Purim story to the American Wild West, where Mordechai becomes a Sheriff and reveals Haman's treachery before he is hung on the town's gallows. Ahasuerus was the town's Mayor, and Esther one of his favorite molls. I wore spurs and a leather cowboy's suit and played Two-Gun Haman. Charlie Becker liked the play and performance so much that he had it filmed.

The religious institution with which I was not associated—the model to be disdained (at least from my mother's perspective)—was Rockdale Temple, one of the two major Reform congregations in Cincinnati. Rockdale of the 1950s represented the ultimate in the embrace of the American Christian tradition and rejection of Jewish ritual. There was no Hebrew language as central to prayer, no wearing of a yarmulke in the synagogue and, of course, no separate seating of men and women. Founded in 1824 as the first synagogue West of the Allegheny, the forerunner of Rock-

---

[3] For more on the history of the Talmud Torah movement, see: http://www.jcpa.org/dje/articles2/hebrew-mississippi.htm.

dale had been strictly Orthodox, employing its own supervisor for animal-slaughter, operating its own ovens for the manufacture of Passover matzot. Then, in the 1870s, under the influence of the famous Reform leader Dr. Isaac M. Wise, the Congregation surrendered most vestiges of Orthodoxy. Over time, it established family pews (where women could sit with men), a mixed choir with organ accompaniment, prayers and sermons recited in English, and a new prayer book. When I was in Cincinnati as a child, the Rabbi was Dr. Victor Emanuel Reichert who was the embodiment of severe and austere Reform. We went to Rockdale Temple once or twice to attend weddings or similar events. It was deemed a danger, I think, even to expose me to the place.

Rockdale Temple was the religious home for one of the refugees in my age cohort, Tom Schaumberg. He and his family had been in a concentration camp, and after the war they had spent a year in Amsterdam before coming to Cincinnati. His father had been Orthodox. But in coming to Cincinnati in 1947, he was determined, for himself and his son, to absorb the customs of the new society and, as Tom recalled years later, "never look back." Rockdale Avenue Temple became their place of association. Schaumberg, perhaps as an extension of Rockdale's teaching, became interested in the English First movement in his later life as a trade lawyer in Washington D.C.

In 1950, when we moved to the suburbs, I became a student at my final Cincinnati Jewish school, Beth Am. Beth Am's philosophy was close to that of Talmud Torah and, in fact, the institutions merged in 1953. The cliché in Jewish supplementary education was that boys, after their bar mitzvah at age 13, stop attending religious school. But I stayed at Beth Am with a shrinking group of compatriots, through the end of high school. The leadership of Beth Am worked diligently to keep our small group engaged. We sang cantatas, had wonderful breakfasts of bagels, cream cheese and lox on Sunday mornings, were sent on conferences through the Midwest. We learned how to lead services, how to take responsibility, how to sponsor or promote initiatives that would create a stronger community. It was wholly recognized that we would soon enter the larger non-Jewish society. We would go to excellent colleges, be broadly educated and in many ways assimilated. All the more reason that we were supposed to remember, as it was incessantly stated, that we were links in a chain. On our personal choices rested, in some non-metaphorical sense, the future of the Jewish people.

During my high school years, I attended services at the Roselawn Synagogue in a former movie theater. The seats were raked, but there was no popcorn or chewing gum underfoot. The fittings of the theater remained in place for a very long time, giving a slight show business ambience to the conduct of services. We went to this transformed structure because it was the closest modern Orthodox synagogue to our new home. By that time, too, I had my first falling in love, and my girlfriend's father, George Rosen, courtly and outgoing, was one of the leaders of the congregation. I could watch him, a slightly Southern accent betraying his Kentucky origins, working to raise funds for a budding institution, weekly conducting an auction to sell off honors for reading Torah or opening the ark.

SCHOOL

For me as a refugee it was the public schools of Cincinnati that were the bridges to secular culture and the most potent instructor of paths for change and self-definition. The first school I attended, Avondale Elementary School, was not inspiring, and, standing alone, would have placed a ceiling on my sense of becoming. Avondale was close to what might be called today an "inner city" school. It was economically mixed, with many of the children poor, though most far from destitute. It was a school that was on the verge of demographic instability. The school was overcrowded as a result of baby booms and other post World War II shifts. In my early years there, I was always in fear of being consigned to what were called "the bungalows," temporary structures, undoubtedly Army surplus, erected outside the school building itself. These buildings were reserved for the harder-to-educate, less promising children. Somehow, and probably not for the last time in my life, I was thought of as a child with disciplinary imperfections, and this reputation or ranking continued through my progression at South Avondale, grade to grade. My strongest memory is of the vice-principal, a cruel man, in my mind, Mr. Nankovich, who walked the halls, tall and powerful, who had a slight limp and used a cane, and who would stop me and dig his fingers into my shoulders in a gesture of disapprobation.

My friends in school were not just the children of refugees, at least not the refugees of the 1930s. For the most part, they were Jewish children whose parents had come to the United States and Cincinnati in the 1920s. There was Elaine Torf, whose father was a pharmacist, and Jerry Rubin, later to become famous as the nation's leading Yippie (whose father worked as a delivery man on liquor trucks and then became a union activist, and whose mother worked for my father). I certainly did not have the sense that I could excel. I received disappointing grades in conduct and fair grades in academic subjects. Even "Shop," a course that involved working with lathes or making things out of wood and other materials, was an embarrassment for me. In the sixth grade, when we moved to Roselawn, I was transferred to the Bond Hill School. The first day I was there, the teacher brought me to the front of the class and publicly asked me to explain why I received an inferior grade in Conduct. Perhaps the teacher decided to take on, personally, the cause of rehabilitation. Whether for that reason or others, my world-view (as developed in school) and my performance shifted with the shift to the suburbs.

Nothing was the equivalent of attending Walnut Hills High School, which seems ideal in retrospect. Entrance was by competitive examination and it had a deserved reputation as one of the best public schools in the United States. All students were required to take Latin during their first three years (from the seventh to the ninth grades). Walnut Hills was a distinctive and privileged place, a meritocracy. *Sursum ad Summum*, rise to the highest, was the school's motto, and the authorities were not engaging in empty rhetoric. We were treated not only as if we were already in university, but also at one that cherished and nourished its students. My teachers relished the idea that they were teaching at the college level. I was on the staff of the *Chatterbox*, the school newspaper and my first school of journalism. I tried, but failed, to be a member of the basketball team (the requirements of Hebrew School interfered with my time for practice, among other more built-in obstacles to my life as an athlete). I acted in the school plays, playing a Capuchin Father in St. Joan and a courtier in Cyrano de Bergerac. I did many of the things, but not all, that teenagers did in the 1960s.

My high school principal was Harold Howe II, who was one of the most distinguished educators of the period, becoming Commissioner of

Education in the Johnson Administration and a high official and architect of the education program at the Ford Foundation. His brother, conveniently, was the Director of Admission at Yale College. My senior year, I applied to Yale because it sounded like a good thing to do, because it was a peer-type goal at Walnut Hills High School and because Doc Howe—my principal—encouraged me. He saw qualities in me that I did not see in myself. When Harold Howe died in 2002, his obituary in the *New York Times* provided some of his history, insight into the qualities that benefited my educational crossing. He was born in Hartford, a son of the Rev. Arthur Howe, a professor at Dartmouth College and president of the Hampton Institute in Virginia. His grandfather Samuel Chapman Armstrong, a Union general during the Civil War, had founded Hampton as a trade school for freed slaves. After graduating from Yale, Howe was captain of a Navy minesweeper in World War II. It was one of the many wonders of America that my young life and that of Howe would intersect in this manner. I was admitted to Yale. My time in Cincinnati ended. I had found my way to a phenomenal new escalator into the culture of America.

6

WORK

I look for traces of my Austrian-ness in the way I have shaped my ambitions, assessed myself against others, valued wealth and chosen paths of education and career. I want to know something rather unknowable. I want to plumb for the ways the events of 1930s Vienna and its consequences for my family meant that a different "me" emerged. I could dwell, though I do not, on what I would have become, and what my trajectory would have been like, had life on Taborstrasse gone on as before, had my father continued to enjoy the Vienna that he loved. I would like to understand the influences of that Vienna, filtered through my parents, when they meshed with the pressures, provocations and customs of the United States of the 1940s and 1950s.

In the 1940s, the decade of my childhood, my family was what might be called decently poor. The decision to move from New York to Macon had resulted in a stable job for my father. My mother had, from the moment of landing, demonstrated her capacity to put aside savings, no matter how small our income. My parents had some financial support from my father's uncle. But we were living the dominant refugee narrative, struggling, strategizing, trying to build reserves, worrying about the future. And there were inevitable comparisons with the Austrian existence, even for those—like my parents—who did not dwell excessively on the past. Like the flocks of refugees who assembled in the Catskills summer or the Gate Clubs of Cincinnati and around the world, my family had lost security-providing wealth, been severed from careers and were trying to find a new place in a shaky universe. It would be more correct for me to think of myself as a child of these regenerating refugees than a refugee myself. My parents did not overtly see themselves as in a relay race, and, in a sense, neither did I. But I was definitely enwrapped in the soft-edged dictates of the refugee corner of the American Dream. My mother and father did not need to say so. But their lives proclaimed something like the following: "we made sure we got out alive, we survived, we scrimped and saved, and worked for pennies, and that was a lot. We triumphed over adversity. The rest is up to you." This was the subliminal text in the Austrian and German community: even if we cannot accomplish the goal for ourselves, our children, the next generation, should become as financially and socially comfortable in the United States as we were in Europe before the rise of Hitler. Indeed, the opportunity in the United States is to become more liberated, more adjusted, and even more secure.

The strength of this imperative had its harsh, sometimes bitter implications. The America that we and other refugees entered was a place of oppression as well as opportunity, of deep economic hardship and deprivation as well as a place of hope and mobility. The refugee community, already shaken by the tragedy that had befallen them, often faced the daunting gulf between the opportunities they were told were all around them and the reality that faced them in the eye. Suicide, breakdown, fracture could be the description of refugee life almost as much as achievement, conquering of circumstance and economic redemption. A hundred times or more I heard a story in the Catskills or Cincinnati or New York City that wrapped struggle in humor and illustrated the ironic memory of the 1930s refugees. Mr. Klein, from Berlin, was walking his tiny dachshund along Broadway in Washington Heights. Mr. Grossman from Vienna, admiringly, compliments him on the dog's qualities. "That's nothing," Mr. Klein replies. "In Berlin, he was a St. Bernard!"

INSECURITY

Throughout his life in the United States, my father was a loyal worker, but I attribute to him a perspective that much of life is illusion and that it should be perceived and played out as ironic and amusing. From my mother I learned something quite different: that ultimately the experience of life is tragic and the illusion of illusion crashes into the reality of reality. This division reflected something more than the differences in my parents' geographical lineage. The two attitudes could be compartmentalized as the environment of Vienna before the 1930s (more my father) and the tense and urgent Vienna of 1938 and 1939 (my mother). My father's family, with greater Austrian roots, reflected more clearly the liberation of the nineteenth century. My mother's family, with deeper pre-Vienna roots in Slovakia, reflected more the extensive history of exclusion and restriction.

While I was writing about these differences, I read a short novel by one of my favorite authors, Anthony Trollope. Trollope hardly ever wrote sympathetically about his Jewish characters, but in *Nina Balatka*, published under a pseudonym in 1866, he actually tried to write a close and compelling psychological profile of the liberated generation of Jews of the second half of the nineteenth century. The novel has, as its nominal central character, "a maiden of Prague, born of Christian parents, and herself a Christian—but she loved a Jew...." The book is also about the young Jew, Anton Trendellsohn, who yearns for a more open environment in which to fashion his career. I wondered, as I read it, whether Trendellsohn's story could teach me something about my father's father—or the differences between my mother's family and my father's. Trendellsohn was the product of a deep-rooted Czech Orthodox Jewish tradition that endured and accepted the ubiquitous and harsh division in social relations and in business between Jew and Gentile. Jews could prosper and become wealthy, but they saw themselves as abused, mistrusted, patronized. Trendellsohn "had heard of Jews in Vienna, in Paris, and in London, who were as true to their religion as any Jew of Prague...[but] [t]hese men went abroad into the world as men, using the wealth with which their industry had been blessed, openly, as the Christians used it. And they lived among Christians as one man should live with his fellow-men—on equal terms, giving and taking, honouring and honoured." For Trollope and for the young Emperor Franz Josef, this more civil society was much to be preferred. Vienna symbolized the opportunities and taste of freedom. "In Prague a Jew was still a Pariah."

In *Letters to Milena*, published more than a half-century after *Nina Balatka* and around the time my father was born, Franz Kafka wrote of a still-oppressive Prague; and as he did so, he described what would be the world view of my mother's family more than my father's: "The insecure position of Jews, insecure within themselves, insecure among people, would make it above all comprehensible that they consider themselves to be allowed to own only what they hold in their hands or between their teeth, that furthermore only palpable possessions give them the right to live, and that they will never again acquire what they once have lost but that it instead calmly swims away from them forever."[1] This background idea—that one's place in the world is transitory, subject to the madness of crowds and the bizarre imaginings of their leaders—must affect attitudes toward property, to wealth, to respect for law.

My father's father, Salomon (Mundi) Preis, could have been the aspirational urban and comfortable Jew who Trollope's Trendellsohn admired. He was, from all I can gather, a cultivated and easy-going man, participating in a growing and more liberal Vienna. One of 16 children, he was a partner in the Viennese forwarding company he had established. He also ran a commercial newspaper whose contents, mostly about trade in Vienna, bolstered the forwarding business. The fact that he married his American cousin, the fact that my rather sophisticated and demanding grandmother chose him, says a great deal for his cosmopolitanism. His portrait, showing a distinguished, open and generous face, hangs in my den. He looks like a man of an expanding world. Among the mementos I have from the Vienna of those times is the special issue of his newspaper, published by Brüder Preis, printed specifically for his wedding to my grandmother. It is a paper composed, in a clever, Viennese way, with humor that employs the vocabulary of shipping, the format of classified ads and the headline format of a regular paper to celebrate the editor's wedding to his American cousin. He embodied the business and social values that were a beacon to Trendellsohn.

After Mundi's death in 1911, my father was much under the influence of his uncle Isidor, a whimsical, rakish figure who was a genius in busi-

---

1 Franz Kafka, *Letters to Milena*, edited by Willi Haas, translated by Tania and James Stern, London: Secker & Warburg, 1953, pp. 50–51.

ness and who expanded Brüder Preis into a larger enterprise, encompassing the spinning and recycling trades. As far as I can tell, my grandmother left most of the rearing to Isidor and to my father's governess. I have a curious album of hand-drawn postcards, prepared for Isidor's fiftieth birthday, filled with gently mocking scenes from his adventurous life. The text on the cards is written backwards so that the pictures can be mirrored and projected. In these cards, a lovely Viennese wit is at play, a wit I would often see in my father. Isidor, perhaps as an homage to his deceased brother, exposed my father to elements of the business and wanted him, when he was ready, to work in his burgeoning and widely spread activities. He encouraged my father to study and train at high school and technical institute to become a textile engineer, not to go to university as my grandfather had. The first time my father had responsibility in Brüder Preis was when he was around 20, but the chemistry between him and Isidor turned sour and the match was unsatisfactory. For several years, my father, perhaps to show his independence, worked outside Brüder Preis though within the textile industry. From my father's recounting of these years, I gathered that while business was important to him, its value was greatest when he could exercise just those personal traits he found most entertaining: his charm, the application of detailed knowledge, the understanding of human behavior. Later, in the United States, wherever we traveled, he would always seek out business opportunities, try to develop new contacts, renew friendships that could ripen into contracts. This trait must have echoed his time selling in the towns and cities of the former Empire.

When Isidor, himself, died suddenly in a tram accident in 1932, all his property was left to my father and my father's sister Alice. As a result, my father returned to take over the company (together with his brother-in-law). This change in his status could have had the most pleasant long-term consequences, but, of course, the Anschluss intervened. Business for the Brüder Preis had been embedded in empire, the Austro-Hungarian Empire or the fresh memory of it. For my father (and for my mother's father, too) the definition of his trading world was very close to pre-Versailles Habsburg, and particularly during his time away from Brüder Preis, his itinerary, as sales person or buyer, ran through Central Europe and the Balkans. Like aspects of Franz Josef's court, much or all of this life was superficially wonderful, but fatally doomed. The operetta of Viennese life had its horrid realities for my father: my grandfather had died when my father was a child, his beloved Austro-Hungarian Empire, so much in the grain of his personality and his identity, had ended, my father's Uncle Isidor had had a fatal accident, and then came the Anschluss. My father's time in charge was abruptly truncated: in 1938, he was commanded to surrender his stock in the company as part of the Aryanization process.

As was the case with many refugee children, I was brought up sensing that my father's slot in the hierarchy of work and compensation here was not the correct one, that some greater approximation of his Viennese professional existence would have been more appropriate. My father's fate was not, as often was the case in the Russian immigration of the 1970s, like that of highly-trained engineers who ended up driving taxicabs. Rather it was that he had to work too hard and had been deprived of the time to pursue his own desires. He did not have the privilege, associated with being an owner, of being idiosyncratic, or playing with and squandering wealth. Unfulfilled, for him, was the opportunity to perform his duty to the memory of his father, or redeem his relationship to his now-dead uncle. He could not go through the familiar exercise of trying to work out whatever problems existed with his family firm in a style that he desired or design his own balance between the necessities of work and the other benefits of a Viennese life.

My mother, as I have already discussed, was an influence on me of a different sort. She had not, of course, worked in Vienna either before marriage or after. Still, she came from clever Ehrenfeld stock. Her Vienna was far more straightforward than that of my father. It did not embrace, at least in my perception, the elaborate pretense and theater of the Habsburg legacy. Work was clear, achievement directly related to input if one was sensible about it. In her consistent way, drawing on these experiences, she ultimately demonstrated her business and financial acumen. The literature and anecdotal history of work and adjustment for my parents' generation does not dwell deeply on the activities of its women. It was the men who were given the task of being primary providers and definers of family and position. But my mother had exceptionally strong ideas, articulated them and was persuasive in making them part of the family ethic. She worked, she conspired, she achieved. Her sense of work was far more transferable to the American context than was my father's.

RECYCLING

One of my father's specialties in Macon and then Cincinnati was the trade in cotton linters. When cotton is pulled from its seed, there are various grades, depending on length and accessibility. After most of the cotton is pulled, what remains are the linters, harder to reach, lower in quality. My father absorbed, as part of his American expertise, the purchase and sale of this material in carload quantities. Another zone of his knowledge involved what was called "wiping waste." This specialized market that expanded in World War II required purchasing remnants from factories, either baled cuttings or baled material that had been used for the cleaning of machines (and had, then itself, been cleaned). The bales, transported around the country or the world, would be recycled for other purposes. The company for which he worked in Cincinnati, the Railway Supply and Manufacturing Company, had started economic life using this material for stuffing seats on railroad carriages.

I carried this idea of recycling and reuse into my academic life and research. The drama of recycling reinforced a narrative: a history of Jews in Vienna (and elsewhere, ultimately including in the United States) that describes particular forms of work, enterprise and aspirations for success. Frequent was the tale and image of the peddler, working the mean streets, purchasing surplus pots and pans on the cheap and selling them more dear. Many of the sons of what might be called peddler-fathers were enabled to go to colleges and universities in the United States, and many became teachers, researchers and professors. For me, rather than represent a disjuncture, the process involved a continuum. At least as I internalized it, research could be viewed as a recycling of old ideas, their refiguring and representation as new. It was wrong too haughtily to ennoble the change. It would be wise to remember that underneath much academic work was the solitary trader, foraging for objects that could be acquired at a low price and sold for a higher one. This idea of transformation was rendered a bit too brutally concrete for me much later when I visited, one day, the Museum für Kommunikation in Frankfurt and, saw, rather by accident, an exhibition of anti-Semitic postcards of the nineteenth and twentieth century. There were definitely a lot of them. One, however, jolted me into bringing up from my mental storage place this notion of the academician as scrap dealer. It was a four panel postcard in which the first showed a stereotypical Jewish figure in the streets, the second as tailor, the third as proprietor of an elegant shop and the fourth as art dealer. "The Emergence of an Art Dealer" was the title of the card.

In a sense, recycling could be a term applied to the considerable effort to rehabilitate the male refugees (mostly the males) of the 1930s period. There was a complex class system or hierarchy to this process, partially reflecting their pecking order in their place of origin and partially reflecting their interactions with the social structure at the US as a place of destination. I certainly didn't have the vocabulary necessary to understand this in the 1940s when I was growing up, but I could see, even in the hothouse of the Warwick in Cincinnati, the interactions of previous life, present connections and the nature of work. Language and adaptation to English was a significant variable. Certain jobs or skills were transferable, but in other cases profession and fame were of little consequence. There were those (they were more likely to be called Exiles), who could, with hardships to be sure, take their European achievements to Hollywood in the 1930s, or find homes in academic life (like the Graduate School in Exile) or as potential officers in large corporations. Laura Fermi's *Illustrious Immigrants: The Intellectual Migration from Europe 1930–1941* and other books celebrated this story of exceptionalism, perhaps out of proportion. It was comforting to many to focus on this class of immigrants who "were different from their predecessors, not only because of the greater concentration in their ranks of intellectual talent, artistic, scholarly, or scientific. They also became Americanized at a much faster pace than any previous group of Americans."[2]

These illustrious ones were in a minority, and not all of those who deemed themselves illustrious in their place of origin could become such in their place of destination. My father bore a different myth. He carried with him, always, an idea of his station in Vienna, not as a matter of arrogance, but as an element of self-definition. He had been an owner in Vienna and there was something always potentially independent about him, and he identified with the owners and managers of the companies for which he worked. He was far from being one of the great figures of the

---

[2]   Laura Fermi, *Illustrious Immigrants*, Chicago: University of Chicago Press, p. 5.

immigrant imagination, but he was never wholly on his own and had the constant reminder of his mother's American past.

This, though, is one of the puzzles about him. Despite the safety net that was beneath him because of his American relatives, he was much like those dealt with by the National Coordinating Council (which I described in Chapter 3), as it sought to provide assistance in getting established. He didn't apply for material assistance, but practices of the NCC might have been meant for him. For example, the Council ran a loan fund to provide assistance where an outlay of funds or an investment could create a bit of stability in tattered lives and some notes from its activities might shed light on attitudes of the time. On October 31, 1939, at the time my father was struggling in New York, the committee decided to recommend a loan of $100 to Ignaz Winkler who had come from Vienna with his wife and their two children on April 7, 1939, about the same time we arrived in New York. Winkler had been a watchmaker all his life—he was 53 years old. He was employed by the Swiss American Watch Hospital in New Haven, but was in danger of being laid off unless "he obtains the necessary tools for his work." The committee concluded that if he received the loan, and could then take the job, his family could be reunited and "Mrs. Winkler and the two children will be resettled in the particular community where Mr. Winkler is employed." The Swiss American Watch Hospital had agreed to deduct the sum of $2.00 weekly from Mr. Winkler's salary to be applied on account of this loan. The "self-support" department of the NCC similarly recommended a loan of $250 to Eugene Feldstein to enable him to buy stock so he could fulfill orders he had booked in the button trade. Feldstein threw in a clinching argument for the loan: according to the minutes of the department, though he had arrived in August 1938 with an affidavit from his wife's sister, she now "refused to assist the family further unless they became converted to Christianity, which they refused to do."

My father was neither a physicist nor a watchmaker. He had been a relatively solid middle class person in Vienna, with a noble, though not great, commercial history. It was never clear to him how to reestablish that in the United States (though it was clearer to my mother as to what steps to take). There were many factors that could have influenced the process of remaking or reestablishing position. My father might have served in the Armed

Forces, but did not. Some of his cohort worked after the War to help with the Occupation or with the sorting out of displaced persons, but that never seemed an option. Ultimately, it was my father's personality, his sense of self, his confidence, whether he had gained sufficient management skills in Vienna, whether he saw himself as broken. Undoubtedly, much turned on how old one was when leaving Europe, where one lived, on whether and to whom one was married, on whether there were children or parents to support, how many and with what needs, and what ties existed to the world of work. But that does not account for the variations of ambition, drive and seizing of opportunity.

TRYING OUT

When I was young, in my pre-career as it were, these patterns, mixtures of memory and experience, certainly influenced me. As must be true of most children, I was a student of my parents' interactions with the world. But I had my own, self-generated influences. For example, when I was around ten, going to the Cincinnati Zoo during its annual summer festival, there was a booth that always fascinated me. There, on a raised podium, with a neatly arranged wooden table in front of him, was the seller of mechanical contraptions to cut, dice and peel vegetables. He mesmerized the crowd by transforming carrots and onions and tomatoes quickly and efficiently from one form to another. He promised some kind of deliverance from the boredom of hard and repetitive kitchen chores. I loved how the barker captured the crowd, his carefully crafted delivery, the coordination of hand movements with speech, and the tangible payoff of sales to customers thrilled at the prospect of achieving at home what they had observed. His art was repeated by the seller of little aluminum tubes and paper nozzles that allowed the production of hors d'oeuvres or multiple cookies from dough. These little devices could rescue cakes from mediocrity through the creation of beautiful toppings, flowers and designs, and fancy inscriptions. We acquired one of these sets, and I spent many hours squeezing batter through silver stars or other metal designs.

When I was 12, I sold my baby sister's bassinet on television. In those primitive early television times, the local station, hungry for content, broadcast a weekly sell-a-thon in which any person could offer goods. I successfully demonstrated the virtues of our bassinet and had the gratification of satisfactorily disposing of it. I did my first fund-raising, to finance the renting of 16 millimeter films that I, with my friends, would show at the Jewish Home for the Aged in South Avondale. It's odd, but I remember the pitch I made to my first board of directors, as it were, a group of men that got together once a week to play cards and gamble. I convinced them to give a portion of the pot to finance the film club. When I was about 13, I acted as one-time artistic manager for Robert Meitus, a talented pianist in my class. In my remembering, I encouraged him to enter a competition at the neighborhood movie theater that, as a way of adjusting to television, had amateur-hour contests on Saturday mornings. I did not have a talent with which to compete directly, but I invented my own category of participation, namely assisting my classmate in exchange for part of the winnings if, as happened, they transpired.

I also had new models of how to behave and what to value. When I was a young teenager, my friend Michael Pichel took me on weekends to the home of his uncle, an underworld figure named Porky Lassoff, who had (so it seemed to me at the time) an impressive estate in the outlying area of Amberly Village. Porky, with his brother Bobby, had invested in illegal gambling casinos in Newport, Kentucky, would later be an investor in the Dunes in Las Vegas, and looked and talked a good Runyonesque game. I had the job, with Michael, of cutting the lawn with the Lassoff's miraculous (to a young city boy) mechanical tractor. I could study Uncle Porky, watch him in his lawn furniture, drinking and eating, imagining, remotely, what he did to produce wealth, and taking in, with large round eyes, how he lived. Another exposure to the ways of wealth came through my job as caddy at the Losantiville Country Club. As with my trips to the holdings of Uncle Porky, work on the golf course allowed me to see how rich people walked and talked. Being a caddy had its intimacy. One goal was to gain the affection of good tippers so they would ask for you especially, avoiding the risk of the draw. In the days before golf carts, the caddy accompanied the player, at a proper distance, and learned the etiquette of pulling the right club and presenting it exactly to the client.

After my first year of college, our family was living (temporarily as it turned out) in Charlotte, North Carolina. That summer I had two jobs that had a pronounced impact on my way of thinking of work. The first—

which only lasted a few days—involved selling multi-volume sets of Colliers Encyclopedia door to door in small Southern towns. From the training session for that task I learned a great deal, but not about the importance of spreading education, or the needs of children in backwaters of American life. First, I was taught that the key problem for a salesman, the thing that should be the initial objective, was crossing the threshold and actually getting into the house. The trainer said that until one was inside and seated, you were a D.P. My association with these initials had been the displaced persons who had left the concentration camps at the end of World War II, but my trainer made it clear that he meant Damned Peddler. Either way, the overarching goal was to be invited, to be admitted. The second lesson from the Colliers training team was that all living rooms were predictable in their content. They distributed to their sales force a small chart of an average apartment, with arrows pointing across the entry, across the living room, to the couch. In front of the couch was the coffee table. Its surface was the domain that had to be captured. The salesperson had to understand the structure of the living room and the relationship of the table and couch to the door. It was a little like a military campaign: The task for the salesman was to get the company's documents on the coffee table, glossy pages splayed with compelling photographs—volcanoes, flowers, battle scenes—that served as soldiers in the process of persuasion. There was so much sociology and psychology packed in this lesson, including, of course, a statement of the common habits and predilections of the population. The third lesson from Colliers would also stay with me. It became clear that, in many of these small North Carolina towns, the World Book Encyclopedia had made deals with the teachers in the schools who, in exchange for a benefit (a commission, for example), recommended this favored encyclopedia to the families of the children over whom they had reputational sway. There were towns where Colliers did not stand a chance because of the nefarious and preemptive actions of this World Book strategy. I learned that it was not the quality of the books that would make a difference (this was probably down the list), nor was it the face-to-face skills of selling and of reaching the couch and exhaustedly unfurling brochures that were important. Rather it was, on a larger scale, an understanding and active participation in the process in which decisions took place. One had to know the competition and one had to use one's skills to eliminate or damage the competition through superior strategies or complex and possibly devious arrangements. The World Book Encyclopedia dominated because of its cleverness at organizing the field of distribution.

As it turned out, I couldn't stay in the Colliers job. My mother thought I was traveling too far away, in places too distant from Charlotte, penetrating unknown American terrains, working too late at night. But the training sessions sank in, meshing, perhaps, with my own inclinations. Somehow I associated the Colliers lessons to its salesmen with the idea of outsiders gaining entry and having to use their skills and wits to do so. The Colliers lesson was a tutorial in the vital arts of persuasion, the basics of marketing, public relations, propaganda. Getting through the door could be viewed as one of the important lessons of the past (finding the right bureaucrat for gaining an affidavit or freedom), and an important lesson for the future. Colliers underscored the importance of having their specially developed brochures actually opened—only this would trigger the magical, mesmerizing impact of their marketing materials. One of the essential projects of mass communication was figuring out how to enter the living room, and, perhaps, my training session in Charlotte helped prepare me for my later studies of radio and television. And also helpful was this Colliers pseudo-scientific observation: that the insides of houses in small towns in North Carolina were more or less all alike, and probably the same is true for the insides of most houses throughout the United States—at least in ways basic to understanding how to reach those who live there and influence their behavior. Finally, there was the Colliers assertion of the power pieces of paper could assume if properly signed (we refugees knew the power of pieces of paper). The most important act of a sale was the contract, its mysteries of words and intimidation not effective until there was an actual signing, the essential magic of turning paper into rights and obligations.

My other Charlotte, North Carolina job was with Sears, Roebuck working in its basement, selling barbecue grills. Sears, Roebuck provided a basic salary and a one percent commission on sales. My self-defined modus operandi was to identify the good customers and move their aspirations up from the basic grill to one that had all the features an American store of the 1950s could offer. These included a fancy motor that activated a glittering spit, oven-black curved top, and special trays or holding areas for raw and cooked meat. I loved doing this job and did it with such enthusiasm and drive that a fellow salesperson approached me and asked—much to my mortification—if I were a Jew. I was mortified, not because I was ashamed, but because, after my process of integration, after a year in college, at Yale no less, to be so easily identified was jolting. Much to my further mortification, I muttered something that could be interpreted as a negative and asked why she inquired. "Well," she said, "you sure sell like a Jew."

ASSIMILATION AND NATIVE AMERICANS

For fifteen years, beginning in the late 1960s, I wrote about or represented Native American groups or tribes. It's hard to think of many areas of study that would have had a more significant metaphorical relationship to the vestiges of my refugee-ness. As a boy, my father had loved the pulp novels of the obsessed and happily fantasizing nineteenth-century Dresdener, Karl May, who wrote dozens of books in German about American cowboys and Indians. In my twenties, as a law student, I read a different set of stories: court decisions of early American history, such as the Supreme Court narratives of the Cherokees, with their Trail of Tears in the 1830s, expelled from their lands in Georgia and Mississippi. It was hardly a stretch, and perhaps a bit of self-reflective indulgence, to see in the group and individual stories of these groups echoes of those in various parts of the Jewish and refugee world. I could see, as my familiarity with these stories evolved, that twentieth century tribes were struggling to maintain traditions, provide continuity, reestablish custom and language. They wished to fashion legal systems in which there was loyalty to tribe as well as loyalty to state, citizenship in both. None of this was distant from some of my own questions of sovereignty and identity, my own witness to the falling apart or dissolution of civilizations, the rejection and reinterpretation of histories of ethnicity or group identity. There, too, was the idea of the victim, not just any victim, but the victims of systematic notions of expulsion, destruction and genocide.

The beginnings of my professional interest in Native Americans—the relationships among the tribes, the individual states and the United States government—had been at Yale Law School in a seminar on Law and the

American West with Professor Charles Reich. An idiosyncratic romantic who later wrote *The Greening of America*, Reich began the seminar by reading a long meditation he had written, long hand, on a legal pad on the underpinnings of law, and its making, especially in the circumstances of the frontier or raw environments. He then dismissed us for several weeks to think about what he had said, to let it seep in like the waters of an underground stream entering crevices of life. Inspired by Reich that New Haven spring, I wrote about a peculiar principle in Western mining law that grew out of the special customs of a "lawless" society. The rag-tag miners were creating their own sense of order and property, namely that the discoverer of the outcropping of a mineral could make a claim to the entire vein. This was in contrast to the ordinary rule of law, that the owner of a plot of land had title to everything below and above it.

Somehow, the existence of this anomaly—how ownership was decided—struck home, and I seized from this research a few things that related to my past. Laws, rules that might ultimately have the sanction of the state, could come out of the chaos of local action. These rules could be arbitrary and still function (in some places minerals would follow title to the land, in others it would go to the discoverer of the physical manifestation above the ground). And the American West (or other places by extension) was a place where law could be viewed as an experiment, could be shaped, and modes of justification could be unorthodox. I myself had been born in a place and at a time where laws of ownership were transformed suddenly and things called "government" rendered arbitrary what had been long accepted and rendered standard what had previously been arbitrary. I could have been responding to an idea of the chaotic and ambiguous sources of legitimacy.

One summer, partly based on my experience in the Yale seminar, and before I went to work teaching at the UCLA Law School, I was asked to provide research assistance for the Agua Caliente Tribe of Indians, a group whose land was intermingled with the fate of Palm Springs, California. I was attracted to the wonders a lawyer could perform, or try to perform, in the contest between authority and weakness. Through legislation and agreement, railroads had come through Agua Caliente land; as a bonus for its work crossing this part of the continent, the railroad received title to every other section along the right of way. The tribe, as a consequence of the "checkerboard" arrangement, retained the rest. Now, in the 1960s as part of a new pattern of benevolence (or malevolence), the land was being distributed to individual members. After a complicated division, the county of San Bernardino decided to impose burdensome property taxes on the lands that had been divided, determining, in the process, new valuations. My first Indian law case was to argue that the federal legislation controlled how and when the county could tax the land. I had an immediate interest and empathy for a group that was asserting claims to property with history as the text for a defense. I was intrigued, as well, by the sound of clashing sovereigns and the issues of social organization that were at stake.

Then, in 1969, I went to work, part-time and largely as a volunteer, for California Rural Legal Assistance, one of the most adventurous programs funded under President Johnson's Office of Economic Opportunity (part of the War Against Poverty). There, I learned to see law as charismatic force, and lawyers as charismatic figures, especially Gary Bellow, later a professor at Harvard Law School, and James Lorenz, the program's founder. CRLA was principally designed to serve Mexican-American farm workers, but much to its surprise found a great demand for legal assistance by the fragments of surviving Indian tribes and groups both in Northern and Southern California. At CRLA's request, together with George Duke, a lawyer working for CRLA in Santa Rosa, I helped establish California Indian Legal Services, which would assume the duty of providing such assistance throughout the state; and, through the California entity I helped develop the core proposals for the Native American Rights Fund.

Throughout I saw more than a glimmer of resemblance between the issues as defined by Native American tribes and the rhetoric dunned into me in my Jewish life. The tribes were coping with problems of identity, of assimilation versus separation. They were striving, often, to maintain physical communities, assure marriage within the group, pass on a culture and tradition to young people who heard the siren song of modernity and the city. Native Americans complained of the destruction they had suffered, the expulsion of many from their original lands, the robbing of their customs and the downgrading of their beliefs. I could find ways of writing about the Jewish people and Jewish history without writing about Jews at all. A casebook I published in 1971 called *American Indians and the Law* has this subtext. Who controls education? How does a fragile society defend itself against the norms of the dominant culture? Can a private, consensual system of rule making and enforcement exist within a fairly hostile state environment? With the drama of Israel being constantly played out, I could ask, for Indians as for Jews, how important it was to have a physical place for a group to have its national identity. It was hardly foreign to ask what it meant to be Navajo if Navajos were in a permanent diaspora without any Indian country to consider their home. Native American groups tried to restrict intermarriage, engage in once-prohibited dancing, encourage the revitalization of languages that were on the edge of extinction. There was the fact, important to me, that the leading lawyer of modern American Indian law was Felix Cohen, with whom I identified because I thought he, too, was projecting, perhaps subconsciously, similar issues of separation and assimilation on a Native American canvas. The predominant view is that Cohen's policies were ideological, not based on anything especially related to his Jewishness. But for me, the connections were strong. It was Cohen who fought successfully for the existence of the Indian Claims Commission, established in 1946, which was to provide reparations for certain actions by the federal government against the tribes, whether violations could be stated as moral or legal in their nature.

Another element of this connection came out of other opportunities I had to put these connections to use and provide actual legal advice. Terry Lenzner, who had been appointed head of the Office of Legal Services nationally, asked me to visit tribes and similar entities throughout the United States to help make more useful the legal services programs that would be established for their benefit. I ultimately traveled from Philadelphia, Mississippi and the Choctaws throughout the Southwest and California, to Pine Ridge in South Dakota, to Alaska and to Micronesia where the Trust Territory was seen to have common issues. Unlike lawyers for the urban poor (whose task might be to move people above the poverty line), I— and other government-funded lawyers for Native Americans—could be considered more like advocats for the wealthy, or at least a kind of landed poor. We could use our skills architecturally to reassert tribal control over their assets and alter their value. Tribes required lawyers who thought creatively about what constituted an asset or an advantage and helped redefine the group's confidence in itself and its functioning as a sovereign manager of its world. Lawyers needed to listen more carefully to the articulation of these issues by the Native Americans themselves rather than accept the status quo. In the late 1960s, I put some of these ideas together in an essay,[3] and that in turn helped inform California Indian Legal Services. I wasn't the only one who held this view, and it was certainly at the heart of the massive legal services program established on the Navajo Reservation and the basis of the strategy of the Pequot Indians in Maine who later negotiated a breakthrough settlement redefining their economic and political relationship to the state. For better or worse, in a kind of enormous legal joke, the approach, using jurisdiction as an asset, led to the extraordinary right of Indian tribes to engage in gaming, establishing casinos throughout the country. By 2000, Indians were among the major contributors to the Democratic Party nationally, and, with mixed consequences, some tribes were transformed.

This philosophy of wealth-accumulation was extended, after 1973, when my main professional focus was on the Natives of Alaska, where, for about a decade, I represented Cook Inlet Region, Inc., a group of Indians, Aleuts and Eskimos assembled into a for-profit corporation by the Alaska Native Claims Settlement Act of 1971. Cook Inlet Region, Inc., which started as a corporation in trouble, with few land and other resources, transformed into a successful seizer of opportunities that distributed $500 million dollars to its 2,000 shareholders in 2001. CIRI began its modern corporate life at a time when the promise of oil development in Alaska gave the Natives substantial leverage. In a settlement that I helped negotiate, CIRI was allowed to exchange its rights to unprofitable tundra and mountain tops that had been foisted upon them for property (real estate, especially) the federal government was declaring surplus throughout the United States and would put up for auction. Instead of having a valueless dowry of land unusable to their members, CIRI ended up with a huge inventory of apartment buildings, warehouses and other structures from Florida to Hawaii. And taking advantage of a regulatory advantage given to minorities so that they could own radio and television stations, CIRI became perhaps the largest minority owner of broadcasting properties in

---

[3] Monroe E. Price, "Lawyers on the Reservation: Some Implications for the Legal Profession," *Law and Social Order*, 1969, 161, 197.

the nation. There were many reasons and many people that were responsible for CIRI's transformation. Senators, governors, the team of Alaskan Natives who ran the corporation, more radical forces that kept pressing for justice, lobbyists, and environmentalists were all part of it. But at the core, I felt the impact of an idea, and, in a way, the playing out of my philosophy.

There were, in this Alaska transformation, shards of my Austrian-ness, tiny extensions of my being a European refugee. I remained the 20-year-old encyclopedia and barbecue salesman I had been in Charlotte, North Carolina, figuring ways of improving the package. I saw myself, in Christian Washington and among my Native clients, as playing the role of the intelligent and crafty court Jew. There was displacement as well. I was trying to reinstate wealth to a group that had been deprived of it by historic circumstance. And I was helping to reposition Alaska Natives as they would function in greater Alaska society. And there's another side, perhaps slightly more Viennese. I saw law—or the application of law—as a kind of theater, a theater that could be tweaked and changed. There was an irony to law, and a place for wit or creativity in altering its impact. Somewhere in the mix of causation was this idea that law could be upended, made to frolic, allowed to turn disaster into an unforeseen opportunity. Somewhere, in the contribution I made to the sequence of events, was the acceptance of the absurd as a potential mode of solving problems.

ASPIRING

I return to the master narrative, the legacy, privilege and burden of many refugees, namely the duty to aspire. An element of "surviving" was, quite definitely, the implied obligation to justify myself in this new place, to compensate for the privilege of our entry, and in the process to demonstrate what could be accomplished in the United States. My parents did not force me to feel I had a special responsibility, but they created the environment in which such feelings would emerge. Responsibility was embedded in the idea that "opportunity" existed in the United States, and in the contrast between the new possibilities of rebuilding as opposed to the social, physical and cultural destruction that had been our fate in Austria. What's the point of opportunity unless it's seized?

My Hebrew school and high school in Cincinnati, my education by my parents, were all classrooms in citizenship. I've written of these earlier bits of Americanization, but my university was, perhaps, a more leveraging force in this process. In a way, the real curriculum of Yale College in the 1950s was not Economics 10 or Art History or Ancient Greek, but what place a particular Yale graduate would hold in the America of the future. The institution and its students knew that within the 1,000 (all male at the time) undergraduates in a class, there was a strong likelihood of a president emerging, certainly senators and congressmen, secretaries of state and other cabinet members and a strong representation in the CIA (which, from the beginning, had strong Ivy League tendencies). For me, coming to Yale, in terms of the opportunities of citizenship, was stepping on a golden escalator (attending Walnut Hills High School had a similar escalator effect, perhaps silver rather than gold). The curriculum of ambition was played against a national and international stage. These were not merely instructions for personal education. Everything at Yale was rehearsal. The Chairman of the *Yale Daily News* was, we all knew, just biding his time to take an equivalent post at the *New York Times* or *Time Magazine* or the *Wall Street Journal*. Those in the Political Union were just trying out their lines for runs for public office in Missouri or Indiana or South Carolina.

There were complicated lessons as part of this curriculum. Yale reflected historic power relationships in the United States and was a cherished home for the offspring of the old elites. Yale couldn't help but provide insight into the cultures of exclusion and the hierarchies of opportunity that persisted in American society. The icons of exclusion were the intimidating mausolea of the Secret Societies: Skull and Bones, Scroll and Key, Wolf's Head and the others. Each one, each year, selected 15 seniors who, in their view, were the true elect. For those not coming from the historic ranks of the American elite, the lesson was quite an interesting one. It was that room could be made for some at the table of power if they played their cards right. Yale could engage in alchemy and, more or less, turn outsiders into insiders.

One of my most important tutors was William Horowitz. He had come to Yale College from modest origins in Kansas City, Missouri, had graduated in 1929, had married and settled in New Haven, and was the father of my friend and classmate Daniel. Each year, Horowitz "adopted" a young Jewish student at Yale whom he took under his wing and tutored. Among those whom he marked were Calvin Trillin, who became the celebrated *New Yorker* writer and author, and Joseph Lieberman, who became senator from Connecticut and nominee for vice president of the United States. As with others in this "club," he saw in me someone who was making a journey similar to his, from a protected but strong identity of the past that could survive and distinguish itself in the complexity of Yale. He owned a major radio station in New Haven and gave me a job, election nights, of helping to collect precinct data as part of an effort to be the first to announce accurate results. He knew everyone, and when I was about to graduate, he introduced me to a series of other mentors—in public relations and in industry—for whom he thought it would be beneficial for me to work. Horowitz very much saw himself as an intermediary, a bridge and a translator between a changing Jewish community and a changing Yale. In the late 1970s, as co-chair of a committee to raise funds for Jewish studies to Yale, he was involved in determining whether a Yale far more plural than the one I had attended ought to have a Center for Jewish Life. Horowitz took the position (a position that did not wholly prevail) that it would be wrong to have a facility that emphasized or encouraged any segregation of Jews at Yale, intellectually or socially. He wished to preserve an environment in which Jewish students gained strength mainly in interaction with others.

In my senior year at Yale, I wrote a column for the *Yale Alumni Magazine* about life in New Haven as it might interest the graduates of the University. Based on my columns there, one of Yale's great journalistic graduates, Oliver Jensen, wrote me inviting me to New York to talk with him about a job. Jensen, an idiosyncratic and intriguing collector of American trams and trains and a long-time writer at *Time Magazine*, had recently relaunched *American Heritage Magazine*. With a small and talented group, he had turned it from a sleepy journal of a society of historians to a luxurious, hard bound, more popular magazine that was designed to appeal to other eccentric lovers of the curious people, objects, industrial processes, quirky religions, military battles and countless other phenomena that marked the American character. Jensen invited me to join, as a very junior editor, an extraordinary group that included Bruce Catton, the civil war historian, Alvin Josephy, a writer on American Indians, and Robert Cowley, the son of the famous critic Malcolm Cowley. Since I was torn between newspaper journalism and possibly going to graduate school *American Heritage* seemed an interesting halfway point. Slight ironies can be significant, and I was moved to take the job in part because of its subject matter.

In 1961, a year out of college, I took a break from my job at *American Heritage Magazine* to work in the first primary campaign of Robert F. Wagner, Jr who was running for reelection as mayor. I loved my job in that election. Wagner, the son of a great New York senator, had been chosen and put in his job by New York's political bosses, but now, partly out of the necessity of popular weariness with those in power, and partly because it was an appealing platform, Wagner was running against them, running, in a way, against his former self. My job was as junior advance man and partial companion of the press corps. A typical foray involved the mayor visiting a neighborhood in his limousine and the press accompanying him in theirs. I would talk to people in the streets, just before the mayor's arrival, and find some locally dramatic subject that would excite them: fixing or agreeing to introduce a crossing signal or street light, unraveling a problem with the local school or something equally inspiring. I would race back to the mayor's car and tell him or someone in his entourage what he might highlight and then retreat to the press car and spend as much time as I could with the mostly cynical press.

That was an extraordinary education in the melding of immigration and elections. I was learning something of American campaigning from streets defined by their melting pot politics. I received a solid and intense, if too brief, education in the ethnic politics of New York. Those were the days of balanced tickets (my year it was Wagner, Screvane, Beame; Irish, Italian, Jew), of local clubs, the power of endorsements, the dying out of ancient bosses. Here, too, I was learning techniques of persuasion: how public opinion was formed, the utility of mundane tasks like putting up posters, and the ways in which reporters decided what to write about whom. My experience involved an immersion in tribal loyalties, the persistence, in New York, of tight local customs and politically coherent and strongly defined communities. As we cruised the streets from morning to night in our black limousines, we crossed border after border of immigrant dreams.

120

I wasn't exactly preoccupied with race, class and immigrant involvement in American history and civics, but the subject certainly fascinated me. Intriguing, always, was the question of when and why young outsiders put themselves forward for positions of civic leadership. I had been impressed, years before, in high school, that our class elected Rossman Turpeau, a black student, as our president. His was a small moment of civic entry and emerging leadership that I would see frequently repeated as part of the American democratic drama. When I was later living in Washington in 1965, there was a lengthy essay in the *Washington Post* chronicling the fact there were many Jewish staff members in Congress but very few Jewish Congressmen. The explicit analysis became, in a sense, an instigation for change; soon more and more Jewish candidates began presenting themselves for office. The only living, breathing Austrian refugee candidate I could identify in New York was Franz Leichter, who worked his way up from City Council to Assemblyman and then State Senator from Washington Heights. He seemed softer, more reflective, more philosophical and more ironic than most politicians—qualities, of course, that I attributed to his Viennese origins. When the media highlights the heroic aspects of Asian elections to local offices, the breakthrough of women into governorships, the drama of rising black candidates in the Senate, I read these events against elements of a refugee past.

After my period at *American Heritage,* I deferred or avoided the opportunity to serve in the Armed Forces, and went off to law school instead. In my final year at Yale Law School, Potter Stewart, who had been appointed Associate Justice of the US Supreme Court by President Eisenhower, chose me for the much-coveted job as his law clerk. Stewart was from a distinguished American family that had moved in the nineteenth century from Connecticut to Ohio. He was, as it happened, from Cincinnati, from Yale and from Yale Law School, a mirror in which my refugee life was an interesting distortion, adaptation or variation (I had written an article about his appointment to the Court when I was a journalist at the *Yale Daily News*, where he had been a staff member two decades before). Working for Stewart was a superb example of the American success story: Refugee boy works for the Highest Court in the Land. The year before my clerkship, another refugee from Vienna, Ian Deutsch, had clerked for Justice Stewart. Stewart undoubtedly chose me on the recommendation of Alan

Novak, his other clerk, who had been a very good friend of mine at Yale. After my clerkship, I worked for another year in Washington, as a special assistant to the Secretary of Labor, then W. Willard Wirtz.

And then I went to California. California, even California of the 1970s, represented a kind of holy grail of American opportunity. So many people were immigrants, even if from some other part of the United States, that fixed and impermeable identities of leadership hardly existed. Things seemed so fluid, so non-hierarchical, so open, that huge shifts in personal careers could occur. Lana Turner could be discovered on a soda-fountain stool in Hollywood and become a star. But it was also true that people could start Savings & Loans and become multi-millionaires, invent housing subdivisions out of the desert, start little law firms that would blossom into powerful empires. In 1972, taking the idea of American democracy quite literally, I, bizarrely, ran for public office in Los Angeles. I was 32, and I had been in California, teaching at UCLA, for just four years. The race was city-wide. The state legislature had established a set of elected boards for local community college districts and the Los Angeles board had seven sparkling vacancies. The unusual absence of incumbents lured 138 candidates, 14 of whom would be chosen for a run-off. I won't go into the details except to say that I finished a respectable 18th (in a ballot in which candidates were listed alphabetically, seven out of the fourteen winners had names starting with A or B). Other ambitions were surely involved, but my running surely reflected my refugee fantasies.

WITTGENSTEIN AND ME

As part of this search for what, in me, is Austrian or Viennese, I read, among other things, *Wittgenstein's Poker*, by David Edmonds and John Eidinow. The book is an intelligent, popularizing treatment of the famous 1946 dispute between the two philosophers, Karl Popper and Ludwig Wittgenstein. It deals with their attitudes towards the world, their origins in Vienna (vastly different, in terms of wealth and class and in other respects, in ambition and education, essentially similar), how they came to leave Austria, how each was affected by his Jewishness and how, shortly after World War II, they met and came to verbal blows in Cambridge. The book helped me, by exploring the conflict between the two of them, to understand some of my own attitudes toward law and my behavior as a lawyer and law professor. I don't mean, at all, that I have been directly influenced by Wittgenstein and Popper themselves (especially because I had never studied their work).[4] Rather I was trying to determine whether some aspects of the life they had led in Vienna, which had differentially shaped their world views, had, on a far reduced, remote and less significant way, influenced me.

Wittgenstein famously said that the purpose of philosophy is "to show the fly the way out of the fly bottle." This phrase stunned me as I read it. True, it captured Wittgenstein's trademark anti-essentialism, his effort to liberate people from what he considered useless metaphysical claims and definitions. But more important for me, though he wrote the words long before the Anschluss, he invented a phrase that captured the late 1930s. This was a moment when whole populations, but especially the Jews of Vienna, became flies in bottles, desperate to find an exit. Families like mine sought meaning in what was occurring, but often couldn't find it; they tried to rely on legal protections and discovered they were arbitrarily applicable, almost totally unreliable or had vanished. What these families learned was that it is never clear what part of escaping the bottle is up to the fly, what to the shape of the bottle, and what factors exist wholly outside the physical world and the exercise of personal will.

I had much sympathy for the absurdist approach of Wittgenstein, since it encapsulated the irrelevance of law and legal structure at precisely that moment when law was supposed to matter. But I could also come away from my reflections sympathetic to the philosophy of Karl Popper. Popper was much more of a positivist. He did not ridicule the idea that morality existed or that there was a fixed vocabulary of meaning. For him, the purpose of the lawyer or legal analyst would be to do more than show each fly its own best exit from its own distinctive fly bottle. Lawyers could work with the actual rules and try to improve them to make a specific positive social difference in terms of human freedoms. He argued for a society in which there would be an active and effective public sphere. Popper's work ultimately inspired his student George Soros to establish the Open Society

---

4   For a person who could seriously and convincingly write about Wittgenstein's influence on her life, see Marjorie Perloff's *The Vienna Paradox*.

Institute, which encouraged a key generation in Central and Eastern Europe to believe that change was possible, that law was significant, and that establishing a reliable legal system could be the foundation of a meaningful civil society. For Popper and for Soros, the claim of logical positivists to some higher claim for particular laws or legal systems was not a set of "foolish errors," in which, to quote Wittgenstein, "they look for an explanation, a universal answer, a theory to cover all cases." Wittgenstein mocked those (like lawyers examining laws) who "stare at objects and feel they can somehow penetrate phenomena and reach an immanent core...."[5] Popper and his followers took law seriously.

So was I a positivist, more like Popper, or a mocker, more like Wittgenstein? Which Vienna was my heritage? When I was 20, I wanted to be a journalist, and when I went to law school, two years later, I still looked at the world through an aspiring journalist's eye. I read law, statutes and cases the way a journalist might see "facts," less as a statement of immutable principles, and more as a set of representations. Wittgenstein said that philosophy was about puzzles, not problems, and I saw law in much the same way. In other words, rather than trying to find out what the law "is" or "should be," I saw law as something closer to what Wittgenstein called a function of altering the grammar of the everyday. For Wittgenstein language operated as an ultimate kind of propaganda, as a lever. The rules of the language game were not determined by the nature of the world, but by interactions among people. "Truth" is not some sort of external reality, not a set of intrinsically correct statements, but is constructed by the coming together of a complex set of factors. Meaning is *usage*.

The marking event of my family's life had been a wholesale revolution in the structure of rules that governed the life of Jews in Vienna. At the beginning of their ordeal, the meaning and protection under existing law was fundamentally altered. Soon after the Anschluss, the new regime announced laws that would make it very clear what status Jews should have. The Popper response to the danger of this kind of outcome would be to fight for human rights principles, for a rule of law in a system that furthers an effective civil society (which implies a flow of information that

---

5   David Edmonds and John Eidinow, *Wittgenstein's Poker: The story of a Ten-minute Argument between Two Great Philosophers.* New York: Ecco, 2001, p. 182.

produces an effective check on authoritarian power). The Wittgenstein response might be to recognize that law will be continuously manipulated, that it is a reflection of shifting politics. The Third Reich is merely an example of the incapacity of law to restrain human behavior. As for me, I find a Viennese solution to the problem I've posed for myself: work for Popper-like outcomes but with a Wittgensteinian skepticism in the fundamental nature of law's dominion. I conduct myself as if law should be taken seriously, but in my bones, I have my doubts.

7

FOOD, CLOTHES, STORIES, SEX

What about the trappings of personality, the things one wears or eats or one's sexual negotiation of adolescence? Perhaps here I can locate aspects of being Viennese, or a particular kind of Jewish Viennese refugee of the 1930s. Blaming or attributing my idiosyncrasies on my Austrian past is neither fair to Vienna or to myself; still it is a way of trying to sort things out and to link the unlinked.

FOOD

Small cooking pots, random kitchen implements and a baby cup were among the objects hurriedly thrown in the crates that followed us from Taborstrasse in Vienna to New York and along the rest of our journey in the United States. These were holy objects, like the gold vessels and trays used in a Catholic communion. And the food we ate, even if it was macaroni and cheese made from a box, had in its composition some derived feeling of our lost household in Austria. Food and the smells of food are part of the intense continuum of identity for every refugee. And for every immigrant, negotiating food is a path forward to assimilation and a path backward to nostalgia. The preparation of food, the mode and context of eating, change over time, or at least they did for me. I become older and marry. My mother's kitchen governs no more and the habits of the society around me change, I move from one part of the country to another. Alternate cuisines from other immigrant and refugee groups begin to replace my own.

We are what we eat, it has been famously said. When I think about food as a guide to my refugeeness, most important are the dishes that originated in Vienna and were prepared wherever we were: Macon, Cincinnati, Charlotte, North Carolina or Forest Hills in New York. My mother prepared Paprikahändl, schwammerln mit Eier, Zwetschgenknödel, Palacsinta, Rizy-Bizy, Topfendenkeln and other foods that were characteristically Austro-Hungarian though with an emphasis on the Hungarian. These dishes still cling to my memory even if I never eat them again.

I loved helping to participate in the preparation of Zwetschgenknödel. My mother would make a yeasty batter that would be placed overnight to rise, with a towel (itself brought from Vienna) on top of it. She would have purchased a large can of sweet plums (or, failing that, have a bottle of apricot jam). The batter would be rolled, and then cut roughly into circles by pressing an inverted drinking glass over it (we specialized in the glasses which formerly held yahrzeit or memorial candles). I or my mother or, later, my sister, would insert the plums and pinch the dough. Then the dumpling would be placed in boiling water. When they were removed, after an anxious determination of the right amount of time of boiling, they would be rolled in confectioner's sugar and bread crumbs. For Topfendenkeln, the rolled pastry would be cut into triangles, and a spoonful of cottage cheese, flavored with sugar, egg and vanilla, would be dropped on top of them. Then, trays of them would be placed in our oven. We had an assembly line for producing these, especially if my parents were having one of their many afternoons for the other refugees of the Cincinnati neighborhood.

One of the exciting, deeply satisfying foods was Grammeless (or Gribbenes or Griven depending on what part of Europe is responsible for the naming). We would get fresh roasting chickens from the butcher and my mother would cut the yellowish fat pieces from the bird, collecting them for their eventual delightful fate. If there was going to be a large event, with guests, my mother might get a greater number of these pieces by gift from the butcher himself. These remnants were then placed in a frying pan over low flame and sautéed (though we didn't use the word) until a magic moment in which they were crisp—all the fat had transmuted in texture—but not burned. Often, my job was to watch for this critical point, and sometimes, but not often, I erred on one side or the other. I so loved these symbols of metamorphosis that I conspired to sample them before the moment of service, but do so in such a way that the whole did not look diminished.

In an art that seems somehow to have gotten lost somewhere along the line, my mother would get baby yolks, yolks in such an early development that they would be still inside the ova. These were delicate and delicious and would often be included, as a surprise, in chicken soup. At Passover the soup course, according to my father's custom, had to include extracting the yolks from normal, hard boiled eggs and mashing them into the chicken broth.

A big event in my early life was the serving of "hoorah Fleisch," a meal in which seasoned rice was prepared with the addition of sweetly roasted lamb or beef. For reasons of economy, the ratio of rice to meat was often quite high and the point was to figure out a way to cherish this fact rather than wallow in poverty. The upshot was to proclaim hoorah! when one found a piece of meat, and hence the name. Paprikahändl was a stalwart of the household, pieces of chicken thrown with abundant paprika, other spices, oil and onions. The chicken would simmer in an ancient saucepan and blend for a very long time, at low flame. This dish, always accompanied by Knockerl (blend flour, egg and water into a paste and then drip into a pot of boiling salted water), made for a satisfying meal especially on a cold Cincinnati night.

For many of these things, my mother used the metal pots that had made the trip from Vienna and the process of using them lent a special dignity to what was prepared. It was as if the pots brought flavors with them from Europe, or allowed for the proper combination or quantity of food to be made. They were slightly blackened, gently misshaped. And there were other Viennese food-related devices or implements. For Passover, there was a wondrous silver Seder Schüssel (or seder plate as it is usually called in English), a complex and stately architectural achievement in which the elements and design fit the ceremonial obligations. Four silver circular trays were stacked, separated and supported by slender silver columns that, temple-like, formed the exterior of the structure. This arrangement created the three compartments or spaces for the ceremonial matzot, unleavened bread, necessary for the performance of the Seder. On top there sat a trellis of interrelated bronze receptacles to hold the other foods symbolic of the Passover meal: bitter herbs, roasted lamb, roasted egg, charoses (a combination of fruit, wine and nuts) and karpas, radishes or parsley. The Seder Schüssel was glorious, but it had been so injured in its passage from Europe to the United States that almost everything was askew. Things that should have been fastened were now loose, and things that were integral might have been missing. The Seder plate stayed the way it was, unreconstructed, a symbol, though not explicitly recognized, of our own flight from Egypt.

When we would visit, each year, my great aunt, Irene Goldstein, in her apartment in the Bronx, she would produce a small museum of foods that were the continuation of Vienna and Slovakia. One hallmark was a home-made muscatel strong enough in character to last in memory from year to year. I was never sure what alchemy converted grapes into wine, or how it was that my relative, unique among all the people we knew, was distilling her own alcoholic beverage, but it was splendid. She collected and informally pressed a particular grade of green grape and then stored it in recy-cled green bottles that must, through constant reuse, have added additional flavor to what was almost a potion. She was an expert, too, in drying sa-lami. Salamis of various ages and moistness would hang in her crowded and tiny kitchen. When I was in college, years later, she would send me packages of them, dessicated to a point of concentrated flavor, together with her home-made muscatel and dry but delicious cookies. I could dis-appear in my dormitory room and recreate the Bronx just by taking a se-ries of bites out of the precious hoard.

In our annual visit to my father's sister, who lived in Newburgh, in up-state New York and then in Jackson Heights, in Queens, the feeling was of a much different Vienna. Here it was the approximation of a bourgeois sitting room that reigned. The silver from Vienna was all in use. We used tongs to take cubes of sugar from a Rosenthal porcelain sugar bowl and lift them to a Viennese cup and saucer. The pastries that were served were acquired from the bakery in the neighborhood that had croissants or petit fours most like those prepared at bakeries near Taborstrasse.

These were the foods of remembrance, but there were also the foods, as a young child, of adjustment, assimilation, transgression. For me, these offerings were, first, from the White Castle, the white-tiled forerunner of a mass fast food franchise located not far from the South Warwick where we lived. I must have eaten there during the time of my soft rebellion from keeping kosher, from the time I was ten to the time I was thirteen. I must have passed the White Castle a thousand times before I succumbed to its five cent hamburger. Later, it was Frisch's Big Boy, the 50s diner in my life, where everyone from Walnut Hills High School went for milkshakes and French fries and hamburgers (fish filets for those of us who persisted in not eating unkosher meat).

It's impossible to separate the Austro-Hungarian nature of our cupboard and kitchen from its Jewish character. My mother, brought up in the Orthodox tradition, had kept a kosher home in the short two years of my parents' marriage in Vienna and, of course, was determined to keep kosher in the United States, whether in Macon, where it was difficult, or in Cincinnati or New York, where it was not particularly difficult at all. What this meant, however, was that adjustment and change for me had to be navigated around the rules of kashruth as well as being a refugee. I had to square the fact that there was one set of rules at home (separating dishes for dairy and for meat), and one set of rules almost everywhere else (being indifferent to which dish was used for what purpose). At home, dishes that had somehow been exposed to forbidden foods, or used improperly, had to be purified again or discarded (though we were not meticulous about this), while in other people's houses, we did not abide by this rule at all. Besides, while my mother adhered to the rules in a mostly comprehensive way, my father openly and notoriously transgressed, in minor rebellion, smuggling forbidden foods into the house, even small but significant pieces of ham (Schinken) which were segregated in the refrigerator and became the cause of internal consternation.

My own practices of kashruth shifted and changed. As a small child, the practices of my household were automatically my customs. But already in Macon, the children with whom I played were of the place, small-town kids of regular folk, hardly Jewish refugees. Their habits were wholly different from ours, and their foods were as well. They shot squirrels, skinned and ate them. That is the most distinctive memory I have of Macon. I recall visiting my best friend and seeing, in his backyard, a galvanized tub filled with water, where dead squirrels were being kept cool prior to whatever process next occurred in their advancement to becoming food. I couldn't escape, totally, the immersion in popular attitudes toward diet propagated by advertising and practiced by my peers. My first idea of an American food was Dr. Pepper, which made its impression on me when I was still in Macon. It's hard to imagine now, but the not-so-subliminal message, underscored by the name of the beverage, was that the drink was secretly medicinal. Its long-running radio advertisement suggested that drinking it, as if by prescription, four times each day would improve one's health. The jingle became one of our frequently sung songs.

At some time, around my tenth or eleventh birthday, I decided to pack it all in, in terms of maintaining any semblance of keeping kosher. I had been in the Cub Scouts and now I was in the Boy Scouts. I wanted, I am sure, to be one of the regular gang. A great part of being a Boy Scout was going away, cutting trees into poles, building fences and camps, putting up tents, and then, of course, eating together. Breakfast was always—always—bacon cooked on camp-made fires. It was too much of a lure. I wanted to belong. I wanted to eat. I ate.

My diet changed again as a result, I'm surprised to say, of my bar mitzvah. There I was at the New Hope Congregation, taking the admonitions of the rabbi and the congregation seriously, and accepting that a significant moment had occurred with my arrival into symbolic and legal manhood. I decided to resume my former practice of keeping kosher, at least the lax mode that was the law of our household. I would eat anywhere, from any dishes, but I wouldn't eat meat that had not been prepared in a properly kosher way, and I would not eat shellfish or fish that were forbidden (catfish being the clearest example). I never understood the complexities of laws governing the delay between eating milk and eating meat, so I never consciously followed them. I fasted on the significant fast days and I abided, wholly, by the laws governing diet during the eight days of Passover. Then for that period, there was no difference between my diet at home and my diet abroad.

These rules that I settled on at the time of my bar mitzvah provided great flexibility and the dual possibility of moving freely in the world and still ensuring difference. I could think of myself as maintaining some sort of integrity and loyalty. Eating was a form of homage. I ate the way I did out of respect for my mother, out of obedience to what I was taught in Hebrew school, out of remembrance of my dead relatives. My eating was an exercise in adapting law and explaining why I had done so. I had to internalize these rules and be conscious of them. I needed to be on guard against accidental violation or the dangers of temptation. And, often enough, I had to articulate, when questioned by my friends, why I could eat one thing and not another. As a result, my status as a person of slightly distinctive background was reinforced for me and for my peers. Eating this way had social consequences, since it meant that there were certain things I did not want to do or explain (I quit the Boy Scouts partly so I didn't have to explain why I wasn't eating bacon any more). It meant, too, that I could see myself, and the small group of my friends who kept similar rules, as something of an elect.

This set of rules followed me until the end of my senior year at Yale. When I first visited Yale, as a Walnut Hills High School senior touring the East Coast with my friend Morry Wise and his mother, it was the week of Passover. I had packed two suitcases, one with clothes and one with foods that I could eat as we traveled through Amherst, New Haven and Princeton by car. In my very first moment in New Haven, as we went to our hotel rooms in an elevator of the Duncan Hotel, my suitcase of food broke open and cans of matzo ball soup and bottles of gefilte fish spilled out and rolled around the elevator floor. I tried to be nonchalant and dignified as I gathered up the food. After I was admitted, I went to the Jewish chaplain, a young Reform rabbi, Richard Israel, and explained my dietary laws. He wasn't sure what should or could be done, since no one or virtually no one had stated similar needs in his memory. He called the venerable Chaplain of the University (Sidney Lovett at the time), who agreed to call the kitchen staff and see how I could be accommodated. My personal laws and Yale's capacity easily adjusted one to the other. I stood in the regular dining queues, but, in those days before the ascendancy of the vegetarian alternative, special arrangement were made to assure that I could have an omelette or some other main course when meat was the only thing being served (which was the norm). And then, half-way through my senior year, my rules changed once again. Steak was given as a reward to the Yale undergraduates once a week, probably Saturday night. For three and a half years I had, in respect for my brand of kashruth, denied myself this treat.

And then, one day, I buckled. It was fine with my friends, my conscience, my parents, but the kitchen staff, who had maintained my discipline for those short, bright college years, were slightly saddened.

I did not and have not abandoned all rules. Now, I will eat the meat of any animal that could be prepared in a way that would be kosher, even if the particular meat I am eating is not. I will not eat shellfish, like lobster or crab, or meat that is forbidden, like pork. This has caused intellectual problems. I did not know, for a long time, in what category goat or venison was. Since these had never, in my consciousness, been prepared and presented to me in their properly prepared form, I did not know whether I could eat them under my invented rules. The first time I was tempted by venison on a menu, I called my friend from Yale, William Cutter, a Reform rabbi on the faculty at Hebrew Union College to ask him whether deer, if properly slaughtered and prepared, could be kosher (if it could be, then I would agree to eating it). Apparently, deer met the standard of having cloven hooves and chewing cud.

All of this rigor or absence of rigor concerning food rules had to be redefined, redefended, rearticulated by me when my middle son Gabriel thrillingly became a baal teshuvah and rigorously observant. Indeed, in a turn that caps this journey, Gabriel became a national expert in the technicalities of kashruth, dealing with difficult problems of definition, such as the acceptability of new chemical additives, the complexities involved in the shipping of raw materials, and the production of kosher and non-kosher products under one roof. I have listened, transfixed, as he explains the composition of coatings used to make apples shiny or preserve fruits, or the administrative problems of negotiating with factory supervisors as food processing innovations change settled presumptions about what quality controls are maintained.

My personal confrontation with kashruth, my playing around with the rules, my pattern of adjustment to them, had interesting implications. I am pretty sure that it affected my attitude to law and jurisprudence, for example. When Max Gluckman gave his lectures on Barotse jurisprudence at Yale Law School when I was a student there, and talked about the relationship between custom and law and how custom adjusted itself to behavior, I could think back to my days passing the White Castle and buying my first hamburger. How I established rules for eating was a little index of my search for modes of socialization, for maintaining some elements of the past without its burden (or benefits) impinging on my exploration and negotiation with the present.

CLOTHES AND CARS

Refugee children from Vienna in the United States did not dress in dirndls and lederhosen, did not do Austrian dances, did not have clubs that recalled Austrian ways; but still, clothes, like food, were markers of adjustment. It is a useful game to play to think of my relationship to articles of clothing and elements of style and fashion in the same way I have tried to remember reflections of identity in recipes or menus or habits of eating. Over time, a chest of drawers, a closet and the armoire of one's family become a particularized museum of sartorial assimilation. Some of these clothes (and my attitude toward them) were related to Vienna. Most, however, resulted from our particular mode of being refugees.

There were many photographs of my father and mother in Vienna in which they present themselves with a comfortable middle class elegance. It was their natural appearance there. My father was in his very early 30s, before he left Vienna, neatly mustached, often with a nicely folded handkerchief in his suit pocket. My mother, who thought of herself as not so slavish about clothes, was meticulously and carefully attired, with dresses made for her or purchased at good shops. There was always a drawer in our apartments in Cincinnati and elsewhere in which unused emblems of an increasingly distant Viennese life were kept: pearl stickpins, tuxedo points, and gold cuff links. My mother had a drawer of jewelry from Vienna, and some jewelry kept in a safe deposit box as well. On the big Jewish holidays, she would take out diamond earrings or another piece of jewelry and wear them. There were other clothes that had followed us from Vienna. My mother brought her bridal gown that stayed, wrapped, through 60 years of moving from place to place. When my father finished school, 16 years old, he was sent for training at the family's weaving mill in the Burgenland, in Neuenkirchen. It was bone-chilling cold. The company bought him a herringbone, fur-lined coat with a fur mantel to protect him from the elements. He wore it only in Neuenkirchen, not in Vienna. But, somehow, it was placed in the crate that made it to the United States. I wore it when

I went to high school, to Walnut Hills. Later I had it refurbished and gave it to my son Gabriel who wears it still.

In 1940, when I was just two, my mother's mother, isolated in Vienna, probably realizing that she may never see us again, sent a package of clothes for me by way of one fortunate enough still to depart at that late date. The family trusted with this task lived in the same building in the Grosse Schiffgasse as my Aunt Irene and Alfred. Included in the package was a dark blue coat with silver buttons, lederhosen for a small boy, and a green Tyrolean hat with a feather extending from it.

Clothes for us reflected a view of reality. Rather than have pretensions upward, we were to be somewhat more modest in appearance than we were in station. For me (and my sister) it was made clear that some things were important in the world, some values, some attainments, and some ambitions. Clothes were not. My mother had a standard answer if I asked for something expensive or unnecessary in the way of shirts or pants: "If you want clothes like Johnny's, ask Johnny's mother if she needs another boy." We did not even believe in investing money in clothes just because they would last a long time (besides my mother was sure I would lose or stain or tear what clothes I had). There were new clothes for school and for camp. Woolworth's was my outfitter and later Robert Hall. My mother was fully aware that clothes were part of the definition of status and one aspect of navigating American culture. For her, in almost everything, the choice was clear: save money, don't be dependent. The clothing manifestation of that approach was a remarkable insensitivity to fashion and a dedication to functionality. Her excitement at finding appropriate clothes in a thrift shop or obtained second-hand never terminated. Indeed, the larger her personal wealth, the greater her gratification at obtaining suitable clothes for next to nothing.

When I think of my chest of drawers and closets even now, there are suits and shoes and shirts that I have acquired because they were available at a bargain, even if they don't quite fit or are awkward or out of style. I don't wear them, but they have lingered in my sartorial armoire for a very long time. I have the white tuxedo that I bought when I was a senior in high school because the purchase price was just over twice the rental. When I was at Yale, it was still the time of compulsory shirts and ties to be worn in the dining hall. But at Trumbull College, where I lived, I must have dressed in a way that severely challenged the rule, questioning by my actions either what constituted a shirt or what constituted a tie. Sometime in my junior year, in 1959, the Master of the College, John Spangler Nicholas, wrote me a letter threatening me with eviction if I continued to flaunt the regulations. I was not politically rebellious, but I was conditioned to think of the minimum approach to satisfying an external rule of fashion.

New Haven, however, was a school in the use of clothes as a new uniform of status, and even I absorbed the lesson. The two most fashionable stores around Yale, J.Press and Fenn-Feinstein, were shops owned and operated by second-generation Jewish immigrants. They were tailors to the rich and privileged and exulted in serving extremely well the class-related norms of Yale (and upper middle class America). From them I learned two lessons: the function of clothes as part of adjusting and the role of immigrants as tradesmen to the court.

It is a bit of a stretch, but I would connect cars and clothes, looking at cars as another form of dress. Used car dealers, car manufacturers and designers know the intimate relationship between selection of automobile and sense of personality and self. So maybe my cars, too, over time, provide an insight into something as obscure as my Austrian-ness. My first car certainly fit this mold. I bought it when I was a senior in high school, or maybe it was when I was a junior. It was a Kaiser. It was not named, of course, after the Austrian Emperor (though could there have been a subconscious association?); rather it was the creation of an idiosyncratic visionary who wished to find a popular car to meet the post-War demand and provide a challenge to General Motors, Ford and Chrysler. Mine was a 1948 Kaiser, and in 1954 or 1955, when I purchased it, the company was either out of business or almost so, and, as a result, their cars were extremely inexpensive. The Kaiser was a luxurious car in many ways, but one of fading luxury. It was comfortable. But mostly it was idiosyncratic. And of course it was cheap. Undoubtedly, I was the only young man in my school who had a Kaiser. I had solved in one fell swoop the problem of desiring a car, not having much money, and not wanting to be ordinary.

The last car I had, 50 years later, was Kaiser-like in a way as well. I was spending two academic terms at the Institute for Advanced Study in Princeton, New Jersey, and I wanted a car for shopping and occasional trips to the countryside or to the airport. I bought, in late 2000, a 1977 Lincoln

Continental for $900. Like the Kaiser, it was luxurious. As with the Kaiser, I was the only one on my block to have such a car. As with those who rode in my Kaiser, my passengers in the 1977 Lincoln loved the experience and saw it as a special thrill. In between, differentiation by car purchase took place in various ways. When we first moved to Los Angeles, and I could barrel down canyons, I actually bought a 1962 Mercedes Benz 190 SL sports car. Just buying a Mercedes Benz, even a used one, was a transgression since many Jews defined their Jewishness by not acquiring a German car. In the late 1970s I acquired a big 1960s Buick convertible, fins triumphant, that ended up being a massive window box for flowers parked outside our house.

I cannot trace all these car choices back to my birth on the Taborstrasse. Every purchase of an automobile is a reflection of the buyer's personality (and the shaping of that personality by the car industry). Were these cars like my clothes? They seemed, as with clothes, to involve decisions, partly economic and partly quizzical: not to be like others (not even to assert one's individuality in the way Detroit deemed proper). I could take my Kaiser and repair it using plastic cement and not care; I could buy my Lincoln Continental and, at the end of the time, drive it into a river. I could think of cars not as status, but as the functional equivalent of clothes bought in thrift shops. This was not true of all my clothes or all my cars, but there was a consistency to be cherished.

ADOLESCENCE

It would be a tribute to that cliché of being Viennese, Sigmund Freud, to try to use my approach to adolescence as a key to my Austrian-ness. It is probably true, and I do not think it was an element of the Kinsey Reports, that patterns of sexual practice can be ascribed to particular refugee groups and, had we the science, to their children as well. Let's take the easy parts—easy, that is, to identify: the expectation of my parents' refugee generation that children should marry, marry someone Jewish, and then, far less stated, to have more than two children to compensate for the depopulation of the Holocaust. Put more strongly, the duty was to recreate, not just procreate, to provide some chance that what had been destroyed could be continued.

Probably the fact that I was an adolescent in the 1950s was far more of a factor in my sexual maturation—or lack of it—than anything related to my Viennese past or refugee upbringing. Of course, Vienna was the city of wine, women and song. And that was something that was reinforced with joy. Those imperial exemplars—the human gods of the Austro-Hungarian court—were famous for their sexual complexities. There were stories—probably told to me as a leitmotif of education—of the more obvious existence of mistresses as a matter of accepted fact there. My father's Uncle Isidor, who had become his protector and his guardian after my grandfather died, was killed, famously, run over by a trolley on his way to see his lover at the Hotel Metropolitan. That was an idea of what it meant to be a Viennese man. My father hinted at acceptable visits to a Viennese brothel as part of his own sexual initiation. He was an *homme a femmes*, happy to banter with women, especially beautiful women, and he was a charming and engaging conversationalist. One possibility—who knows whether it was a factor—was that I considered myself a refugee from my father's sexual world and not yet comfortable in the new one. My sexuality could not be the same as if it had been developed as a young person in Vienna. Nor was it clear which Vienna I should emulate—the urbane Vienna I attributed to my father, or the Orthodox Vienna of my mother. My models, images of the mind, would not be the Crown Prince or the implicit wooing and indiscretions of the operetta. But I was not sure I could make it all the way over to the models and images of American song, of Frank Sinatra and later Elvis Presley.

Since it is difficult to locate and describe, in my particular refugee-ness, a specific subtext of attitudes toward sexual passion and sexual practice, I could try starting the other way around. Perhaps my pattern of learning about sexuality can cast light on the meaning of my Austrian Jewish refugee-ness. Over the years, perhaps through my own particular refugee lens, I have thought a lot about the structure of Jewish fraternities at my high school, Walnut Hills. There were two, Round Towners and Phi Rho Delta. Of course, the existence of the Jewish fraternities *qua* Jewish implied that they were a minor part of a larger set of fraternities that did not have many Jewish members. As I came to understand it, Round Towners was the fraternity of the German Jews, and principally German Jews who were not children of refugees. This was the establishment fraternity, the fraternity with boys who dressed well, had new cars, knew exactly what to do, and had the preferred girlfriends. Phi Rho Delta seemed to be the fraternity of Jews of Polish and Russian origin, largely (in my non-sociological mind of the time) non-refugee, but certainly more open, and less definitive in terms of its criteria of membership.

I was not a member of either. It's not clear to me why. I am pretty sure it was because I was not asked, but I may not have put myself in the way of involvement either because of uncertainty about the virtues of belonging or about fear of cost. Another explanation, and probably the most accurate one, was that there was something about my being, my dress, the classmates with whom I associated that sufficiently branded me as an outsider (to myself as well as others). I was not high on the ladder of the clubbable. I would have a hard time capturing who I was at that time. I loved my friends, but maybe, they were, a bit like me, at the margin. I think of Richard Portnoy, smart, fat, messy, not one who played the games of the majority. There was Mark Schulzinger—son of a butcher who collected Duesenberg automobiles—who became a minor cult figure in the world of science fiction before he died in 2000. And there was Jerry Mork, painfully gawky. None of these were fraternity material, none seemed preoccupied with girls, as opposed to stamp collections, or science, or ping-pong, or other forms of sublimation.

I tried to be an athlete, a kind of gateway to a vaunted American sexual identity, but I was a horrid one. Fairly tall, I tried out for the basketball team. But I was clumsy in a way that Sid Bass, the coach (this is true, not purposely self-deprecating), feared that using me in practice might endanger the other players on the team. I was the only person on the basketball squad who never was asked even to dress for a game, who never even made it to the bench.

On the other hand, I had a girlfriend in those years, and a great and gifted one, and she was a significant figure in much of my developing life. We became girlfriend and boyfriend, at least from my perspective, in the high school sense of the 1950s, sometime in the ninth or tenth grade at Walnut Hills High School and stayed in the awkward intimacy of that category until half-way through our senior year in college. I worked hard at winning her. When I first began to court her, or the equivalent of that in 1953 or 1954, Jeanne was the accepted girlfriend of Rusty Frankel, who was (in a view clarified by the distance of time) very much the successful, adjusted Cincinnatian. Of course, he was not a refugee, and of course, he would be, easily and comfortably, a member of one of the fraternities (Phi Rho Delta, I think). In the fabulous custom of the 1950s, one that probably persists, he, like all his fraternity mates, could offer his pin to a girl, "pin-ning" it to her blouse, where she would wear it proudly. Maybe Jeanne was "pinned" in this way. To win her over, I did all the awkward things love-torn teen-agers do. I wrote poems and I parked outside her house looking at her window. I tried to demonstrate in Latin class or math or English that I was worthy of her respect and love. More than this, I went to synagogue at the converted movie theater in Roselawn where her father was one of the leaders and demonstrated my religious fervor in a way that would be totally acceptable in a son-in-law.

It's a hypothesis, but one I find worth considering: marrying (and the idea of marrying and sexual intercourse were, it should be remembered, pretty clearly bound together) was a final defining act of a post-refugee life. Through it I would form a wholly pervasive new alliance and alli-ances, in my personal life as well as my external one. It is one thing to say I did not know what that life should or would be; it's another to imagine, and it may be true, that I was not ready, and would not be, to leave the self-definition and insular protection of my particular refugee identity. Jeanne represented some form of connection to a different world, but there was a trap in this: was it too different or not sufficiently different? Not being able to answer this question restricted me, obstructed me, and impeded my capacity to be sufficiently present and whole. Undoubtedly, this process of searching and defining is true for everyone, in the awkward, halting way of the semi-blind young, where infatuation and reason clumsily interact. My only claim here is that my special awkwardness arose (as is also univer-sally true) from my particular circumstances, the way I became 15 or 16 as the background for my beginning stages of contemplating adulthood.

Who knows what I have suppressed that is relevant to an understand-ing of these questions? I can add a few instances of relevance. When I was at Walnut Hills, I acted in plays, and in my senior year was asked whether I'd be willing to be "lent" to a private girls' academy, the Hillsdale School for Girls, to perform one of the male roles in Jane Austen's *Pride and Prej-udice*. This experience was a revelation. Walnut Hills High School was a blessedly diverse place with Cincinnatians of all backgrounds and degrees of wealth. But this was different. I was admitted to an extraordinary new world: a world of privilege, of wealth, overbrimming with young women in the splendor of their uniforms and practices and in Anglo-Saxon ease (or seeming ease), many of them preparing to become debutantes (a category of achievement or privilege that had probably previously eluded me). I immediately had a crush on one of them and fantasized that the feeling was reciprocated. I luxuriated in my brief, intense time there. I actually attended one or two debutante balls at the invitation of girls I had befriended. I was a besotted student of the new customs and possibilities and thunderstruck by the way these young women could open the way for a crossing of religious and other lines.

Five years later, already graduated from college, I became drawn, fairly passionately, to a graduate student in Cambridge, Massachusetts, a colleague in school of Helen Lefkowitz, then the partner and now the wife of my closest friend, Daniel Horowitz. In fairly short order, I was swept away. I went to visit her and her parents in Pennsylvania Dutch farm country, and was convinced I wanted to marry her. I went to my mother to speak with her of the possibility. With enormous emotion, she delivered the atomic-bomb Holocaust speech (in so many words). "Hitler destroyed our family. You cannot marry a woman who is not Jewish. This is your immutable, unchangeable obligation." Of course, I obeyed.

In 1963, I met and fell deeply in love with Aimée Bertha Brown, with whom I have now had more than four decades of glorious adventure (including the pleasure of three sons and six grandchildren). When we met the two of us were in that moment of maximum promise, I in my last year at Yale Law School and Aimée a young Ph.D candidate in art history. That first date, I inveigled our way into the Elizabethan Club in New Haven, in a quaint eighteenth-century house, where the tea was complimentary, and the cucumber sandwiches were on neat wedges of white bread. This was an excellent site for an initial interview. When that went well, I immediately asked her to continue to dinner at the city's only Hungarian restaurant (we drove in a car I borrowed for the occasion from a classmate).

I had already learned that Marthe, her mother, had been born in Transylvania, of an assimilated Hungarian Jewish family, which accounted for

my choice for our first meal together. I learned, that evening, about Aimée's gifted father, Adolph, who had died at age 56 of a heart attack the
spring before. He was from Toledo, Ohio, but when he was a child, his
mother had been sent to Colorado because of tuberculosis. The family
was wretchedly poor and his father was without the capacity to take care
of his children. Adolph and his sister and brother were sent to the Cleve-
land Jewish Orphanage (much later I would see the kinescope of a television program the Bell Telephone Hour made in the 1950s from his script;
the program, called "The Frying Pan," was a wholly fantasized episode in
Adolph's life at the Orphanage, suggesting that he secretly kept a chicken
and hoarded eggs, and yearned for the gift of a way to cook them).

There were brilliant and ambitious boys at the Orphanage and Adolph
was one of them. He worked his way through Case Western Reserve Medical School and in the 1930s he was in Paris receiving specialized training
in the relatively new field of plastic surgery. In that romantic French environment, he met the striking, athletic, vivacious Marthe, a Hungarian-Pa-
risian in the making, who was also studying medicine there. He soon asked
her to marry and join him, after their studies, in Chicago, where he would
begin his practice. She accepted and arrived in 1936 with a very limited
command of English, a charming accent, and a guaranteed round-trip
ticket in case she found Chicago impossible to bear (by the time I came on
the scene, Adolph had shifted his practice to Beverly Hills, largely for reasons of his health, and Aimée went to high school there).

The transition had its complex dramas. Before Aimée was born in 1939,
her grandmother arrived from Transylvania to see the new child and help
Marthe take care of her. But this visit had its hurtful, tragic side. With
the outbreak of war in Europe, Mitzike, as she was known, could no longer return home to her beloved husband. He and one of Marthe's brothers were sent to the camps and killed, while other close relatives became
survivors.

In later years, Aimée reproached me (she viewed it as a reproach) for
marrying her because she was tall, nice and Jewish, or at least that I saw her
as fitting these three criteria of appropriateness. This was not quite right.
She represented some combination of attributes that fulfilled my unfin-
ished, unfulfilled, not well understood refugee yearnings. True, she passed
the religion test in a way that could raise no objection, but, and I won-

der if I viewed this as something positive, her understanding and practice of Judaism was practically non-existent. I think the first thing she served me in her little apartment in New Haven was lobster soup (I refused it). It was significant to me that she was, in some respects, Austro-Hungarian. She represented some confirmation of my situation and status. I could search for her Hungarian-ness in the way I rifled through my own refugee past. But she also represented a rejection of all that as well. True, she had Hungarian songs sung to her as a child, as had I. Her grandmother prepared Hungarian foods for her and mailed them to New Haven much as my great-aunt did for me. Yet, it was pretty obvious that her family's was not my refugee narrative. Much more was it about traditional American success. Her parents seemed to live a life more of ease, of privilege, a sort of life of society. Adolph had risen from the Orphanage to town house in Chicago and then Beverly Hills and Malibu.

Fourteen days after meeting her, I proposed.

8

OBJECTS OF REMEMBRANCE

My father and mother both enjoyed recounting their happy European days. The time they spent there together, as a young married couple, had been only two years and their courtship was not so long, so that most of their Viennese tales were of their earlier, separate lives. My mother loved to talk about her grandfather's farm in Nyitra in Slovakia, her travels with her mother and her emergence as an independent young woman. My father sought to impart, what was, to him, a blissful time—the late period of the Monarchy and the Austro-Hungarian Empire before World War I. He adored talking about Franz Josef, the members of the imperial family, their Lipizzaner stallions. He also wanted to remember, as deeply as possible, a debonair and charming father who had died so young (one memory, he reenacted, was his father's habit of dividing his salted *Butterbrodt* into half-inch strips, a custom we followed).

Stories my mother told and stories my father told were different for a fundamental reason. So many of my mother's family died in the concentration camps that every word, every anecdote, carried that sad future with it, but this was not true for my father. When my mother told stories of Vienna, in the background of her voice and thought were her parents, her cousins, her uncles who had been killed. Every telling was an act of memory. When my mother lit her many ceremonial *yahrzeit* candles, the 24-hour lights in a simple embossed glass, it was an event of extraordinary solemnity and sorrow. My father's grandmother, Charlotte, had had 16 sons and daughters. Few of them had children, some of the family had already died by the early 1930s, some had migrated, and almost all the others of his relatives left Austria in time.

Through my own experience as child, father and grandfather, I know how styles in children's stories have changed. I have a sense, too, that the set of stories a mother tells a child helps shape his or her attitude toward the world. Certainly, choice of story and cohort of stories provide a rich source of information about the relationship of mother to child, and mother to a sense of self. I have thought, though not carefully enough, how the idea of a former world was inflected on my consciousness through the close and emotional mechanism of my mother's storytelling to her son.

My mother told stories of the kind a mother tells a child: nursery rhymes, fairy tales, morality tales, not particularly Austrian or Viennese, but more Germanic or European than American. They had a significance, in their place and time, and it is useful to think of how they were received by me. Take, as an example, that sweet Scottish nursery rhyme:

> *My Bonnie lies over the ocean,*
> *My Bonnie lies over the sea.*
> *My Bonnie lies over the ocean,*
> *Please bring back my Bonnie to me.*
> *Bring back,*
> *Bring back,*
> *Oh, bring back my Bonnie to me, to me.*
> *Bring back,*
> *Bring back,*
> *Oh, bring back my Bonnie to me.*

For me, even as a child, this poem and song immediately had a wistful quality. "Over the Ocean" meant volumes, meant so clearly the ocean we had crossed together. Who was the Bonnie who was over the ocean? Was this my mother's mother singing about her daughter? Was I the Bonnie who was over the ocean apart from someone, someone or somewhere? Was the Bonnie who lived over the ocean the younger aspect of my mother, or was it my mother's mother trapped and then killed in the war?

My mother read *Struwwelpeter* to me, a book of very Germanic morality wrapped in threats that would be ignored by a child at the greatest of risk. *Struwwelpeter* was hardly a set of fairy tales. Mystery or distance of time and place did not exist. The book involved personal discipline related closely to the day-to-day. The stories were a plea for good behavior wrapped in the horrific and macabre. Little Robert, who did not obey the rule that he stay indoors on rainy days, was carried off, never to be seen again, when the wind caught his umbrella. In this world of rules to obey, punishment followed directly and ruthlessly from violation of norms. As for the behavior that was condemned, I particularly remembered "The Story of Cruel Frederick":

> *"This Frederick! this Frederick!*
> *A naughty, wicked boy was he*
> *He caught the flies, poor little things,*
> *And then tore off their tiny wings;*
> *He kill'd the birds, and broke the chairs,*
> *And threw the kitten down the stairs;*
> *And oh! far worse and worse,*
> *He whipp'd his good and gentle nurse!"*

Or of "Augustus Who Did Not Have Any Soup":

> *"Augustus was a chubby lad;*
> *Fat ruddy cheeks Augustus had;*
> *And everybody saw with joy*
> *The plump and hearty healthy boy.*
> *He ate and drank as he was told,*
> *And never let his soup get cold.*
> *But one day, one cold winter's day,*
> *He threw away the spoon and screamed:*
> *"O take the nasty soup away!*
> *I won't have any soup to-day:*
> *I will not, will not eat my soup!*
> *I will not eat it, no!"*

I sympathised with "Fidgety Philip" ("Let me see if Philip can, Be a little gentleman; Let me see if he is able; To sit still for once at table") and, of course, Johnny-Look-in-the-Sky:

> As he trudg'd along to school,
> It was always Johnny's rule
> To be looking at the sky
> And the clouds that floated by;
> But what just before him lay
> In his way,
> Johnny never thought about

All the ill-behaved, neglectful or thoughtless children in *Struwwelpeter* get what is due to them. Cruel Frederick was bitten by his dog and Augustus, who ceased eating his soup, wasted away. Johnny tripped and fell and almost broke his bones. Pauline, who was warned against using matches, ignored her lesson and:

> She was burnt with all her clothes,
> And arms and hands, and eyes and nose;
> Till she had nothing more to lose
> Except her little scarlet shoes;
> And nothing else but these was found
> Among her ashes on the ground.

How could I ever forget the mother's threat in "The Story of Suck-a-Thumb":

> The great tall tailor always comes
> To little boys that suck their thumbs.
> And ere they dream what he's about
> He takes his great sharp scissors
> And cuts their thumbs clean off, - and then
> You know, they never grow again.

148

I adored these stories, I think, for their very German-ness. We had an old copy in German, and I knew that my father and mother had each been an audience for their reading. Because these were tales that came from use in Vienna, I could imagine how children were disciplined there and what dangers and flaws children were suspected of having. My mother told these stories with great gusto.

Of the fairy tales, one of my mother's favorites was the very complex Rapunzel, a tale of the Brothers Grimm. Here, a very poor couple stole vegetables from a neighboring garden, hidden behind a wall. The enchantress who owned the garden discovered their violation, and told the poor husband she would forgive the trespass and allow the man and wife all the food they needed if they agreed to give up their first child, a child yet to be born. A beautiful daughter arrived, the enchantress made good on her claim, and, ultimately, imprisoned the girl in a tower. Only by climbing the girl's beautiful tresses could the enchantress gain entry. A prince came through the forest, saw the witch calling for the tresses and mounting to the tower chamber. He called to the damsel, and was allowed access, with the inevitable result. The evil witch discovered the pair, banished the maiden and put out the eyes of the prince. But love triumphed over the tragedy of blindness and the young couple was reunited. My mother also told me the story of Rumpelstiltskin, the dwarf who helped a miller's daughter spin gold out of straw, a miracle that paved the way for her to become married to the king. There was one condition, agreed to by the young woman: the dwarf, at some unknown time in the future, would have the right to take the queen's first child from her and claim it for his own. After the marriage, and after the birth, he came to seize the baby, but, out of pity, allowed the desperate young queen three days of grace. If she discovered his name, she would be released from the obligation. Frantically, she sent her messengers around the kingdom, and because of the dwarf's own bragging, learned the dwarf's true name, just in time, thwarting him forever from taking her child. In a rage, he stamped the earth so violently that he tore himself in two.

Who was the Rapunzel of my specific imagination and what were the undercurrents of the story for a refugee mother and her Americanizing child? In Cincinnati, in Eden Park, there was a tower we frequently passed when I was a child that we called Rapunzel's tower. "Rapunzel, Rapunzel" we said as we passed, with me playing the part of the prince charming, "let down your hair." I suppose, as for almost all boys, my mother was the nearest thing to the Rapunzel figure, though I probably could not work out all aspects of what trap installed her in what tower and what it would take for me, as young prince, to release her. Yet, there was more in the metaphorical telling of the imprisoned maiden, and the seeming marks of irretrievable tragedy. Was Rapunzel, for my mother, a story of those who had been left behind, in an unknown and unknowable tower, their families roaming through the forest seeking to locate them, free them, take them down from their cells in the sky? In both Rapunzel and Rumpelstiltskin, a terrible shadow (loss of a future child) floated across an idyllic possibility (marriage to the king in Rapunzel or the very birth of a child in Rumpelstiltskin). Both in Rapunzel and Rumpelstiltskin this almost inevitable threat to a seemingly satisfactory status quo is foolishly forgotten or suppressed. And in each story terrible things occur because of a bargain that seemed expedient at the time but, morally, should have not been made. Was there something like that lurking in our Austrian past, or the past of all the Jews? Had there been complacency in the face of predictable and cyclical oppression? These stories implied one further and relevant lesson. Escape from the consequences of evil might be possible or inevitable given sufficient innocence, good fortune, cleverness and persistence. This lesson of avoiding death through brilliant initiative or magical intervention was an attribute, too, of Hansel and Gretel (another of my mother's favorites) where two clever children outsmart the witch who imprisoned them and who wished to fatten them up to make a satisfactory meal. The children avert death by extending a bony finger when the witch seeks to see if their arms are sufficiently fleshy and corpulent.

There were Austrian stories of trolls and mountain stock, including the tale of six baby goats instructed by their mother not to admit anyone to their house unless the visitor showed a white knuckle. The wolf, overhearing this speech, rubbed his paws with chalk and, when the mother went away, gained entrance and ate the kids. When the mother came home, she discovered that her children were missing. She raced to the water where the wolf was sleeping, slit his stomach, recovered her children, and filled the wolf with stones before sewing up the skin. The wolf, on waking, moved slightly and sank, drowning in the river.

I don't know how vivid and active my imagination was at the time. I, or my mother, could imagine that our family in Vienna was like the goats, with the wolf coming to our door at 11A Taborstrasse in November, 1938. This wolf used power, not subterfuge; fear, not chalk. Perhaps we, as a family, were cleverer than those goats, escaping the wolf, not devoured the way others were. Certainly it was a moral that one could always count on the mother to rescue from the certainty of tragedy. Could one hope that it would be the case in life that the wolf, or the witch, or the troll, or the dwarf would have only a temporary victory, even a seemingly satisfactory one, only to be outsmarted or outwitted at the end? There had been an evil enchanter in our lives, a major, functioning witch who had caused calamities without number. Our little family had escaped, had a victory over power. My mother must have been conscious of parallels between stories and life, intertwining fairy tale with the reality of the events of the 1930s.

Other tales may have had different motives. My parents loved the stories of Mount Olympus and talked with me about its gods and goddesses often. And it was up to me to reconcile this discourse of the gods of Greece (or Rome) with the master narratives of Jewish history. One possibility is that my parents wanted, through these stories, to provide a subversive deflection, a kind of Viennese skepticism, about the claims to truth of any religion, including Orthodox Judaism. Much of the Jewish narrative was "true" in the sense of being about events in the world (including our expulsion from Vienna). Judaism was ours and was important, but something short of "belief" in the divine claims of a true religion was warranted. The stories of Pharoah or Abraham, Isaac and Jacob were surely different from those of Rapunzel and Rumpelstiltskin or Zeus and Hera. The Torah was central to our Jewishness; but in a modern turn, the centrality had to be defined in some way that winked slightly at the highest set of claims—the existence of God—while still taking narratives seriously.

I could question whether my father's family, more anchored in society, may have been drawn to the sections of Torah on Joseph in Egypt or the account of Mordechai in the Megillah Esther (the Purim story). These were Court Jews, men of the present: Joseph helped run the empire of the Pharoah, and his equivalent could certainly be found in the empire of Franz Josef. Mordechai was the intermediary, the trusted official, sometimes misunderstood, sometimes tarred with being Jewish, who could explain his beleaguered people to Ahasuerus, the King. In the family of my mother, the focus may have been on the patriarchs and matriarchs. My mother's family would more surely think of an idealized future, a time when the Temple would be restored, and the Kohanim and Levites would resume their proper roles. After the war, when I was growing up, the Holocaust affected the way everyone read the Torah and its stories, and this process could be said to have been influenced, again, by the establishment of the State of Israel. But however these emphases altered, they were always variations on power and responsibility.

This question of the relationship of the Jewish story to all other stories was especially significant for me on Yom Kippur, the Day of Judgment. I recall, as a child in Cincinnati, how, halfway through the communal fast, Cantor Rosen held Feinberg Synagogue in awe as he pleaded, in one of the most famous prayers, for God's permission to intercede and carry forward the Congregation's requests for forgiveness. The prayer always seemed quite long (it was a star turn for a professional cantor) and it sought to invest a special belief in the mystery of the moment. For me, no Yom Kippur of this period passed without my wondering about this intercession, the personal and transparent request for authority to be the carrier for the community to God. This, too, was a special moment in which I came closest to having actually to wrestle with the idea of belief and not treat everything as either a recounting of events or one possible explanation of the spiritual. Yom Kippur was when the specific question might most deliberately arise about God and the Holocaust. On that day, the most extraordinary statement about the power of God and the intensity of prayer is uttered:

On Rosh Hashanah it is inscribed
And on Yom Kippur it is sealed
How many shall die and how many shall be born
Who shall live and who shall die
Who at the measure of days and who before
Who by fire and who by water
Who by the sword and who by wild beasts
Who by hunger and who by thirst
Who by earthquake and who by plague

Who by strangling and who by stoning
Who shall have rest and who shall go wandering
Who will be tranquil and who shall be harassed
Who shall be at ease and who shall be afflicted
Who shall become poor and who shall become rich
Who shall be brought low and who shall be raised high.

We are told, in the Yom Kippur service, that "repentance, prayer and charity avert the severe decree." As a child, in Feinberg Synagogue, I found it impossible to believe that, in the 1930s, there was a Yom Kippur in which the fate of my grandfather and grandmother and six million others was sealed. By seeing these narratives as somewhat, even if not wholly, like fairy tales, I could get through the afternoon.

VITRINE

As I study the memoirs of refugees, I almost always see reference to some object or practice that was carried from the place of origin, cherished along the refuge-seeking route, and held dear at the site of resettlement. Families have altars, shrines and arks of such objects and memories of them. These can be immaterial, embodied in a dance step, in speech or dialect or in the form of religious observance. There can be small things—letters, stamps, photographs, a matchbook or piece of cloth. On the walls of our apartments were pictures and paintings that had come from Vienna. One of the first things my father did when we moved to a new place, after placing a mezuzah on the doorposts of the house, was to hang the picture of his most honored and most respected antecedent, his great grandfather Gabriel Engelsmann, the Oberrabbiner of Rechnitz, and, as well, a portrait of his father and his grandmother. My mother would hang, in almost a set arrangement, a group of miniature portraits, jewel-like paintings about a half-inch in diameter, that represented women of stature, of origins unknown. She would prop up photos of her family in their country farm. In the dining room and halls would go the five or six drawings of Viennese and Austrian town neighborhoods, urban scenes or crowded courtyards that had made it across the sea. And every living room in which we lived had several paintings from Austria, landscapes or interiors.

153

In its silent way, our vitrine, the glass-fronted cabinet that had come from Vienna in one of the sacred crates packed on the Taborstrasse, served the purpose for us of shrine of remembrance. Carrier of memories and past dreams, it was a bulky, looming, sometimes messy presence in our lives. It had been shipped to the United States just before my parents left Vienna with little expectation that it would make it through the Nazi bureaucracy. But, astonishingly, the vitrine-laden crate arrived in New York and my parents picked it up shortly after we landed. Whatever else happened in our American lives, whatever was lost, or ruined or bought, the vitrine accompanied us from Manhattan and Lawrence, Long Island, where we lived briefly after arriving in the United States, to Macon, Georgia, where we moved next, to Cincinnati, Ohio, then Charlotte, North Carolina and back to Forest Hills, where it has been sitting for almost 40 years. For us, as refugees, it was a vernacular Aharon Kodesh, the traveling ark that held (and holds) the scrolls of the Torah.

The vitrine is a large piece of furniture, over six feet tall, a Biedermeier derivation, nineteenth century in its origin, with mahogany wood of light and dark hues. It is a piece of Vienna, not a memento, more like a cubic meter of Viennese earth, or, to mix a metaphor, an iceberg's tip of memory in one's own living room. It always held a mysterious collection of things representing some life that had been boxed into the past, a life of silver trays and crystal vases and of porcelain figurines and delicate mocha cups and creamers. Crowded in the dark vitrine, they performed some sacred function of remembrance, investment, promise, intimations of a better life in the past and in the future. In our world of uncertainty, the vitrine and its contents were something of a constant. The apartment could change, even the city or region of the country. The refrigerator could become more modern. A television set with its images of everywhere would appear. I would grow older, gain a sister, change in relationship to my neighborhood. But the vitrine would endure. Objects would be taken out from time to time, for special events. Mysteriously, small items would sometimes topple or shift. But the entity, the composition, remained as is. It represented a world of different habits, different qualities, mainly the fact that another world had existed, and this was evidence of the fact that my parents had been part of it. The vitrine was my first museum.

The vitrine, as a concept, as an object, seemed to have its own history. It was furniture made to hold some of the passions of the times: the exchange of tokens of friendship: small porcelain vases, teacups and saucers. My father and mother's family were hardly alone in having such flotsam and jetsam of identity in Vienna. Factories had flourished in Germany, Austria, Hungary and Czechoslovakia to meet the demand for such goods. Many years later, my wife and I would visit Pécs, in southern Hungary, where many such objects had been manufactured (ceramic lamps and vases and figurines). For the Habsburgs, at the end of the nineteenth century and the first decade of the twentieth, one way to dampen the possibility of revolution was to encourage a dense family life in the image of the state. A scholar wrote of a slightly earlier period: "Denied a public forum, the honest and industrious citizens of the Biedermeier age turned inwards, making the family home a focus for cultural life. They mounted home theatricals, combined to form musical and literary clubs, and cultivated hobbies such as needlework, drawing and painting, writing poetry and reading aloud. They loved their gardens and flowers exploded into the house, on cushions, porcelain, textiles and elaborate greetings cards to which they were much addicted." This collecting urge required a domestic vehicle for display, usually a cabinet with three glass sides with a wooden or mirrored back. Our vitrine and the objects in it were a consequence of this gestalt.

In its place, in its time, such a cabinet and its contents were elements of a conversation between its owners and the society around them, and undoubtedly performed the same function for our family in Vienna. In New York or Cincinnati, our vitrine was a vessel of people and events already a shadow, and a token of a place that, for us, no longer existed. Somewhere along the line, maybe when I was not yet five, it occurred to me what an odd thing it was to have such a thing as this vitrine. I could see each object as metonymic (not conscious of the concept), standing for some other thing, some activity that had disappeared. It was a collection of signs whose referents now had changed meaning. I could take a silver napkin holder and think of the complex set of implements to which it belonged, the table it adorned, the house in which the table existed, the people around the table, the conversations and lives in which they indulged. What I learned later was that Hilda and Joseph, my grandparents, understanding the future, gave my mother many of their objects from the Unter Augartenstrasse to take to the United States.

155

Looking back, there were objects within the vitrine that were especially important to me. One such object was a small white porcelain cigarette holder, a clown surrounding and holding a short support for 17 pods or apertures (each gold-tipped, in the style of elegant cigarettes). When there were especially fancy parties in Cincinnati for our refugee friends in the Gate Club, I would be charged with taking the holder out of the vitrine and filling it with cigarettes. I was fascinated by the vitrine's small mocha cups, used in Vienna, but never or hardly ever used in our lives in the United States. Before I knew what mocha was, I knew about these delicate cups. As I grew up and looked at the objects, I would discover a fancy creamer or a tiny Murano vase from Venice, or tucked in the back, a lace fan. Many of these were mementos of travels my mother took around Europe in more normal times with my grandmother. We were schooled to think reverently about Rosenthal cups and saucers and serving platters, each almost a badge of honor. One beautiful piece of Rosenthal was a plate, broken at some stage of our voyages, wired together and then placed in the vitrine, balanced precariously. Ceremonially important was an imposing silver menorah, given to my mother by her parents before we left. They recognized that if this object were to have a future life, a purpose, it would have to be in the world to which my parents were going. Each year, I was responsible for digging wax from each candle holder, not knowing the menorah's history or what must have been the consciousness at the time my grandmother handed it to her daughter. There were other objects: an ornate silver coffee pot that had existed and been used in Nyitra, Slovakia for a century and, the story is told, had been periodically buried in earth to protect it from roving thieves. There were the ceremonial candlesticks. My Slovakian Ehrenfeld great grandparents had one pair for each of their daughters, and this was the set that had been for my grandmother.

A different set of objects came from my Uncle Isidor's possessions at the Taborstrasse (the apartment that became my parents'): a bronze raised art nouveau plate, held up by a swooning nineteenth century goddess, used by us, in a different time and place, for piles of ambient mail including the endless appeals from yeshivas and rabbis and organizations that purport to help the Jewish poor. One of my favorites was a silver inverted umbrella, a couple of inches high, that was used to hold toothpicks. And there were a variety of salt and pepper shakers, some stately and tall, some silver, some crystal.

Not all of the objects from Vienna were in our vitrine. A collection of small bronze figures would be used as decoration in the kitchen or living room. I was particularly affected by a massive desk set that belonged to my maternal grandfather. This bronze arrangement includes a lion standing athwart a semi-circular blotter that could rotate back and forth absorbing ink. The set had an inkwell and a sturdy outsized bronze base. Some nineteenth-century allegory seems to be in play, in which beasts of power are associated with the signing of contracts and the transaction of business. In Cincinnati, this slightly overpowering set was occasionally in use by my father. Now, it sits on a table, crowded with other objects, mostly a shrine to my mother's parents, together with other vestiges of Vienna. On a table near the front door of my mother's living room is the lamp given to my parents on the occasion of their wedding in 1936. It is Augarten porcelain, large in scale, about 18 inches high, with two frivolous, courtly women and a man, dancing around a may pole (which holds the lighting paraphernalia). The lamp, crammed in the back of the car when we moved from Cincinnati to Charlotte, suffered a major crack, now crudely repaired. On a nearby table is a beautiful ceramic standing maiden coquettishly holding a nicely figured basket, her hand broken off, and her basket badly chipped, all damage that was part of the transfer to the United States. Drawers and closets were stuffed with other remnants. There is a photo album of the early twentieth century, bound in fabric, with thick pages in which elegantly posed professional photographs are mounted. They are of my father's family, but few are marked with any indication of name or identity. Either as part of our shipment or that of my great aunt or grandmother's, there were Persian carpets and runners. One reiterated task, as we moved to each of our successive apartments, was to find which floor could best accommodate which carpet.

Time has erased the possibility of any true recreation of an exact order reflecting a Viennese heritage. My great aunt, my mother's Aunt Irene, had her own object-laden vitrine, and after she died, her silver trays were mixed with ours. My mother, in the 1960s, worked for Tiffany's in New York City, and one of the perks of the job was to get slightly damaged, but still unusual, Tiffany objects. They, too, are now crammed in our vitrine or the two additional cabinets from my great aunt. As time went on, the top of the vitrine became a place for accumulation. Surmounting the vitrine were always one or two outsize crystal vases, blue glass or clear, capable of receiving monumental flowers, but hardly ever used. In addition to vases, there were clocks. Two clocks had fallen apart, and much later, I had one repaired and used the other one as a mode of payment for the other's rehabilitation. There was a walnut clock, strong, an object that was to clocks what consoles were to radios, that had been given to my parents for their wedding, and a gilded pink porcelain clock that had come to our family when my father's mother died. Other things found their way to an increasingly dusty top as well: old mail, ignored tzedekah holders, other mysteries.

Almost all these things, the vitrine and many of its objects, came to the United States packed in straw, with porcelain or small paintings wrapped in Viennese newspapers and buffered by featherbeds and pillows. There were three crates, specially built. Bits and pieces of this packaging stayed with us for years. In Cincinnati, in my bedroom in the South Warwick, one of the crates served as a pedestal for our manual typewriter, with a small throw rug from Vienna acting as cover.

I had stages of relationship to these objects. I would bring some of the more exotic exemplars of my Viennese past to elementary school class for show and tell. Once I took examples of inflationary currency, once rustic costumes, lederhosen, pictures in a scrapbook. My sense—perhaps false— was that I left them, sometimes, at school, or lost them on the way home. Maybe I was shedding them (though I lost other things as well). In these elementary school years, I did not understand their significance even when I showed them as a badge of myself, and I am not clear how these objects were received. For a long time afterwards I had dreams of their loss, nightmares perhaps. Later, certainly through my twenties and thirties, I had a stage of ignoring these objects, parking them somewhere in my consciousness. I had a loden hat, with a feather, that had been my father's in Austria or sent by my grandmother to Macon, Georgia in 1940. It languished in closets and finally disappeared.

Then there was a stage of repairing or restoring. There is a painting of my grandfather, my father's father, who died when my father was six. It was crumbling and the frame was broken. I brought it to Budapest for restoration, partly because it was less expensive to restore it there, but partly for the poetry of having the work on its refurbishing be done in part of the former Austro-Hungarian Empire. My father's winter coat, bought for him when he was a 16-year-old working in Neunkirchen, had begun to disintegrate and my wife had its fur trimming repaired for one of my sons. I sent a beautiful Haggadah used by my father's uncle Isidor, which was falling apart, to a special paper restorer in Northampton, had it carefully cleaned and strengthened, and placed it in a specially built box.

OBERRABBINER

If there is a single object of remembrance that represents the contradictions of my identity, it would be an oval inked impression on now-yellowed paper, the portrait of Gabriel Engelsman, my father's great-grandfather. He was our most distinguished forbearer, a scholar and teacher who had held the position of Oberrabbiner—chief rabbi—of Rechnitz, a small town of typically complex history in the Burgenland south of Vienna. I have mentioned that this picture, its battered frame stuffed in our suitcase leaving Vienna, was the very first thing nailed to a wall when we moved from place to place, apartment to apartment, city to city. Gabriel Engelsman was the scion of our family, but it was for me to figure out what lessons I was supposed to take from the invocation of him as a model. He was from a distant place and time, not exactly from Austria, not from Vienna, but the immediate bridge to it. He was deeply religious, but the threshold to a much more secular family future. He represented the idea of authority and conviction in a world where those qualities were fractured and disappearing.

Looking at the slight, almost frail figure in the picture, I know far less than I would like about him given the importance he has in the identity fashioned for me. An entry in the Jewish Encyclopedia (under Gabriel ben Reuben Israel Kohn) reports that he was a Hungarian Talmudist born in 1765 at Vágújhely (a town known—in that complicated Central European way—as Neustadt an der Waag or in present-day Slovakia as Nové Mesto nad Váhom). He was called to the post in Rechnitz in 1822 and died there on December 29, 1850. According to the encyclopedia entry, Kohn (his family took on the vernacular name of Engelsmann) was of the very Orthodox camp in an increasingly contested sense of religious practice and opposed significant change in ritual usage. An example: Kohn maintained the traditional view in a debate, then rampant through Ashkenazic Jewish communities, was over the physical position of the "almemar" or pulpit-desk from which the Torah was read on the Sabbath, during several occasions of the week and in religious festivals. He opposed modernizers who wanted to move this central icon from its traditional place in the center of the synagogue (possibly mirroring the considered structure of the ancient Temple) to a user-friendly more frontal location. Engelsmann wrote books still available in print and opinions on significant doctrinal questions. He had important disciples. The Hebrew inscription on the portrait I have calls him "a true genius, clear, decisive and well-respected." When my second son was born, I named him Gabriel to honor the family tradition, and I hung a Xeroxed version of the portrait near his crib. Far be it from me to attribute too much influence to a name or a picture, but that son has become, in his turn, against the odds, a learned Talmudic scholar and Orthodox Rabbi.

Like countless other diaspora Jews who have visited their place of historic roots, I went to Rechnitz (in 2003) to see where the Oberrabbiner functioned and to get some greater insight into who he was (and indirectly something of who I had become). I flew to the Vienna airport, rented a car and drove partly through Hungary to the small towns of the Burgenland, each with its own distinctive Jewish histories: Eisenstadt, Mattersdorf, Schlaining and other castle villages, in which under complex arrangements, the reigning proprietor or feudal family allowed Jews to live. I passed through Siegendorf, where a town fair was in process, its local band oompahing into the twilight. A block away, between wonderful ladies selling typical Austrian food and a hokey carousel, Nazi memorabilia was for sale among used books and other collectibles. I passed through Stadt Schlaining where the medieval castle had been snatched from oblivion and banal development and converted to a university and Peace Studies Center with a complicated but mission-driven Peace Museum as a means of defining itself for a larger, hard to find audience. Off the square, behind cafes and a hotel, was the former synagogue, now tastefully used as a library of books relating to the town's theme of peace research.

Rechnitz had one of the largest of the Jewish communities in the nineteenth century Burgenland, numbering 800 or 900 souls in the total population of several thousand at the time my great-great-great grandfather was there. Rechnitz (called Rohoncz when it was under Hungarian aegis), like so many other such communities, was an incubator of future striving and achievement, a tight reservoir for energy expended (often on assimilation) when Jews were given greater rights to live in Vienna. I bought a small camera to take photographs of my trip, but I found it hard to match the images I could see with my eyes to the images I wanted to find and memorialize. The twentieth century had too desperately intruded. Though a Judengasse remained, there were no more Jews. The castle or manor of the Batthyánys, the Hungarian noble family that had permitted Jews to live and work in their domain, had been burned, almost to the ground, as a last and departing act of the German troops upon hearing the Soviet soldiers coming near. Buildings, crowds of men, the nature and content of stores, the heavy burden of absence—everything spoke of the events of the late 1930s and 1940s and the erasure of my great-great-great grandfather's legacy. Everything was neat and carefully organized, but the very order added to my own sense of loss. A clean, efficient, village of wineries and shopkeepers smothered a multi-ethnic, difficult to manage past. I went up and down streets looking for the dusty paths and elemental buildings of Gabriel Engelsmann's time. I wanted to see where he or his successors studied, where boys with long sideburns ran and were mischievous, where my great-grandmother may have gossiped with her friends and decided to move to Vienna and make her life there. There was little to see. The last surviving synagogue building had been converted to a puce, conventional and undistinguished building of offices and apartments, its only sign of a radically different past being the dutiful brass plaque affixed to its walls. The old yeshiva or place of study had been resurfaced with white stucco, remodeled with large vertical windows cut in its side, converted into a store and yard for the selling of building materials. The cemetery, several times vandalized, had been restored by the people of Rechnitz, and now the stones stand clean and marching as if there had been no intervening history.

I like the symmetry between Gabriel ben Reuben Israel Kohn, my ancestor, and Rav Gabriel Price, my son. From the children of that first Gabriel came the experiment in modernity, life in a secular Viennese world.

And now, five generations later, this new Gabriel has entered the grammar of the Oberrabbiner's existence. Somewhere in between my own Austrian-ness was just barely locatable.

COLLECTING

There is no vitrine like that of my parents in my own family apartment in New York City. Instead of the kinds of objects collected by them, I have gathered photographs and prints and drawings, ending up with hundreds, possibly thousands, of works, mostly of the twentieth century. Just as my interest in the objects in my parents' vitrines was not in their market value, not even, so much, in their aesthetic significance, I have something of the same attitude toward the things I gather and acquire. Perhaps I am preparing them to be the equivalent of the things from Vienna, precarious, ephemeral, things to be venerated, unclear how and why. And, perhaps, they are objects at risk of destruction and unknowing distribution. Almost always I acquired work at the margin, art by little known artists, or art in which the name of the artist was unknown, or works that may never have been intended as art. I collected inexpensive *ex libris,* the printed name-plates that were artistically constructed in the 1920s and 1930s by bibliophiles in Central and Eastern Europe to celebrate the books they had. I saw these small works and others as remnants of a prior culture. I was also, in part, engaging in an act of recycling: finding things that were virtually cast off or on the verge of destruction and trying, by placing them in my drawers and in my collection, to give them renewed meaning or another chance at an economic life. I was saving them the way objects in the crates from Vienna were saved.

There's an influence beyond the vitrines. I hold and categorize prints and drawings in a way similar to the system my father used for the samples of cotton he needed for his business. These samples, arranged by quality, country of origin, length of staple, would line a wall, with a cubby-hole for each one or cluster of things similarly situated. In his mind, he kept control of the whole system, knowing, often without reference to paper, which sample could be located at which part of the wall. I arrange my prints and drawings in much the same way. They are in three sets of massive drawers, with the overflow stuffed under beds or lining opportune places in closets. They have an arrangement (usually by country or region), but the arrangement is not marked down anywhere, there is no full inventory and the information about names, origins, prices, and iconography is primarily in my head. I know this is not the best way forward, but perhaps my perception of my father's habits remains the template for my actions. Of the fruits of my collecting obsession, there are only three prints from Vienna. For about 15 years, I collected photo albums that contained carefully assembled black and white pictures of families. I collected them with a certain voraciousness, wanting to have a hundred, two hundred, three hundred such albums. I must have originally come across such an album serendipitously, looking for prints and drawings in an antiquarian bookstore or in a thrift shop. Then, for a while, I collected them, not determining, in advance, what criteria I was using to decide which ones I wished to own or collect and which were outside my interest. It was only later that I understood, more, how this aesthetic of the vernacular, the interest in photo albums, was connected to some notions of identity.

In my home, growing up, we always had photos, black and white photos, pictures of my mother's idyllic grandparental haven in Nyitra, my mother and her mother traveling in Venice, my mother with her loving cousins, pictures of more remote relatives whose names I could not remember, whose role seemed an endless mystery, whose very context, place and function was beyond capture. For my father's side the photo-montage of the past was different. There was not the womb of a Slovakian farm for perennial visits. Besides, his photos did not carry with them the overlay of Holocaust-related tragedy. They were pictures of people who lived, conducted their business and, only in the regular course of events, died.

Several photos have made a particularly strong impression on me: a picture of my father and his sister when he was a child of two and she a girl of five or six, overpowering him; a picture of my mother's grandfather sitting, with his pipe, wearing a ceremonial hat and waiting for his grandchildren; a picture of my mother and her mother, Hilda, walking, in vacation, along a canal; a photo of my grandfather, as a young married man, standing behind my American great-uncle, A.D. Engelsman, sitting athwart a chair; a marriage picture of my great aunt Irene and her husband Alfred unaware of the complexities that lay ahead. For the most part, these photos were not organized, not placed in schemes or narratives, just as the lives they represented could no longer be organized. Photographs of these families, my mother's and my father's, were, like the images of all such families, supposed to be part of a very long future, an extending narrative. Now, however, these pictures are detached, increasingly without an understandable history and without a coherent future. The only narrative of their continuity is through the existence of our fragile nuclear family.

The albums that I have superficially imply the illusion of continuity. I know that ultimate destruction, the dissolution of the ideal depicted in the photograph, is an inevitable fate of all families. Mirroring that quality of the inexorable, almost all twentieth century family photos can be purchased now only as single pictures, kept in shoe boxes, stored in drawers, ripped from albums by those engaged in selling them (the earlier photos embedded in velvet-colored nineteenth century volumes are the exception).

I did not like these disembodied photos, photos ripped from the environment in which hope and promise were represented. What I sought was an imposed (even if unrealistic) order, a hoped-for notion of control and optimism entrusted to a person or sequence of individuals who initiated and completed, through photos, chapters in the life of a family. I wanted to see beginnings and middles, or middles and declines.

These albums are from several countries, and from regions of the United States. They are not, or not obviously to me, of families that are Jewish or of families that are refugees. They are not chosen because they represent accidental beauty or are the work of photographers who have advanced the art of representation or any particular aesthetic. Instead, collectively, they seem merely examples of trudging through various chapters of ordinariness. These are albums of families that live in modest one family homes in some small city of the 1940s or 1950s. They have children, young men go off to military service and come back, they take summer vacations and sit at the beach, they have picnics in the countryside, they are proud of their new car. It gave me particular pleasure, for some reason, to collect albums that showed American soldiers and sailors, usually younger than my father, experiencing military life, visiting European attractions and sending snapshots back to their families, and then returning themselves.

I didn't want albums that were costly or fancy, or depicted lives of privilege or showed extensive visits to forests or European cities, or, as so many of them do, what people did on their vacations. I wanted the record of their everyday life, the pictures of family in front of their house, in their living rooms, sitting at dinner, recording graduations or communions or other significant events. I did not look for albums that had surrogates of me, specifically. Maybe I would have been startled to find such a figure, a rough equivalent living in a different context, born at the same time (or just going through life, photographed at age four or five and then again at intervals to give the illusion of a record of development).

My favorites, as is clear, are ones that show families negotiating the late 1930s and navigating through to the early 1950s. This is a period in which the act of taking a picture (or having one taken) was already intensely common, but not yet quite rampantly commonplace. I love the black and whiteness of the contents of these albums, and love, as well, that these photos were held and cherished, were composed and gathered into a record. I love albums where the organization of the photos is done with dedication and the white borders are scalloped or otherwise serve as frames. I specially gathered albums where the person who composed them took the time to write capsule narratives under each of the photographic entries.

I remember a time when I saw a photo album I especially coveted in an unusual museum near Kyiv, Ukraine. It was in 1992, in an extraordinary extensive terrain, a museum in the countryside to which a hundred or more examples of Ukrainian houses, of ancient, folk and Soviet origin, had been moved as an institution marking Ukrainian domestic architecture. Each house was furnished appropriately and each house had a keeper, usually a Ukrainian babushka-wearing woman, who guarded the premises. In one, a modest Soviet house of the 1950s, among the artifacts was what might have been the photo album of its one-time occupants, registering a life like the one that interested me, but under the extremely different (and yet, perhaps, essentially equivalent) circumstances of a Communist order. I wanted to climb into that Russian town, the one in which that family lived, and gain an understanding of its idea of continuity, its aspirations, its own combination of optimism and its hidden terror or anticipation of disasters that would be masked by the usual normality of the album format.

I don't have any photos of myself as a child or of my parents as I grew up. My mother is the custodian of these. One is a picture of me, holding a ball, when I am about one year old in Lawrence, Long Island. I read it as a picture of promise, of simple happiness, of joy between me and the ball. I read it as it was intended to be read, not showing scars of the past or complexities of the future, not telling of place or circumstance. I see it as showing a child well-adjusted, protected from the turbulence of the world, from flight, from the uncertainties of the Depression.

It is the start of an album that could still be assembled, and, perhaps, that is what I have been doing by writing this book.

SETTLEMENT

As I was finishing this book, I found myself in conversation with Austria in a new way, having to engage in renewed state offerings of settlement, reparations, financial and emotional repair. I have had to talk to officials in Vienna, find out about places and dates and styles of living, fill in gaps about family and events and reassess as I go. A kind of conversation occurs, and through it, I am forced to imagine what it would have meant to remain in Vienna and have a life in its precincts. I have made my first friends who are contemporary Austrians, with me talking freely about my past in the United States, as if I were returning home from a great voyage, and they responding, as if telling me tales of what happened while I was away. This accelerated stage of reparations exists for many reasons: the aging of survivors, the contemporary aesthetics of collective guilt, the role of the media, politics within the United States, the balance of power among nations, shifts in litigation jurisprudence and the attention of a few key organizations. A thunder of reckoning, apologies, arrangements, and lawsuits has rolled from the clouds in the last decade and from it a dramatic culture of desired closure has suddenly taken hold. At times, these reparations processes become the therapeutic reformulation of tragedy as litigation. And it is possible that the world has to address its previous debts as it moves on to other theaters of destruction. It would be a peculiarly ironic achievement if societies tried to come to grips with old persecutions before incurring the moral debts of new ones.

The 1990s burst of massive lawsuits and negotiations that dealt with the complex vestiges of the Holocaust ultimately reached down to touch me and my fragile connection with Vienna. The sweep of litigation involved far more than Austria; it attacked, among other things, Swiss banks, the French reading of their own history, German and multinational exploitation of slave labor in World War II, museums that held plundered art, and insurance companies that had failed to redeem abandoned policies. At the same time, books, often reinforcing the lawsuits, explored the same subjects. The publishing industry found a niche with books about IBM and the war, looted art, American indifference, German popular involvement. There was a small riot of financial exposure. American politicians used the nation's superpower status to exercise leverage to achieve "settlements," approximations of closure. Austria, too, was caught up in the geopolitics of this calling to accounts. It was a time of political, historic and forensic marathons with lawyers, diplomats, museum directors, survivor representatives and national spokespersons as the dramatis personae. And the script for Austria was particularly interesting because during the key years, as it was negotiating formulae to acknowledge the past, it was simultaneously undergoing a right-wing renaissance, with strong elements of anti-Semitism.[1]

Every refugee had his or her own relationship to these processes of redressing the past. While I was younger, growing up in Cincinnati, I had little understanding of the letters my parents wrote to Austria after the war to see if their property and some of their interest in their business, seized from them in 1938, could be regained. All of that, not the irreplaceable loss of life, but the loss of apartment, economic opportunities and the mundane objects of life, seemed behind them by the late 1950s. My father and his brother-in-law had hired a lawyer in Vienna in the 1940s to determine their rights under Austrian legislation, probably required by the Allies, that seemed to annul contracts of sale in 1938 that were the result of

---

[1] In 1998, the Historical Commission of the Republic of Austria was established, and it submitted its final report in 2003. Information on the Historical Commission may be found at http://www.historikerkommission.gv.at. Through this Commission, the discourse over Austria's role and its representation became a matter of governmental inquiry, of specifically public history and public remembrance.

the cruel and bizarre duress of the times. They also wrote to the few individuals in Vienna who lived through the war and with whom they felt they had a connection. These were discouraging and unproductive efforts. The lawyer recommended that they take a small settlement provided by the Austrian government and get on with their lives. My father agreed though over my mother's fervent arguments that we should press forward.

I had lived a more than satisfactory life in the United States and was not prone to linger on the severe iniquities that had brought us to New York, Macon, Cincinnati and back to the East Coast. For reasons reflecting my absorption into an American self, I was not determined to seek "justice," nor was I captivated by the idea of compensation, possibly because, in either case, it would be more symbolic than real. I was, mentally, not sufficiently an Austrian refugee to see myself as part of the injured class. I could make myself a surrogate for my parents, supporting them in vindicating their rights, but this seemed hollow to me as well.

Parallel with these steps in the claims processes, Austria began more actively to nourish its relationships with its refugee diaspora. It did a number of things in the 1970s such as inviting the human vestiges of the 1930s to visit Austria as guests of the government and, under certain circumstances, to become citizens again. My parents' first trip back to Austria occurred under such an arrangement in which Austria provided them with airline tickets and a few days stay as guests in a hotel in Vienna. My father and mother, somewhat incredibly to me, went to Austria almost annually for about five years as a regular element of their summer vacations. They would spend several days in Vienna and then a few days in the Austrian Alps before going somewhere else in Europe. My father loved returning and relished his time in Vienna. My mother had a different reaction. She sought to avoid an emotional reaction (not always successfully) by locking out history to the extent possible, and to tread in paths carefully chosen. She did not engage with Austrians, did not then go back to the home of her past or try to trace her old haunts. She tried to make a trip to Vienna into a trip to anywhere.

Whatever her emotional attitude towards Vienna, my mother was acutely attentive to changes in the legal environment affecting our past, changes that accelerated after my father's death in 1983. When Austria offered a benefit—whether it was free travel for children of refugees, or newly available social benefits, or altered terms for asserting claims to property—she knew of them immediately and called me when she thought the benefit might be of use to me. She did not look at these Austrian measures, concessions or invitations with an eye to retribution or fulfillment. She realized that she could never obtain what she "deserved," and never could there be a reversal of history. Rather she absorbed the Austrian actions mundanely. Seizing these benefits was an act slightly more significant than redeeming coupons in newspapers. Certainly, they touched upon history. As well, these changes offered a chance for the two of us, my mother and me, to interact in a manner that provoked our common past and provided some greater guarantee of an understanding of my family and its history. She could gently spur me to take on responsibility. Finally, she could reengage with Vienna in a manner that had relatively low emotional cost. Engaging in the process of obtaining entitlements meant finding bits and pieces of our family's factual ephemera, not reopening the highly-charged cultural and historical whole.

CITIZENSHIP AND PASSPORT

In 1989, my mother called me with one such opening. That year, when my son Joshua was 22 and my son Gabriel was 19, the Austrian Consulate in New York published an announcement of a trip, sponsored by the Austrian Jewish Community of Vienna, for children or grandchildren of Austrian refugees. It was an important event in the lives of both Joshua and Gabriel and, as well, their trip was a slight step in my reengagement, as their impressions and experiences were quite strong. My son Joshua, already an anthropologist and skeptic, sought to unwrap the purposes of the sponsors—especially the organized Jewish Community of Vienna—and see whether it encompassed goals other than those stated, namely to build ties between young Americans of Austrian descent and the land of their parents or grandparents. His conclusion was intensely interesting. Right or wrong, he concluded that episode was directed to what was becoming the new (small) community of Jewish settlers in Vienna, people moving into Vienna from the East (the former Soviet Union, for the most part). The designers of the voyage wished to show these unassimilated Jews of the new Vienna how assimilated young people, contemporary Americans of Viennese descent, conducted themselves. For him, the trip sprang, in some ways, from a crude echo of the 1930s. The new Jews of Vienna were not sufficiently Viennese, not sufficiently normalized. Exposure to these children and grandchildren of more "authentic" Viennese Jews might provide a dramatic model for behavior. The visit was intense, too, for my son Gabriel. Visits to Mauthausen and his reaction to Vienna may have been one of the first steps toward his later, mature and intense religiosity. Gabriel wrote me later about his reaction to the attitude of his fellow young American tourists, the children of refugees: "most of them got a wonderful kick out of riding down the Danube on a yacht while the Blue Danube Waltz blared out of the boat's speakers. In that context young Jews were quick to forgive the Viennese for any crimes that they had done 50 years earlier, and give voice to their feelings to radio or television interviewers."

This trip was followed by another invitation that my mother noted. In 1993, the Austrian government had extended an offer of renewed Austrian citizenship, without any requirement of residence, to a group that seemed to include me. The law required that the applicant should have been forced to leave Austria as an Austrian citizen "before 9 May 1945 because he or she feared persecution by organs of the National Socialist Party or the authorities of the Third Reich."[2] Not much had to be done. A small set of documents had to be assembled, and a short statement had to be signed. I had qualms about eligibility and qualms about applying. I was, as usual, on some kind of margin. I could ask myself whether I was really legally and morally entitled under the program. True, I had been ejected, and I *would* have 'feared persecution' even if I, protected by my infancy, actually had not. And, I asked myself, was I technically an Austrian citizen before 1945? When I was born, Austria was already part of the Third Reich and I was a German before I could become an Austrian. These were foolish concerns, linked to doubt about the meaning of an added citizenship itself.

I applied, but kept getting things wrong on the application form, leaving some spaces blank, or failing to have every document in order. I kept making errors in the declaration I had to sign indicating that I fulfilled the requirement of flight from Vienna, that I had never been convicted of legally

---

[2] Another ground, that a person was persecuted because he or she stood up for the defense of a democratic Austria, did not apply to me.

punishable behavior, either within or outside of Austria, that there was no pending criminal proceeding against me, that I wasn't banned from Austria and that nothing in my life would damage the interests of the Austrian Republic. Forms and letters moved back and forth between me and the consulate in New York and the appropriate office in Vienna. What should have taken a few weeks took more than a year, not because of dilatory bureaucracy on the Austrian side, but because of my *Schlamperei* or slovenly errors. Somehow, I wanted to extend the process. I wanted to test the desire and endurance of Austria. I wanted it to be an effort on their part for me to become a citizen, rather than merely an application from me.

The Austrian law may have been enacted as an inexpensive way to regain some global favor or it may have been part of a negotiation, an element of reparations policy, or it might well have been a symbol of an actual changed attitude toward public responsibility, an authentic embrace of previous citizens. If Austria was seeking to do something positive, then it was up to me to decide whether I would participate, collaborate, as it were, in this process of change. Ultimately, I took what I deemed to be my mother's view. This was a potential benefit (unclear how at the time) to be obtained at little or no cost. I was not to think of it as a sign, as a concession, a formal element of recognition, an agreement that suitable amends had been made. I did not want to vote in Austrian elections (and I assumed that doing so might be an act inconsistent with my American citizenship). I could arrive at the formulation that I was an Austrian citizen from birth, that it was never validly removed from me and that what I was experiencing was a correction or restoration. Or I could consider that I was gaining a document but not becoming a part of Austrian civil society. I was becoming a perfunctory Austrian, Austrian for purposes having nothing to do with Austria. If anything, I was going to have the benefits of being a European, the additional virtues of the European Union. I could go through favored lines in airports or qualify for jobs in Europe or be a part of applications for funding from the European Union or the Council of Europe. Austria would be granting me citizenship and a passport, but in my hands it would transmogrify into something more technical and impersonal.[3]

---

3 In 2003, my third son, Asher, then a student at Oxford, wondered about his entitlement to be an Austrian citizen, partly because of a desire to live and work in Europe. He had the following exchange with the Austrian Embassy in London:

One subconscious concern was that Austria would use the application and grant of citizenship for a kind of propaganda (not my particular application, but the fact of returning refugees in general). If I asked my friends what they thought of my actions starting the process, that is what some of them mentioned. Later, as I studied how these processes were treated by Austria, I came across this press release on an Austrian government information page:

Lena Gitter's 91st birthday was an exceptional one. On July 17, the Viennese-born lady was given back her Austrian citizenship and passport. It was the explicit desire of the Holocaust survivor and human rights activist. When she got back her Austrian citizenship and passport, Lena Gitter received some hate calls. "People insulted me anonymously: how can you accept citizenship from this country of Nazis?" But Lena Gitter did not waver. She was looking forward to getting what was taken from her and she recognizes Austria's changed atti-

---

To Whom It May Concern:

I am writing to inquire whether I qualify for Austrian citizenship. My father, Monroe E. Price, was born in Austria in August, 1938 to Viennese parents. He and his parents (my grandparents) fled the country in 1939 after the Anschluss. They settled in the United States: he and his parents became American citizens. His Austrian citizenship was restored in the late 1990s under a special Austrian law that restored citizenship to Austrians who had fled the Nazis. I was born in Los Angeles, California on Feb. 14, 1979. According to your website: "A legitimate child born before 1 September 1983 obtains citizenship if the father was an Austrian citizen at the time of the child's birth."

At the time of my birth, as I explained above, my father was not an Austrian citizen. Now he is an Austrian citizen (and would have been at the time of my birth had he not been stripped of his citizenship when he fled Austria).

Do I qualify for Austrian citizenship? Is there someone I might speak with about this matter? I can be reached by email or telephone. I write, incidentally, to the Austrian Embassy in the UK because I am currently a graduate student at Oxford.

Thanks for your consideration.

Sincerely,

Asher Price

He received the following reply:

Referring to you e-mail, the Embassy is sorry to inform you, that according your explanations and according to the Austrian citizenship law, your father lost the Austrian citizenship at the time he applied for the American citizenship and regained the Austrian citizenship on that date of his report to the Austrian Authorities (in the late 1990s). During the years in between, your father held only the American citizenship. Therefore, you could not obtain the Austrian citizenship at your birth.

Yours sincerely

Miranda Grogger

Consular Department

Austrian Embassy

tude. She thinks "You always have to learn from mistakes. It does not help to be angry." Lena Gitter celebrated her rebirth as an Austrian at the Austrian Embassy in Washington, D.C., thus on the territories of her old and new home countries...

I did not think I would be "reborn" as an Austrian, nor did I want to be cited that way. On the other hand, I wasn't 91, and I wasn't going to appear, in a celebratory mode, at least not yet, at a local Austrian consulate. In 1997, I received my restored, or reinvented, or newly created citizenship. And shortly afterwards, my passport arrived.

REPARATIONS, OBLIGATIONS, AMENDS

As I became more enmeshed in the conversation of change, I began to find bits of how Austria reinterpreted its history and engaged with these issues of a deeply suppressed past. At the same time I was rather trivially engaged in trying to deepen my understanding of how my life and that of my family had been changed by the events of the 1930s. Austria was, in some halting ways, recapitulating, revisiting and reinterpreting the entire World War II experience. Its search for identity involved justification, introspection, intensive wielding of legal precedent. It involved the balancing of internal moods and international mandates. I understood from my parents that there could never be full Austrian self-awareness though there might be abject confessions concerning the wrongs of the past. Whatever catharsis might take place, either for Austria or its dying refugee diaspora, that catharsis could not be complete. I was becoming, slightly and slowly, an actor in this play of recovered shame, compensation and something like forgiveness.

Austria seemed to be generationally, fitfully, moving a half-step forward, sometimes several steps back over the years since World War II. Any theory of compensation required acknowledgment of responsibility, recognition of national involvement and some degree of self criticism. Willingness to meet legal and moral claims required a sense of history in which Austrian liability was admitted. If Austria had been "annexed" or absorbed into the Third Reich, then it ceased to exist in 1938. Even if it remained merely "occupied" and continued to exist, under this theory, Austria was not capable of acting as a sovereign state during 1938 to 1945. This view dominated Allied thinking during the war and Austrian thinking afterwards, and was encapsulated in the idea that Austria was "the first free country that fell victim to Hitler's aggression" rather than a willing member of the Axis. When my father's property was seized, when Jews were rounded up and sent to prison or to Dachau, it was on Germany's watch, not Austria's. This was a powerful, absolving, almost cleansing idea. Austria was not only a victim, but the "first" victim. This "victim" theory was enshrined in the Moscow Declaration of the Allied Powers, of November 1, 1943. Franklin D. Roosevelt invoked it in his public addresses. The challenge, over six decades, was to find an avenue to responsibility in this narrative or change the collective perception.

The impact of the story was significant, and there were several corollaries to the notion of Austria as victim, especially Austria as annexed or occupied state. Most important, as Austria was incapable of acting as a sovereign state under international law, it could not and should not be held responsible for war crimes and violations of human rights more properly attributed to the Third Reich. As a symbol of this interpretation, since Austria was not a defeated state, but one liberated from Germany, it was not the subject of a peace treaty, but rather a State Treaty. In an important way the theory mitigated the imperative of a claims process and systematic efforts at restoration or compensation. Still, reflecting the ambiguities of the situation, the State Treaty, signed in 1955, provided some duty to provide compensation.[4] And, in the half century after the War, Austria did, in fact, provide opportunities for claims. Just after the conclusion of the War, on May 10, 1945, those who held property taken from previous owners after March 13, 1938,

---

[4]   It provided that "In so far as such action has not already been taken, Austria undertakes that, in all cases where property, legal rights or interests in Austria have since 13th March, 1938, been subject of forced transfer or measures of sequestration, confiscation or control on account of the racial origin or religion of the owner, the said property shall be returned and the said legal rights and interests shall be restored together with their accessories. Where return or restoration is impossible, compensation shall be granted for losses incurred by reason of such measures to the same extent as is, or may be, given to Austrian nationals generally in respect of war damage."

According to Article 26, para. 2, Austria was vested with the responsibility of taking "... under its control all property, legal rights and interests of persons, organizations or communities which ... were the object of racial, religious or other Nazi measures of persecution where, in the case of persons, such property, rights and interests remain heirless or unclaimed for six months after the coming into force of the Present Treaty, or where ... such organizations or communities have ceased to exist."

were required to register that fact. An Annulment Act of May 15, 1946, declared null and void transactions during the German occupation—irrespective of any payment—if carried out in the course of the financial or political penetration of Austria by the German Reich in order to seize property or property rights.

In the apparent effort to make these laws somewhat enforceable, various other laws were passed between 1946 and 1949. The "Third Restitution Act" was the law for the return of property wrongfully taken from its owners that had been transferred to private individuals or businesses, including forced sales or "Aryanizations." The putative effect of these provisions was that the unlawful holder no longer had a title to possession of such property, and the property, under general principles of civil law, was to be restored to the previous owner. But the law seems to have been a general failure. Claimants under the Third Restitution Act had somewhere between seven and nine years to bring their claims for restitution.[5] In those post-war years, the complexity of psychological adjustment by the refugees, the biases of the Austrian system itself, and the local sympathy to the current occupants made fulfillment of the letter of the laws arbitrary and uncertain. It was these laws, often leading to modest settlements (the result in our case), which were the subject of letters from my father to Vienna in the late 1940s and early 1950s.

---

[5]   In 1961, a Compensation Fund was established with about $6 million for those, like my parents, whose rights had been forcibly transferred or confiscated between 1938 and 1945. No compensation was due in cases where such property, rights and interests had been restituted or re-established. It is to be noted that there was no legal entitlement to the payments; rather, the award of compensation was at the Fund's discretion (§1(4)). Compensation was awarded in cases of loss of property in one of the following categories: bank accounts, securities, cash, mortgage claims and payment of discriminatory taxes (e.g. "Reichsfluchtsteuer", "Judenvermögensabgabe/JUVA") . The Compensation Fund was managed by a "Kuratorium" which also included Jewish representatives such as Simon Wiesenthal. The Fund conducted an extensive advertising campaign throughout the world to inform people who had suffered losses in Austria during the Nazi era of this opportunity to apply for compensation. Between September 1, 1961 and August 31, 1962, a total of 10,666 applications for compensation were received and examined by the Fund. The Fund carried out extensive investigations of these claims, in particular by examining the archives of the Collection Agencies which had been put at the Fund's disposal. I have taken this information from material supplied by the Austrian National Fund. That source also indicates that in 1958, the Insurance Indemnification Act ("Versicherungsentschädigungsgesetz") was enacted to compensate for life insurance policies confiscated by the German Reich. "Compensation under this law followed legal guidelines established after 1945 and in 1955, respectively. The guidelines provided that all payments for insurance policies—irrespective of the holder—were to be reduced in view of the collapse of Austria's financial system after the end of the war. The reduction was approximately 60 per cent of the surrender value.

NATIONAL FUND

Because there had been little Austrian acknowledgement of responsibility, these conceptualizations about historic roles and collective guilt fed, for a long time, a national calculus that Austria had met its obligations and the state should not be subject to further requirements for compensation. The overall atmosphere changed somewhat during the Austrian election campaign in 1986 when the presidency of Kurt Waldheim and the intense disclosures of his Nazi past were a national issue. And in the mid-1990s, the tone shifted further. A new formula was legitimated, through the former Chancellor, Dr. Franz Vranitzky, namely that Austrians were not only victims of National Socialism but were active collaborators. In 1995, the Austrian government established a "National Fund of the Republic of Austria for the Victims of Nazi Socialism." The motto of the National Fund would be *"To help in the quickest, most flexible and unbureaucratic manner possible."*

The language surrounding the Fund showed how difficult was the coming to terms. At some times, wording was circumscribed, coming close but not totally embracing an acceptance of responsibility. The fund, one official noted, was in "recognition of our moral joint responsibility and the wrong inflicted on humanity in Austria by Nazism, and recognize that special help should be given to the victims." This was still a remembrance of harm inflicted by a force, Nazism, not the state, Austria. Changing that template would be shifting core beliefs. A later Austrian negotiator, Ernst Sucharipa, speaking of the establishment of a somewhat different fund, demonstrated the difficulty of shaping self-scrutiny: "Like all nations, we have to live up to our past, the deeds of all Austrians bad or good, the fact that Austrians were perpetrators, onlookers and victims."

Within the one-year period for presenting claims 456 policies were compensated. The rather short period as well as lack of publicity could possibly explain the relatively modest number of claims. Whenever new claims were brought in the following years, insurance companies, conscious of the difficult legal, political but also moral background, made every effort to process them in an amicable way.

In line with the handling of insurance claims in the past, those companies which did business during the times of the Third Reich will continue to consider every claim individually and will try to settle it within the legal framework for restitution and compensation. Being part of international insurance groups, leading Austrian insurance companies take part in the activities of the International Commission on Holocaust Era Insurance Claims (ICHEIC) via their parent companies and in this way support the tasks of that commission. Furthermore the insurance companies, conscious of their own responsibility in this context, have asked a reputed Austrian historian to investigate the role of insurance business from 1938 up to the 1960's."

Why does Austria have to live up to the *good* deeds of the past? It may be relevant that Austrians were perpetrators, but onlookers? And *victims*? This is the syntactical desire to maintain the old story of limited liability and balance within the new representation of acknowledged responsibility.

There were other significant aspects of characterization. The Fund would provide a one-time amount, uniform and therefore by definition somewhat arbitrary, to every eligible applicant. By rendering the award impervious to individual circumstances, it was deemed "not a form of reparations." It would be merely a symbolic gesture on the part of the Austrian Republic, "in recognition of its active role in persecuting a great number of its citizens, and in memory of the terrible tribulations they have had to suffer." Another part of the rhetoric was the customary, almost formulaic, acknowledgement "that the suffering can in no way be 'repaired.'" Dr. Heinz Fischer, President of the National Council, said: "In short, it is clear to me that the suffering and injustice that National Socialism guaranteed in our land cannot be satisfied by money." In addition, Austria should be perceived as welcoming back its long-lost representatives. This should be a process not just of providing money, but making Austria whole again:

> "The National Fund should thus, represent a gesture, for people who were expelled from Austria, or who suffered in Austria to show that we are still thinking of them; that they have not been forgotten and that there is a will to rebuild their ties to their former country. Fifty years hence Austria has become a developed and respected democracy at the heart of Europe. This country wishes, that with the establishment of the National Fund, people that are today spread out across the earth will feel that they once again belong to us.... For me it is always moving to see with what emotion and solidarity people react when they return to visit the land from which they were forsaken."

As an applicant, I have read some of the speeches of the Secretary General of the Fund, Hannah N. Lessing. It fell to her to represent an altered spirit of Austrian inclusion. Lessing fought tirelessly to convey this message, and as one of the people constructed as "the audience" I appreciated the sentiment, though I sometimes had difficulty with the tone. I wanted to hold on to my indifference and think of transactions with Vienna as a kind of business matter, not an emotional rejoining. Providing people with "closure" is important, perhaps giving them a connection with Vienna is healing. But it remains to be evaluated what constitutes the appropriate words and inflections in this most difficult of contexts. Here are some examples of Hannah Lessing's rhetoric, heartfelt, to be sure, conflating reparations and settlement with partial reunion:

> The individual stands at the forefront for us: the person who has suffered, the person who was driven from his home, the person who was unable, by any means, to continue his lifestyle as he or his parents had planned it for him. The person who escaped the hell of the concentration camps, the person who lost all his loved ones, and those who defined their very existence by living in this inferno. Those who had to leave their homeland, their roots, their city, and everything dear to them in order to travel to a destination where everything was unknown, and where they had to start their whole life over again.

> The hundreds of positive responses the Fund has received are convincing evidence that the National Fund has been successful in its aims and purposes. An example of a letter written states that: *"Aside from the financial side, I would like to thank you for expressing your compassion. It feels like a healing balm on old wounds. I have loved my hometown, the Alps and also the people, now I don't have to be ashamed of this love anymore."*

> We have often encountered people who under the pressure of a thousand repressed thoughts, talk with us and cry. Some of them for the first time in 50 years. We see people who never wanted to deal directly with the authorities, but after visiting our office in Vienna, tell friends and family "that its a place you can go to, there are women (our office is comprised mainly of women) who understand, who care about your troubles and desires. Our main wish is to re-build a connection to these individuals and their homeland. We do recognise that it does not redeem Austria's sordid role during the War, but nevertheless, the people that had to suffer under Nazi persecution must never be forgotten. In this way we hope to do justice to the remaining survivors, and pay tribute to the individuals that we are no longer able to reach.

I applied to the National Fund long before the deadline. By the end of 2002, the National Fund had made payments to 27,000 people. We, I and my mother, had qualified for this fund because we were "forced to leave the country in order to escape persecution," and I was the child of parents who had lived in Austria for ten years before the Anschluss. If Austria was prepared to make this additional gesture, I was willing to accept it. In July 2002, I received a letter from Dr. Fischer, the President of the Fund's National Council, and Ms. Lessing, informing me that I would receive $7,000. "We would like to take this opportunity to reassure you," the letter read, "that we are well aware that all the injustice, wrongs, and terrible events of the National Socialist era can never be repaired. Still, we are of the opinion that we should continue to discuss the injustice. Therefore we are also trying to make amends in a material form... In conclusion we sincerely hope that the positive completion of your application is seen as a sign that—in the name of the Republic of Austria—the wrongs which harmed you and your family in the darkest days of Austrian history have been remembered."[6]

GENERAL SETTLEMENT FUND

Bewildering to me, yet another set of negotiations, another case for reparations, led, after 2000, to a new set of claims opportunities. A new fund was established by the Austrian government, called the General Settlement Fund, and this meant that I had to reengage, reexamine, to go through the process of filling out an application. This time, I too, was a claimant, on my own behalf and as an heir to my father. This new fund, perhaps the final one, was the culmination of the intense activities of groups dedicated to obtaining more proper compensation from Vienna for those whose property had been seized and lives disturbed. These groups, many unknown to me, included the Conference on Jewish Material Claims, the Central Committee of Jews from

---

6 Dr. Wesley Fisher, Director of Research for the Conference on Jewish Material Claims Against Germany, has commented: "Financial settlements and restitution ultimately were more important for the insights they provided on family and general history than for the money obtained (the 'restitution of history'). Some of the major developments in research and education on the Holocaust have come as a result of property restitution issues. Thus it was in the context of the protests against the Swiss banks that Prime Minister Persson of Sweden proposed what has since become the Task Force for International Cooperation on Holocaust Education, Remembrance and Research—a grouping of 27 governments, including Austria."

Austria in Israel, the American Council for Equal Compensation of Nazi victims from Austria and the Austrian Jewish Community (or Israelitische Kultusgemeinde). Intermediate steps by Austria—the creation of the National Fund and the extension of citizenship—had not diminished the drumbeat of claims, nor should it have. Almost a half century past the war, these organizations and others argued forcefully that Austria had not approximated Germany in terms of coming to grips with its obligations. The illegal transactions, such as those that had taken away my father's property, had been theoretically annulled, but for many of those affected, like my father, the results had been insubstantial and this was a last chance to make amends.

The pre-existing history of Austria as "first victim" was transformed with the rise of class action litigation as a technique in the 1990s and massive lawsuits against Austria and Austrian banks, insurance companies and other corporations. In 2001, after drawn out and difficult negotiations, the parties reached a settlement. It was a strange political moment: the Clinton administration had devoted a good deal of energy to the issues and wanted to have closure. So did the Austrian government, then in the middle of a period of Austrian isolation from the European Union that arose when the Austrian Chancellor, Wolfgang Schüssel, included the far-right party of Jörg Haider in his ruling coalition. Two specific parts of the Settlement would affect me. One provision extended social benefits to Jewish children who fled Austria because of the persecution (I would be one of them). And Austria and the participating companies agreed to establish a general settlement fund to satisfy all the long-standing claims.

It was my mother, as usual, who was attuned to the creation of the Settlement Fund and she called and got the application forms. I volunteered to fill them out, figuring that I should begin to take my own responsibility in these tasks and that the very act of filling them out would help with my self-education. The form asked for very detailed information about our lives, our property, our insurance policies—details that would be sunk in history. My mother could remember much of this information, but not with the precision that would be desirable in completing the application. The Fund provided someone who would provide assistance to applicants; I called and was informed that there were documents from the archives that I could request that would be useful. Indeed, the Fund's representative volunteered to have information reproduced and sent to me.

After requesting this data, I received in the mail a copy of a remarkable document that my father had had to sign, in common with all Jews in Vienna with assets of more than 5,000 Reichsmarks. This was called the Verzeichnis über das Vermögen von Juden, or Inventory of Assets of Jews.[7] He filed it July 16, 1938, a month before I was born. It listed everything he owned: the half interest in the two family businesses he had, just six years before, inherited from his uncle. It also listed his bank accounts. These assets included a spinning mill, a wiping waste factory and the forwarding company his father had started and so much enjoyed at the beginning of the twentieth century. The form listed stock interests my father had that were held in a blocked account in Hungary. (Certain assets could never be listed: At Trumau, in addition to the factory buildings, there was a Herrnhaus, the building for the owner. In the residential grounds, my mother had, shortly after her marriage, planted a white lilac bush, which she received from my father for her engagement. In the short months of promise, in their early time my mother and father had together, the bush had been transported from Vienna to the place they thought would help nourish them.)

Of course, the main point of the inventory had to do with the divestment of property. The Germans were interested in Aryanization and also in capturing funds for the benefit of the Reich. My father, and so many like him, had to demonstrate that they had sold their property before they would be permitted to leave Vienna. As a result, the Registry or Inventory not only listed assets but also documents that demonstrated the disposition of those assets. For example, there is a letter that describes how much my father was paid for his interest in Brüder Preis. The letter is on stationery with a Brüder Preis letterhead but is signed by the new officers of the business, with the stamp of the company under the signature. Above the corporate seal is a typed phrase that had not been there in the months before: "Heil Hitler."

---

7   Dr. Wesley Fisher notes that "in regard to the Inventory of Assets of Jews, originally this documentation was kept classified in the Austrian archives. In the 1990s, however, two of the archivists went against the rules and published the list of names of Jews who had completed the questionnaires, and this led to pressure on the Austrians to make the documentation public. Similar inventories were, of course, completed by the Jews of Berlin, Hamburg, and many other cities, but these have remained, to this day, difficult to access, a question rased in 2009 at the Holocaust Era Assets Conference held in Prague as part of the Czech Republic's Presidency of the European Union."

There were other assets. My father had a life insurance policy, as did many in Vienna (and elsewhere) who left and forgot or died or for whom figuring out which Austrian insurance company had what kind of policy made little sense in their newly complicated lives. US politicians and US state insurance commissioners launched an extraordinary effort in the late 1990s to bring pressure on the successor companies to deal with "unaccounted for" insurance policies.[8] In 2001, the Austrian insurance industry published a list of such policies (my father's name was on it), with the following statement:

> The Austrian Association of Insurance Companies (VVO) and its member companies regret the atrocities of the NS-Era and are aware of the general injustice committed by the "Third Reich" and its racist legislation, in violation of human rights, directed against Jews and others. On account of this injustice, the legal entitlements to benefits under insurance contracts, especially of Austrian Jews, were impaired or confiscated. The Companies facing lawsuits or Holocaust-era claims—insurance companies, banks, industrial enterprises and other businesses—are currently seeking protection from legal actions and sanctions in the U.S. The achievement of "legal peace" for the companies entails agreements with some plaintiffs to voluntarily drop pending suits and/or gaining the active support of the U.S. government in dismissing other suits against them. Such a role by the government contesting current and future suits by Holocaust survivors and heirs raises troubling issues.

My father's Registry of Assets also lists stocks and bonds he owned and bank accounts he had opened. Some of the stocks and bonds, according to the Inventory, were held in a blocked account in Hungary. These securities bedeviled my father in late 1938. It was impossible to sell them. But unsold, they kept my father hostage. Only when he could resolve their disposition was it possible to get an exit permit and for our family to leave. Now these same stocks were reappearing in the world as evidence for a claim.[9]

---

[8] http://www.insurance.wa.gov/holocaust/finalreport12_00-full.pdf

[9] I received a similar statement, somewhat less complex, declaring the assets of my mother's father, Josef Diamant. It contained the following information: He was engaged in the export business (Kurzwaren), at Börsegasse 13–15. There was a valuation of the assets of the store, dated July 14, 1938. This included:

What had happened to these things: the apartment, the spinning mill, the factory in Trumau, my grandfather's shop on Börsegasse, the commercial journal and forwarding business in Vienna that my father's father had started around the turn of the century, that had produced witty special occasion newspapers for family weddings? To file a claim properly with the Settlement Fund, I needed to know something of the fate of these assets. Out of the maw of historic bureaucracies, official documents spewed forth. Tools for repositioning history were made available. I was becoming a more precise, but still largely involuntary, historian of my own past. Ephemera of my family's existence were floating before my eyes. It was almost too much. I wanted to be a responsible chronicler for the purposes of filling out the necessary applications. I wanted to put my own past in a more precise context. But I resisted becoming too absorbed, trying to recreate, master, and almost relive the way of life that had so suddenly terminated.

As to the fate of my family's assets, a series of inquiries produced helpful official responses. We received a letter from the Regional Archives of the Government of Lower Austria, telling us the fate of the factory in Wollersdorf. Of course, the factory was sold (Aryanized) in September 1938. But then, the letter, to my mother, went on, "As you yourself know, a request by your husband...for the return of the factory was refused in 1950." As to our other assets, we received a letter from the archives of the City of Vienna saying that the delivery company, Donau, lost its value on December 12, 1938 when its license to operate was withdrawn. A similar result summarized the destiny of my grandfather's imported embroidery business on the Börsegasse: "On June 10, 1940, the permit for the firm of Josef Diamant, E 40/172, was extinguished by order of the concerned agency."

DIE STADT OHNE JUDEN

One of the consequences of writing this book has been to learn how honey-combed Austria had become with institutions that are committed to studying Jewish life. It plays with irony to call this state of affairs ironic.

Store Fixtures 200 Reichsmark, Inventory 8,443.25, for a total of 8,643.25. He had debts or bills payable of 27,835.55, and payments due or credits of 30,272.18. The Net Value of the store was 6,306.62. In addition he had as objects of capital (checks, etc) 27 RM; things of value gold, silver, etc: Gold Pocket Watch 150 marks, Wedding Ring 10 marks, Silver 234 for a Total of 394 RM.

In 1922 a book by Hugo Bettauer was published in Vienna, called *Die Stadt Ohne Juden* or *The City Without Jews*. The book was written to show how important to Austrian culture Jewish life was at the time (in 1924, the book was made into a mediocre film that crops up at festivals). In Bettauer's eyes the book was "an amusing little novel" about what would happen if the government were to acquiesce in demands for the systematic expulsion of an "undesirable element," namely the Jews. Bettauer says he got his inspiration to write the novel after frequenting public washrooms and reading graffiti on the walls saying "Hinaus mit den Juden!" (Jews Be Gone!) According to a reviewer, Murray Hall,

> The plot is simple: post-war Austria is suffering from economic misery and the Jews are to blame. They own and control everything and even take the Christian sweethearts away from their lovers. Parliament passes the "Anti-Jew Law," the Jews leave the country and things get progressively worse, industry and commerce fail because Christian businessmen don't have the knack, Vienna turns into a hick town, theatres close because Jewish authors have been banned and there are no good plays by Gentiles around anymore, fashion becomes very provincial and so on. A young Jew who has left for France returns to Vienna in the disguise of a French painter to reunite with his Christian girlfriend. He launches a campaign to foment protest in the population which has already begun to suffer from the expulsion of the Jews and parliament rescinds the "Anti-Jew Law," the Jews are invited to return, the population rejoices and Vienna is once again Vienna. The city mayor greets the "painter" on the balcony of the Town Hall with the words "My dear Jew!"

Vienna is not now a hick town, and the return of its Jews, except for a small number, is impossible. So the invocation of Bettauer and his book strikes a dramatic but slightly oblique point. Still there is a yearning, differently manifested. I corresponded with Ursula Seeber Weyrer, the director of Exilbibliothek, an Austrian library established in the context of "Austrian exile research." I asked her about a massive book published in 1992 by the Austrian government to celebrate Austria's "great gift to the world:" the intellectuals who left in the 1930s. I had gone, by chance, to a reception in New York where the Austrian Consulate was promoting this volume, redefining the events of the 1930s as, unintentionally, advancing Austrian culture, enriching academic faculties, and by so doing spreading literary talent, redefining psychoanalysis and psychiatry and underwriting science all over the world.

The Exilbibliothek is related to this project. The library in Vienna is part of a movement, started in Germany, to establish libraries of exile and refugee literature. The University of Hamburg had a small research center, and one existed, after 1972, at the German Institute of the University of Stockholm. Soon there were International Congresses, with strong German backing. From a time of post-war taboos, there was a pendulum swing to a kind of cultural expansionism, as the subject of the Exile found its place in the mind of the Austrian public, the concern for the missing Jewish population, the amputated limb, became more present in the Austrian consciousness. Now documentation of the exile experience includes books, brochures, catalogs, handbills and magazines from more than 20 countries, newspaper cuttings and photo archives. There is a series of volumes published on "Austrians in Exile 1934-1945," with books on France, Belgium, Great Britain and the US. Chairs have been established at Austrian universities for the study of the exile experience, and research programs as well.

I also made contact with the Institute for Jewish History in Austria, located in a beautiful, abandoned synagogue in St. Pölten, 60 miles south of Vienna. The Institute was founded by a scholar named Klaus Lohrmann with the assistance of federal and regional authorities in 1988, precisely 50 years after the Anschluss. The location of the Institute in the former synagogue in St. Pölten gave a new use to this previously abandoned building. Through its research and adult education it attempts to counteract anti- and pro-Semitic prejudices and misinformation. Like other institutions in Austria, it organizes talks and conferences on Jewish religion, culture and history, subsidizes publications on the history of the Jews in Austria and helps maintain the synagogue structure. There is corporate sponsorship that brings its own odd history: as an example, the Institute has published a book, sponsored by Deutsche Bank, on *The Jews of Central Europe, Past and Present*. Its journals are troves of self-examination, with articles such as "From Habsburg Jews to Austrian Jews: The Jews of Vienna, 1918–1938."

In Vienna, there is the Vienna Jewish Museum in the Seitenstettengasse Synagogue filled with memorials to those significant in the course of Austrian Jewish history such as Theodore Herzl. Simon Wiesenthal opened a Jewish Documentation Center to concentrate exclusively on the hunting of war criminals. It is in a nondescript, sparsely furnished three-room office with a staff of four. There is an organized Jewish Community (Gemeinde), run by the Bundesverband der Israelitischen Kultusgemeinden. All Jews active in the Community pay a percentage of their annual income tax to the community to subsidize its services. The Gemeinde helps fund an old age home, the Jewish day school, kindergartens, the Austrian Jewish Students Union, Jewish student organizations and several Zionist youth groups such as B'nai Brith, B'nai Akiva, and Hashomer Hatzair. The Gemeinde maintains the Jewish cemeteries. There are other institutions such as the Coordinating Committee for Christian–Jewish Cooperation of Austria,[10] the Jüdisches Institut für Erwachsenenbildung,[11] and the Institut für Judaistik der Universität Wien.[12]

Austria even has had its own internal convoluted controversy over Jewish attitudes towards philo-semitism, all in the person of Peter Sichrovsky. Sichrovsky was born in Vienna in 1947, the son of Jewish Communists who fled to England just before the Holocaust and moved to Austria immediately afterward. In his book, *Strangers in Their Own Land*, he ridiculed "friendly, kind, genial Viennese" as closet Nazis. Later, he began to complain that his parents tried to instill in him a view that he could never "feel at home in the country of my birth." That contempt began to ease when he wrote *Born Guilty*. He discovered an unexpected sympathy for the children of Nazis, considering them also victims of their parents' era. "I learned to stop judging people because of what their parents did," he says. "The experience also freed me from a false solidarity with children of survivors. I began to be able to relate to people just as they were, regardless of their family histories." In the 1990s, Sichrovsky became the ally of Jörg Haider and a member of his far right People's Party. Sichrovsky told the Jewish Reporter that in Haider, he

---

9   http://www.christenundjuden.org/english/entrance.htm
10 www.jud-institut-wien.at/jiw
11 www.univie.ac.at/judaistik

found the antidote to the "hypocrisy" which he'd detested most about Austrians - the post-Holocaust Austrian pretense that the country had been Hitler's "first victim," as the popular expression went, rather than his most enthusiastic accomplice. "I always hated the false philo-Semitism of the (mainstream) Austrian parties. The Socialist Party has been in power since 1945 and still never paid any reparations to my family... Once I'd made the decision not to hide in the Jewish community but to help Austria get out of the bureaucracy and political control that have frozen this country's development, the question was, With whom? I'd rather work with people who say, `Yes, my father did terrible things but he's still my father,' than with those who tell me their parents saved Jews or how many Jewish friends they had before the war."[13]

TABORSTRASSE MAY, 2002

In May 2002, I arranged to come through Vienna on a trip from London to Kosovo and back. I had decided to write this book and wanted, at least in an exploratory way, to visit Taborstrasse 11A, where I had lived those few months of my Austrian existence, and Untere Augarten Strasse 2, where my mother's parents lived and where, when my father was arrested, my mother went, taking me, for shelter and support. I had been on Taborstrasse—as I barely recalled—a quarter century earlier. But this memory hardly stuck. It didn't burn into my mind. Perhaps it was too complicated, too soon. What I remembered was coming to the apartment with my mother and my son Joshua, then in his early teens. Joshua accidentally leaned against a car near the building in which we lived. The owner came and complained, and my mother, with the deep anger that was bottled within her, unleashed a torrent of abuse, condemning the Austrians, reminding the somewhat surprised Bürger of the role he and his antecedents had played in throwing the Jews out of Vienna.

As it happened, on my brief return in 2002, I was spending the night in Vienna on the 57th anniversary of the end of World War II. I learned that there had been weeks of controversy over the event and demands for a government ban of a proposed march involving veterans and

---

[13]   Yossi Klein Halevi and Vince Beiser, "Peter and the Wolves," *Jerusalem Report*, February 2000.

far-right students to commemorate Austria's war dead. The city was filled with people; streets were blocked, cars were stuck in traffic jams. I didn't try to mix with the crowd, but I caught a glimpse, in reality and on television, of old men walking with candles, and, elsewhere, masses of students and others from Vienna, marching in counter protest. I was neither frightened nor angered by the vigil; if anything, I was moved by the spirit of the protest.

In notes afterwards I asked myself why I visited Taborstrasse. How does it explain anything about my Austrian-ness? I wanted to see the relationship of the physical to the imagined. I wanted to see where my mother and father walked, the windows they looked out, how long it took to get from our apartment to that of my mother's mother. I wanted a better sense of the physical relationship of the District (the Second District) to the city as a whole. I felt a need to see the way people looked who were my age now and my age then. I wondered at the way young people looked as they grew up and the way I might have grown up. I wanted to see the station where my parents left for Cherbourg and imagine the last ride, by taxi, from Taborstrasse to the train.

I wanted to see the streets and imagine looking out the window at the transformation from what was (and is) to a scene of flags with swastikas and windows marked with Stars of David. I wanted to know where various other family members lived, and where the synagogue to which we belonged might have been. I wanted to know to which park my mother took me in the stroller when a soldier said, looking at me with my sweet face and blond hair, "Another one for the Führer!" I wanted to know where my father had coffee and sat and read newspapers. I wanted to know where I would have gone had I stayed, what bridges across the Donau Kanal I would have taken, and for what purpose.

As I turned from Obere Augartenstrasse into Taborstrasse, one of the first things I noticed was that Taborstrasse had become an area of guest workers or immigrants from other countries. A Turkish restaurant or coffee house faced the intersection. I tried to find our apartment, but I had the precise number wrong. I had come all the way to Vienna, all the way to Taborstrasse, but had managed to misremember the actual digits of the building in which I had lived. On the way, past the jewelry shops and the clothing stores, I saw the kind of modest shop which caters to immigrants everywhere wanting to make inexpensive phone calls home. I called my mother in New York and, of course, the address was engraved in her memory. Just before I got there, to Taborstrasse 11A, I had an Italian ice, across the street, at Taborstrasse 11B, to gain some energy, some time, some perspective. The view of the building was hardly more than a footnote to my brief visit. It is a noble building, but I did not scrutinize the nameplates of its occupants to try to fashion some story of significance. I did not try to see my old apartment, nor did I want to know who the current occupants were. I did not feel possessive or try to imagine my parents in their late twenties, starting their household there. One or two people came out of the building; I walked around the neighborhood. It was enough for this visit.

Of course, I wanted to see if I could tell who were the Austrians, those Austrians who had acted with such frenzy in the 1930s, who would still be there, in their eighties and nineties, or those, younger, who might have or would again if they had the chance. Walking through the streets of the neighborhood where I was born, at each antique store I wondered what the provenance was of a clock, or an old chair, pieces of silver, a mediocre painting crumbling on the wall.

Later, when I wanted to eat dinner, I stopped in the phone shop, run by Nigerians, where I had called the United States less than an hour before. It was getting dark. I asked the owner to recommend a restaurant. He wondered if I wanted to eat Austrian food. I thought a minute and declined. He recommended Emmy's, an African restaurant two blocks away. I found it, went through the door and felt transported in time. The owner looked at me suspiciously, as if there was a fear that someone unknown, not African, could do the restaurant damage, didn't belong, and might be the precursor of undetermined violence or bureaucratic punishment. By presenting the business card of the African Internet owner, I was rendered acceptable and welcome. But this reminded me, in a flash, of fears, early on, that Jewish shop owners must have felt in 1938 when a threateningly unknown person might have appeared.

Afterwards I walked through the Second District, a District that had been largely Jewish until the end of the 1930s. I saw a monument, near Schiffgasse, clearly a monument to the Jews who had fled or died, but its exact significance was hidden from me. I wandered in the quiet back streets, seeking directions to the place where my Aunt Irene and Uncle Alfred lived. Looking for guidance, I stumbled on a friendless and dispirited pub. I asked an old man how to get to the street I wanted and, in his attempted instruction, I read the history of the earlier times. He became for me, just for an instant, the face of the violent ones, the eager joiners, those who zealously supported the Nazi regime. Whatever he said, I could not absorb, and continued, somewhat aimlessly, to wander.

INVENTING TRADITION

I thought during this trip into Vienna of a book that's been long important to me: *Invention of Tradition*, edited by Eric Hobsbawm and Terence Ranger. Hobsbawm and his colleagues sought to show that many hallowed traditions are of far more recent vintage than would be popularly believed. What a community considers the sacred elements of its past are not necessarily the result of history only. Rather the precise contours are reinvented, reemphasized, remade to meet the needs of those who are celebrating or "remembering" them. People desire a certain version of the past, and the past can be manipulated to satisfy those needs. In Bosnia, Serbia, Rwanda, in Scotland and in France, indeed everywhere, "traditions" have been wheeled into place to mobilize feeling and drive public opinion.

Refugees are hardly immune from the invention of tradition. They must cobble together their past from the scraps they can find, rejecting those they suppress. Hobsbawm was himself a refugee and, perhaps was, himself, writing about the refugee's special need to hold on to (or repel, which may be the same thing) stories and practices of his former existence. I have always found something perceptive, and simultaneously something disturbing, about the concept of inventing tradition. Just as we are all refugees, we all have a need to provide a story of our own past. We all engage in self-discovery but also, to varying degrees, self-deception. It is often a constructive self-deception grounded in the impossibility of filling in the many blanks where facts are undiscoverable (or unbearable). And as memory disappears or recedes, the process of reclaiming and institutionalizing it becomes increasingly a matter of large-scale organization. Not only the Holocaust Museums but many other efforts walk this line between actual forgetting and corporate remembering: the Video Holocaust Survivors Project at Yale, initiated by Professor Geoffrey Hartman, or the massive Survivors of the Shoah Visual History Foundation, the gift of Steven Spielberg, where elements of this process of reinvention occur. The Shoah Foundation can claim that it has "collected more than 50,000 eyewitness testimonies in 57 countries and 32 languages, and is committed to ensuring the broad and effective educational use of its archive worldwide." Much of what is recorded as "eyewitness" evidence is the product of a specific reality; but it also often reflects the complexity of anguished pasts. "Facts" exist, but they are also selected, emphasized and recited to honor a tradition, to reinforce it, to assure that it is remembered by others. Jonathan Webber has explored this problem in his writings on Auschwitz as he tracks the painful contest between professional historians and those who have the claim of being witnesses. Refugees are engaged in inventing a life as an imperfect archaeology, a biased self-ethnography.

When I wandered Vienna, I was living this tension. I was looking for places where there would have been memories had there been occasions and time for moments to remember. I could not be satisfied going to places where I was taken as an infant to a park, but wanted, rather, to wander to places where I would have gone had we stayed. I was trying to establish a tradition, to create memories, or, more likely, to prove to myself, once and for all, that such memories or tradition had no relevance to me. Hobsbawm, in his preoccupation with creation, had missed a point: memory is destructive as well as inventive. Actual pasts, what might be called earlier imaginings, are replaced by new ones. I could see that for all of us—for me, for the refugee community and for the Viennese themselves—reimagining the past was a combination of foraging for truths, rescuing them from the tattered state in which years of forgetfulness had left them, and creating from the residue a story that could be cherished and nourished. But different truths produced different stories. I had to find out how, or to what extent, my being Austrian was a "truth" significant to my own idea of my history.

Some months after my short visit to Vienna, I went to the Neue Galerie, the new jewel-box museum of Austrian painting and design that opened to acclaim in 2001 in New York City. My heart did not beat faster, as an Austrian, for seeing the splendid Klimt and Schiele paintings. I was not moved, as an Austrian, by the intrigues, the secret romances, the tragedies of their lives. I would rather see the house of Dostoevsky in St. Petersburg, or the place Van Gogh lived in Montparnasse, than the house of Freud in Vienna. I feel more at home, oddly, in the rice fields of Thailand than on the Taborstrasse of my infancy.

ACKNOWLEDGMENTS
AND
POSTSCRIPT

Memoirs are odd art forms: a rummaging through one's past, usually in a search for significance, a try at linking one's personal story to a greater, more encompassing narrative. It's understandable that people with any link to the Holocaust—the survivors, the generations whose families were affected, the soldiers who liberated the camps, Righteous Christians—try to come to grips with their relationship to what seems so wholly inexplicable and complex. In my case, I am sure there are many motives, many reasons to explore these links. It is my way to understand a history of a family that was so suddenly and irreparably torn asunder; it is a way, more particularly, to understand my mother and my father and, by extension, myself.

When I was engaged in writing and thinking about the structure of the book, I had lunch with the gifted writing teacher, William Zinsser, who kindly agreed to read the manuscript and who was encouraging at an important moment. He has inspired many struggling memoirists with this pronouncement: "Writing is a powerful search mechanism, and one of its satisfactions is that it allows you to come to terms with your life narrative. It also allows you to work through some of life's hardest knocks—loss, grief, illness, addiction, disappointment, failure—and to find understanding and solace." I had virtually completed the draft when I read his reassuring words that "The strongest memoirs, I think, are those that preserve the unity of a remembered time and place: a book...[that] recalls what it was like to be a child or an adolescent in a world of adults contending with life's adversities."

As I shepherded the book through its original publication in German, and now through this current edition, I have struggled with a question that must concern many authors: how one's idea of one's past changes because of the new encounters involved in the writing process itself. My sense of what I had lost and what I might have enjoyed as an Austrian—my very perception of Vienna and Austria itself—has been altered through the experience of writing and publication, as should be the case. I decided, however, to maintain my original text—to indicate, to the extent possible, what I perceived, what I had been educated to feel, what I had learned to be, prior to the book's first publication. Also, even in the decade since I began writing this book, the place of the Jewish refugee in the modern imagination has changed: all the vectors, all the reference points, all the symbolic forces. No matter how many museums are built, no matter how many books are written, the stories of the 1930s, World War II and its aftermath are receding in prominence.

There are many people to thank in the creation of a manuscript that spans so many years, so many lives. Most of the credit for the book goes to my mother, Alice Mary (Diamant) Price, whose extraordinary memory, dedication to family and longevity made her a partner in my research. I have been astonished at the living memory of her childhood, of her coming of age and early marriage in Vienna and Nyitra, Slovakia. I am grateful for the time we have spent together talking about her past and that of my father and for the trove of letters and other artifacts of the past she so carefully retained. Both her mother and father had been killed in Hitler's concentration camps, and my sister and I discussed how to talk about history with her in ways that would inform and comfort, but not needlessly open wounds that could never be fully healed. My sister, Vivian Price, was exceedingly collaborative, and we spent many hours comparing our perceptions of growing up in this refugee household seeking its American footing. Eleven years younger than I, her childhood was different from mine, from various perspectives, but also remarkably similar. Now a professor in California and a documentary maker, she has been both devoted daughter and keeper of the details of our family, and, as such, was a trusted voice in getting many parts of the story right. My great thanks to my extraordinary wife Aimée Brown Price who knew when the text rang true or not and told me and who helped wrestle the title to the ground. Because this is a memoir of my childhood (and its relationship to Vienna), it does not even try to capture the full nature of our rich, long and rewarding marriage and her generous contributions to it. Joshua, Gabriel, and Asher Price lived parts of this book and each contributed in his own spectacular and individual way.

My biggest regret is that, because of his relatively early death, I was not able to interact with my father in writing this book. He is so significant a figure in the story that I wish I could have captured him more carefully, more strongly. He was also a person who would have relished responding to the questions I now felt prepared to ask, and the issues that I now wish to discuss. I have a photo of him, at an age a bit younger than I am now, taken lovingly by my mother, in Venice. Born in Vienna of an American mother and an Austrian father, he was enamored of his family's history and would have wanted to contribute to recapturing their lives and vividly memorializing them. I grew up in the imagination of my father's family—trying to put together its various parts and its various journeys. Undoubtedly, the impetus to write this book arose from the process of seeking to resolve ends that can never be other than loose and incomplete.

A cup of coffee with Arthur Samuelson, a friend and talented publisher, launched this project when he suggested that I write about the decision, in the 1990s, to apply for an Austrian passport. I am grateful to Ralph G. Engelsman, Jr. for sharing documents and perceptions of the historically American part of my father's family. Dr. Peter Marcuse's long discussions with me in the mid-1990s undoubtedly facilitated my thoughts about the manuscript, and Robert Friedman of the Center for Jewish History was generous with his time and the Center's extraordinary genealogy facilities. The Austrian Consulate General has also been a source of information, and I am particularly grateful to Irith Jawetz and Sylvia Gardner-Wittgenstein there.

Viktor Bőhm, who has served as my guide to Central European University, helped midwife the current English-language manuscript as has Rebecca Markovits, Péter György and Linda Kunos, Krisztina Kós and György Lissauer with the CEU Press. I also wish to acknowledge the support of Yehuda

Elkana, who was Rector of Central European University and whose open and expansive spirit suffused the institution. Luitgard Hammerer single-handedly transformed my idea of the Austrian experience. Her friend Renate Korber was my dedicated guide to Rechnitz, the home of my great rabbinical forbearer, in the Burgenland. Hannah M. Lessing, the dedicated Secretary General of the National Fund and of the General Settlement Fund, provided backing for the German edition and, more satisfying to me, assured that copies of the book would be made available to libraries and schools throughout Austria. Dr. Wesley A. Fisher, Director of Research for the Conference on Jewish Material Claims Against Germany, generously read and commented on Chapter 9.

Publishers Thomas Busch and Helena Mracnikar of Drava Verlag were enormously supportive in publishing the original 2006 German language edition, *Born in Vienna; Versuch einer Annäherung.* They also assisted in bringing the book to the attention of the Jewish community in Vienna and to institutions connected to memory and exile. Eric Frey, managing editor of *Der Standard*, provided a provocative and thoughtful introduction at a Vienna event marking the publication of the German edition.

For that event, in January 2007, my visit was sponsored by the Jewish Welcome Service, organized by the municipal authorities, to honor the "great cultural heritage of Judaism" and to contribute to "international public relations work on behalf of Jewish culture in Austria." For hosting the launch, I am thankful to Esra, an organization created to provide assistance to the "new" Jewish immigrants, many from Eastern and Central Europe and the former Soviet Union, with the goal of integrating them into Austrian society. Esra is also there to provide counseling and treatment... for problems and disorders caused by the Holocaust." After Vienna, I went to Budapest, where the German edition was introduced at Central European University by Dr. Ferdinand Mayrhofer-Grünbühel, then Austrian Ambassador to Hungary, with a perceptive discussion by Anna Gács, a faculty member at Eötvös Loránd University.

There is one thing more. In 2008, I was sitting in Budapest with Kato Kenedi, my mother's first cousin, wondering with her about the whereabouts of Milan Ehrenfeld, the only other living offspring of their common aunts and uncles. I wrote about him briefly in Chapter 5. His parents had been killed in the early 1950s when they sought to leave Slovakia during the Communist period. Little Milan, who was shot during that border attack, was rescued and taken to an orphanage in Bratislava. There, about a year later, he was adopted by the Javors, a Slovakian Jewish family who felt he should be brought up in a Jewish environment. Even before the Javors moved to Canada, Milan had visited his Hungarian relatives, but as he grew older the contact ceased. Through the miracle of Google, we located him in Canada and my mother, my sister and I met him that September in New York City. My mother showed him photographs of his father and told stories about his father's youth and young manhood in the house of their grandparents. For me, this meeting was a great gift and a useful postscript to this book. But it did not mean there are happy endings, only more and different threads of emergence.

A reunion of the Engelesman-Preis family, around 1900. My grandfather is on the far right, my grandmother, Gella, in the back row to his right, and my great grandmother, Charlotte, seated on the right.

My father's Uncle Emil, popular *fiaker* driver, in his glory

Business card for Preis & Co. in its heyday

My great-uncle A.D. Engelsman, visiting from the United States, with my grandfather (standing), just before my grandfather's marriage to A.D.'s sister Gella.

My grandmother, Gella, around the time of her wedding

My father and his sister Alice, 1906

My father about 1909

My father, on the left, his Uncle Isidor, his sister and his Uncle A.D. (about 1920)

An Ehrenfeld wedding portrait, 1922. My mother is the young girl in the front row, between cousin Klari to her right, and her mother and father. My great-grandfather is in the front row, and my great-grandmother standing behind him. My mother's Aunt Irene is standing on the far right.

My father, in Nice, during his honeymoon, 1936

My mother showing a golden feather to her grandfather, at his home in Nyitra, 1917

My maternal grandmother, 1919

My mother and her favorite cousin, Klari,
in front of the kitchen door in Nyitra, 1929

My mother, appearing in an amateur theater
evening, with cousin Klari, 1932

My mother, age 22, with her mother, visiting
Opatija (Abbazia) on the Dalmatian coast

Wedding of my parents in Vienna, March 15, 1936

My parents on their honeymoon in 1936

My mother and father, Baden bei Wien, 1937

My cousin, Herbert, 6 years old

Bor Ausfüllung des Bermögensverzeichnisses ist die beigefügte Anleitung genau durchzulesen!

Zur Beachtung!

1. **Wer hat das Vermögensverzeichnis einzureichen?**
Jeder Anmeldepflichtige, also auch jeder Ehegatte und jedes Kind für sich. Für jedes minderjährige Kind ist das Vermögensverzeichnis vom Inhaber der elterlichen Gewalt oder von dem Vormund einzureichen.

2. **Bis wann ist das Vermögensverzeichnis einzureichen?**
Bis zum 30. Juni 1938. Wer anmelde- und bewertungspflichtig ist, aber die Anmelde- und Bewertungspflicht nicht oder nicht rechtzeitig oder nicht vollständig erfüllt, setzt sich schwerer Strafe (Geldstrafe, Gefängnis, Zuchthaus, Einziehung des Vermögens) aus.

3. **Wie ist das Vermögensverzeichnis auszufüllen?**
Es müssen sämtliche Fragen beantwortet werden. Nichtzutreffendes ist zu durchstreichen. Reicht der in dem Vermögensverzeichnis für die Ausfüllung vorgesehene Raum nicht aus, so sind die geforderten Angaben auf einer Anlage zu machen.

4. **Wenn Zweifel bestehen,** ob diese oder jene Werte in dem Vermögensverzeichnis aufgeführt werden müssen, sind die Werte aufzuführen.

31312

Verzeichnis über das Vermögen von Juden
nach dem Stand vom 27. April 1938

des   P r e i s   Harold Gustav   Kaufmann
der   _____
             (Zu- und Vorname)   (Beruf oder Gewerbe)

in   Wien, II.,   Tabor   -Straße, Platz Nr. 11a
     (Wohnsitz oder gewöhnlicher Aufenthalt)

Angaben zur Person

Ich bin geboren am   29. Juli 1905

Ich bin Jude (§ 5 der Ersten Verordnung zum Reichsbürgergesetz vom 14. Nov. 1935, Reichsgesetzbl. I S. 1333)

und — deutscher [1] — _____ Staatsangehörigkeit [1]) — ~~staatenlos~~ —.

Da ich — Jude deutscher Staatsangehörigkeit [1]) ~~staatenloser Jude~~) — bin, habe ich in dem nachstehenden Vermögensverzeichnis mein gesamtes inländisches und ausländisches Vermögen angegeben und bewertet [1]).

Ich bin verheiratet mit   Alice Mary Preis   geb.   Diamant
                                                                  (Mädchenname der Ehefrau)

Mein Ehegatte ist der Rasse nach — jüdisch [1]) ~~~~ — und gehört der   jüdischen
Religionsgemeinschaft an.

Angaben über das Vermögen

I. Land- und forstwirtschaftliches Vermögen (vgl. Anleitung Ziff. 9)

Wenn Sie am 27. April 1938 land- und forstwirtschaftliches Vermögen besaßen (gepachtete Ländereien u. dgl. sind nur aufzuführen, wenn das der Bewirtschaftung dienende Inventar Ihnen gehörte):

Lage des eigenen oder gepachteten Betriebs und seine Größe in Hektar? (Gemeinde — Gutsbezirk — und Hofnummer, auch grundbuch- und katastermäßige Bezeichnung)	Art des eigenen oder gepachteten Betriebs? (z. B. landwirtschaftlicher, forstwirtschaftlicher, gärtnerischer Betrieb, Weinbaubetrieb, Fischereibetrieb)	Handelte es sich um einen eigenen Betrieb oder um eine Pachtung	Wert des Betriebs RM	Bei eigenen Betrieben: Wenn der Betrieb noch Anderen gehörte: Wie hoch war Ihr Anteil? (z. B. 1/4)
1	2	3	4	5

II. Grundvermögen (Grund und Boden, Gebäude) (vgl. Anleitung Ziff. 10):

Wenn Sie am 27. April 1938 Grundvermögen besaßen (Grundstücke, die nicht zu dem vorstehend unter I und nachstehend unter III bezeichneten Vermögen gehörten):

Lage des Grundstücks? (Gemeinde, Straße und Hausnummer, bei Bauland auch grundbuch- und katastermäßige Bezeichnung)	Art des Grundstücks? (z. B. Einfamilienhaus, Mietwohngrundstück, Bauland)	Wert des Grundstücks RM	Wenn das Grundstück noch Anderen gehörte: Wie hoch war Ihr Anteil? (z. B. 1/4)
1	2	3	4

[1]) Nichtzutreffendes ist zu durchstreichen.

...ensverzeichnis (BO v. 26. 4. 38)

Verzeichnis über das Vermogen der Juden (my father's property filing from 1938)

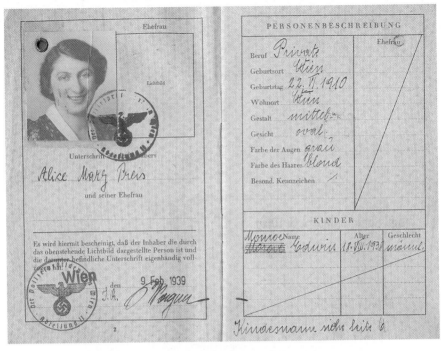

My mother's passport, 1939

Playing in the garden in Lawrence, Long Island, summer 1939

A favorite picture, with my favorite ball, 1939

With my mother around 1941,
Macon, Georgia

My mother, her Aunt Irene, Irene's husband,
Alfred Goldstein and me (wearing Tyrolean
hat from Austria), 1941, Macon

A studio portrait of our family in Cincinnati, 1946

Clutching my father's leg,
Macon, 1942

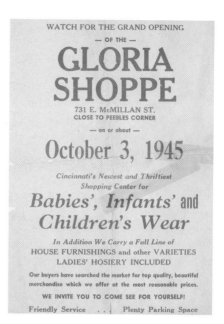

Announcement of my mother's retail business, Cincinnati, Ohio, 1945

Waterside frolicking with my sister
in the early 1950s.

With my sister Vivian,
1957

My mother and father in the backyard
of our Cincinnati house, 1954

Aunt Irene and Uncle Alfred in the Bronx,
around 1950

With my mother at Yale, 1959

My wife, Aimée, during our engagement,
1964

As a law clerk at the United States
Supreme Court, 1965

Ralph Engelsman and his wife Nao in the late 1940s

My mother's cousin Kato and her daughter Marika in Budapest, 1959

My namesake, my father's uncle, Monroe Engelsman